the Culture's Technology

POETICS AND LINGUISTICS ASSOCIATION

1

Editor-in-Chief:

Donald C. Freeman, University of Massachusetts Amherst

Editorial Board:

The Writer's Craft,
the Culture's Technology

Edited by

Carmen Rosa Caldas-Coulthard
and Michael Toolan

Amsterdam - New York, NY 2005

03-1010214

Cover design: Aart Jan Bergshoeff

The paper on which this book is printed meets the requirements of
"ISO 9706: 1994, Information and documentation - Paper for documents -
Requirements for permanence".

ISBN: 90-420-1936-0
Editions Rodopi B.V., Amsterdam - New York, NY 2005
Printed in The Netherlands

CONTENTS

Acknowledgements

The authors and publisher wish to thank the following for permission to use copyright material:

In Chapter 5, James Thurber, *The Pet Department*, for the use of the illustration 'The Thurber Carnival'; The *Times*, London, for the reproduction of the Queen's picture, published on April 22, 1999; ©Pugh/The Times, London, 1999, for permission to reproduce the Pugh cartoon from The Times published on April 22, 1999, page 1; TIME Reprints and Permissions for the 'Image of House' from TIME, September 29, 1997.

Efforts have been made to trace copyright holders of all material reproduced in this volume, but if any have been overlooked the publisher will be pleased to rectify matters promptly.

Notes on Contributors

Anna Elizabeth Balocco is an Associate Professor in the Graduate Programmes in Linguistics and in English Language Literatures at the State University of Rio de Janeiro, Brazil, where she teaches courses on discourse analysis and on writing. Her published research includes: 'Identity in Academic Discourse: Constructing an Insider's Ethos in Prose about Literature' in *Trabalhos em Lingüística Aplicada* 40 (São Paulo: Unicamp: 17-28 [2002]) and 'Zones of Discourse Turbulence in Narrative and Non-Narrative Texts' in *Crop* 8 (São Paulo: University of São Paulo: 297-309 [2002]).

annabalocco@superig.com.br

Mirjana Bonačić is Head of English Studies in the recently established School of Humanities (Studiji humanističkih znanosti) at the University of Split, Croatia. She teaches courses in textual interpretation and literary stylistics and translation. She has publications in the areas of applied linguistics, stylistics, and translation studies (among her articles in English are 'Context, Knowledge, and Teaching Translation' in de Beaugrande, Robert, et al. (eds) *Language Policy and Language Education in Emerging Nations* (Stamford, CT: Ablex: 37-48 [1998]); and 'Some Reflections on the Relations between Language, Writing, and Translation' in *Studia Romanica et Anglica Zagrabiensia* 42: 37-48 (1997). Her current research interest is in figurative language from the perspective of translation.

mirjana.bonacic@st.htnet.hr

Joe Bray teaches at the University of Stirling. His research and teaching interests are in literary stylistics, narratology, and the 18th-century novel. He is the author of *The Epistolary Novel: Representations of Consciousness* (London: Routledge [2003]) and co-editor (with Miriam Handley and Anne C. Henry) of *Ma(r)king The Text: The Presentation of Meaning on the Literary Page* (Aldershot: Ashgate [2000]).

j.d.bray@stir.ac.uk

Rosario Caballero is a lecturer in the Department of Modern Philology, Universidad de Castilla-La Mancha, Spain. She is particularly interested in discourse and genre analysis, and applied cognitive linguistics (metaphor research in discourse contexts). Her recent publications include: 'Técnica del argumento y argumento de la técnica: heterogeneidad, intertextualidad e interdiscursividad en un texto informático' in *Revista Iberoamericana de Discurso y Sociedad* 3(3): 11-37 (2001); 'Metaphor and Genre: The Presence and Role of Metaphor in the Building Review' in *Applied Linguistics* 24(2): 145-167 (2003); and 'Talking about Space: Image Metaphor in Architectural Discourse' in *Annual Review of Cognitive Linguistics* 1: 87-105 (2003).

MRosario.Caballero@uclm.es

Carmen Rosa Caldas-Coulthard, Professor of English Language and Applied Linguistics at the Federal University of Santa Catarina, Brazil, is now Senior Lecturer at the University of Birmingham, England. She has published widely in the areas of critical discourse, media, narrative, and gender studies. Her current research interests are in social semiotics, visual communication, and identity in discourse. She is the author of *News as Social Practice* (UFSC, 1997) and co-editor of *Texts and Practices: Reading in Critical Discourse Analysis* (London: Routledge [1996]). Her forthcoming edited book (Basingstoke: Palgrave [2005]) with Rick Iedema is *Identity Trouble: Critical Discourse and Contested Identities*.

c.r.caldas-coulthard@bham.ac.uk

Robert Cockcroft taught in the School of English Studies, University of Nottingham, from 1965 to 2002. His research interests include rhetoric and rhetorical stylistics, sea literature, and epic. He has recently published *Rhetorical Affect in Early Modern Writing: Renaissance Passions Reconsidered* (Basingstoke: Palgrave [2003]); 'Putting Aristotle to the Proof: Style, Substance and the EPL Group' in *Language and Literature* 13(3): 195-212; and an enlarged second edition (with Susan M. Cockcroft) of *Persuading People: An Introduction to Rhetoric* (Basingstoke: Palgrave [2005]).

robert.cockcroft@ntlworld.com

Ulf Cronquist teaches in the Department of Literature, Gothenburg University, Sweden. He received his Ph.D. in English from Gothenburg and an M.A. in cognitive science from Lund University. His current research project involves a re-evaluation of the role of literature with special interests in hypertext, prosthetics, simulations, and cognitive modeling. Some of his most recent writings are *Erotographic Metafiction: Aesthetic Strategies and Ethical Statements in John Hawkes's 'Sex Trilogy'*, Acta Universitatis Gothoburgensis: Gothenburg Studies in English 78 (2000); 'Introducing Cognitive Poetics to Literary Onomastics: The Example of John Hawkes's Latin Flower Names in *The Blood Oranges*' (forthcoming in *NAMES: A Journal of Onomastics*); 'The Posthumanist Body in the Flesh: Hypertext, Simulation and Prosthetics' (forthcoming in *The Flesh Made Text* 2003 conference proceedings).

ulf.cronquist@spray.se

George L. Dillon is Professor of English Language and Literature at the University of Washington. He has written books on semantics, the reading and writing of literature, expository prose, advice books, and the discourses of academic disciplines. He continues to work on the intersections of visual and verbal meanings and on electronic writing. A good bit of his recent work has been published electronically, such as 'Dada Photomontage and net.art.'

dillon@u.washington.edu

Donald C. Freeman is Emeritus Professor of English at the University of Southern California, Adjunct Professor of Linguistics at the University of Massachusetts Amherst, and co-director of MICA, the Myrifield Institute for Cognition and the Arts in Heath, Massachusetts. His recent work has been in cognitive metaphor.

d.freeman@direcway.com

Geoff Hall is Senior Lecturer at the Centre for Applied Language Studies (CALS), University of Wales Swansea. His research interests are in discourse stylistics and language education. His recent publications are: 'Poetry, Pleasure and Second Language Classrooms' in *Applied Linguistics* 24(3): 395-399 (2003); 'The Year's Work in Stylistics: 2002' in *Language and Literature* 12(4): 357-372 (2003). His forthcoming book, *Literature in Language Education,* will be published by Palgrave in November, 2005.

g.m.hall@swansea.ac.uk

Donald Hardy teaches courses in linguistics at Colorado State University. He has published widely in the areas of linguistics and stylistics. His book, *Narrating Knowledge in Flannery O'Connor's Fiction*, was published in 2003 by the University of South Carolina Press. His research interests are in computational stylistics and Perl programming for natural language processing. He is currently at work on a book on grammatical voice and the body in the fiction of Flannery O'Connor.

Don.Hardy@colostate.edu

Masahiro Hori is Professor of English Linguistics and Stylistics at Kumamoto Gakuen University, Japan. His recent publications are: *Investigating Dickens' Style: A Collocational Analysis* (Basingstoke: Palgrave [2004]); and 'Collocational Patterns of -*ly* Manner Adverbs in Dickens' in Saito, Toshio, Junsaku Nakamura and Shunji Yamazaki (eds) *English Corpus Linguistics in Japan* (Amsterdam: Rodopi: 149-63 [2002]); he is also the co-translator (into Japanese) of Tobias Smollett's *The Adventures of Roderick Random*.

hori@kumagaku.ac.jp

Susan Hunston is Professor of English Language at the University of Birmingham. Her main areas of research are discourse analysis and corpus linguistics. She has written *Corpora in Applied Linguistics* (Cambridge: Cambridge University Press [2002]) and is co-author of *Pattern Grammar* (Amsterdam: John Benjamins [1999]).

S.E.Hunston@bham.ac.uk

Anita Naciscione is Professor of English and Head of the Department of Foreign Languages at the Latvian Academy of Culture, Riga, Latvia. Her research interests lie at the interface of phraseology, stylistics, and cognitive linguistics. She is concerned with the cognitive processes of the mind, creative thinking, the role of associations and the creation of a novel form and meaning in discourse. She is the author of the book *Phraseological Units in Discourse: Towards Applied Stylistics* (Riga: Latvian Academy of Culture [2001]) and many articles on various aspects of the stylistic use of phraseology. She is also the co-author of two Latvian-English dictionaries.

naciscione@parks.lv

Ken Nakagawa is Professor of English Philology and Stylistics at Yasuda Women's University, Hiroshima, Japan. His major publications are: *The Language of William Wordsworth: A Linguistic Approach to Poetical Language* (in Japanese) (Hiroshima: Research Institute for Language and Culture, Yasuda Women's University [1977]); 'The Vocabulary that Constitutes The Prelude' in *Studies in Modern English: The Twentieth Anniversary Publication of the Modern English Association* (Tokyo: Eichosha: 457-47 [2003]), and '"Through" in The Prelude' in *Voyages to Conception: Essays in English Romanticism* (Tokyo: Kirihara Shoten: 118-33 [2005]).

knakagaw@yasuda-u.ac.jp

Marika Schwaiger is a research assistant at the Department of Phonetics and Linguistics of the University of Munich. For her M.A. dissertation at the University of Munich, she is researching the integration of young refugees, using sociological and political theory. She is the author of *Multimedia Training Materials on CD-ROM* for the publishing company Langenscheidt (Munich) and of *Interactive Training Materials for the Online Language Course uni-deutsch.de* of the Department of Language and Communication, University of Munich.

marika.schwaiger@stud.uni-muenchen.de

Michi Shiina teaches at Hosei University (Tokyo, Japan) and is currently a Ph.D. student at Lancaster University. Her main areas of research and teaching are historical pragmatics, stylistics, discourse analysis, sociolinguistics, cultural studies. Her main publications are 'How Spouses Used to Address Each Other: A Historical Pragmatic Approach to the Use of Vocatives in Early Modern English Comedies' in *Bulletin of the Faculty of Letters* 48 (Tokyo: Hosei University: 51-73 [2002]); and 'Cultural Studies and Linguistics' in *Gengo* 29(3) (Tokyo: Taishukan: 30-35 [2000]).

michi-s@air.linkclub.or.jp

Michael Toolan is Professor of Applied English Linguistics at the University of Birmingham. A current research interest is patterns of coherence and expectation in the reading of narrative fiction. His *Total Speech* (Durham, NC: Duke University Press 1996) explored aspects of integrational linguistic theory. Other recent books include *Language in Literature* (London: Hodder [1998]), *Narrative* (2nd ed.; London: Routledge [2001]), and the editing of a four-volume anthology of seminal papers in critical discourse analysis (London: Routledge [2002]).

M.Toolan@bham.ac.uk

Preface

This book inaugurates *PALA Papers*, a series of volumes comprising essays selected and edited from presentations at the annual conferences of the Poetics and Linguistics Association. It appears in the 25th anniversary year of PALA's founding; its geographic and intellectual range reflects the extraordinary growth of what began as a small group of like-minded scholars, mostly from Great Britain, a quarter-century ago.

The authors included in this volume, *The Writer's Craft, the Culture's Technology*, represent countries from Brazil to Sweden and from the United States to Japan; their essays discuss issues ranging from Jakobsonian poetic analysis to textmontage on the World Wide Web. Several of these papers discuss the phenomenon of globalisation; the volume itself is a prime example of scholarly globalisation both for PALA and the academic profession in general.

Books like *PALA Papers* are necessarily cooperative undertakings. I am grateful to the contributors for their patience while we all coped with the steep learning curve of contemporary technologies of scholarly publishing. I am especially grateful to the volume editors, Michael Toolan and Carmen Rosa Caldas-Coulthard: PALA is fortunate to have scholars of their standing as editors of this first volume in our series. Thanks are also due to Margaret H. Freeman for help in the final stages of preparing the manuscript.

Donald C. Freeman
Editor-in-Chief, *PALA Papers*
University of Massachusetts Amherst

Myrifield Institute for Cognition and the Arts
Heath, Massachusetts, USA
May 2005

Introduction

The essays published here derive from papers given at the **Twenty-Second International Conference of the Poetics and Linguistics Association (PALA)** at Birmingham in April 2002. They address, directly or indirectly, the main theme of that conference: the interaction between literary creativity and a culture's technological affordances. The collection reflects the diversity of approaches sponsored by PALA conferences, where the chief stipulation is simply that a focus on the language of texts, systematically studied, is maintained. We have divided the book, loosely and chiefly as a way of postulating main trends, into four parts.

In the first part, **The Writer's Web,** appear two papers, by Dillon and Caldas-Coulthard, which were originally given as plenary lectures at the conference, together with essays by Cronquist and Caballero.

In 'Anti-Laokoön: Mixed and Merged Modes of Imagetext on the Web', **George Dillon** investigates the affordances of hypertext reading. He begins by reminding us of the authoritative influence once wielded by the high modernist segregation of words from visual images (they might be 'equal'; they had to be separate). In recent decades, but obviously hastened by the accelerant digitisation, words, images, sounds are mixed and merged in sense- and cognition-taxing mélanges. The new media facilitate the handling of text, image, and sound in ever more ingenious and widely available ways (every [western] woman her own movie-maker). Here Dillon begins to spell out some of those ways, and begins to think about the stylistics of digital imagetexts. He describes in illuminating and entertaining detail three particular tactics that move toward equivalence and fusion of text and image (and sound). These he terms *textmontage*; the chaining of words and images as hypertext anchors (*image-text chains*); and the rendering of text as visual event through animation (*dynamic textmontage*). An inescapable preoccupation is with the kinds and functions and effects of links, and how they 're-establish the readability of the visual world, at least in places, and the seeability of words, to which we can add the hearability of words and images: we can make literally speaking pictures'. One of the affordances of hypertext links, then, is to weave fragments together into complex signifying structures and to make us alert to how we are constantly shifting interpretive rules and frames to make sense of our world. The Web artworks scrutinised here, Dillon concludes, amount to multimodal metaphysical conceits. And they seem to foster two contrapuntal shifts: the physical/visual elements tend to be apprehended as more metaphorical, while the textual/ verbal ones are taken up as more a matter of design and performance, than they would do elsewhere.

Carmen Rosa Caldas-Coulthard's paper, 'Personal Web Pages and the Semiotic Construction of Academic Identities', examines the effect of culture and gender on the discursive strategies used by Web page writers to present themselves in terms of the narrativisation of their lives and in terms of the multi-modal choices that help to create a particular identity. She discusses in particular how participants in this new genre of internet pages recontextualise in the public sphere a fictionalised representation of themselves. In a virtual age, people construct their identities through different media, and the internet is a powerful source of self-identification. Identity construction is a complex phenomenon, and people project in public spaces idealisations of what they 'think' they are. The multitude of formats, photographs, colour choice point to the hybrid formation of identity. The online construction is an extension of the offline persona. Institutions, she concludes, cannot control these self-representations. There will always be a way out of the institutionalised corporate 'image'. She also emphasises the importance of the study of multimodality in the new communicative genres, since Web pages combine language, image, and graphics into a single integrated text structure; Web pages are *interdiscursive, intertextual, dialogical,* and are also *sites of engagement*. It is through breaking down the traditional hierarchical separation of different modes of representation, Caldas-Coulthard claims, and focusing more on their roles in *social actions*, *social identities,* and *social practices* that we will achieve a true understanding of the society we live in – and virtuality for her, is here to stay.

In 'Hypertext, Prosthetics and the Netocracy', **Ulf Cronquist** asserts that the postmodern world of firewall-to-firewall technology causes both autocracy and democracy to be supplanted by a 'netocracy' (of which we are the 'netizenry'). Relatedly, the old borders or identities, (pre-)determined by nationality, sex, class, etc. are dissolving. The last such frontier is our body itself. Cronquist sees all this being worked through in Jeanette Winterson's internet-set novel *The PowerBook*, in which the multi-voiced narrator offers the reader 'freedom for just one night'. Cronquist examines the layered hypertextuality, extensive prosthetics, and positional Netocracy that such 'temporary freedom' entails. But he does not want to overstate the case; he points out that '*The PowerBook* turns out to be a printed text that mimes hypertext – the novel never radically questions its ontological status as a printed text that *mimetically* represents reality'.

Rosario Caballero probes the influence of hypertext on genre, specifically by examining some of the techniques and structures found in a small corpus of 80 book reviews taken from online sources. Do (online) reviews comprise a unified genre, or are they rather a group of writing practices that might be regarded as genres in their own right? The use of hypertext technology in online book reviews highlights divergences already existing in practices of review-writing and stirs them into new life. A particularly revealing aspect in this regard is the system of links used by the online reviews in the corpus, which are discussed in relation to two central parameters of genre – audience and communicative purpose – and are found to play a similarly significant rhetorical goal in hyperdiscourse interaction.

Part II of the collection, **Textual and Technological Transitions**, comprises six papers which explore kinds of crossing or crossover in a variety of texts and by various means.

Anita Naciscione discusses creative aspects of textual and visual saturation in a multimodal discourse. Her approach is cognitive: it proposes that the perception of an image, whether it is lexical or phraseological, is a cognitive process, which creates a mental picture in one's imagination, a kind of visualisation in one's mind's eye. Naciscione looks at some of the ways that familiar (even relatively dead) metaphorical phrases get exploited, extended, glossed by visual accompaniment, and so on, on particular occasions of use. Thus a phrase like *family tree* is played with in a darkly humorous way by

Mark Twain when he suggests that his own family tree took a distinctive shape (and then confirms this with a sketch unambiguously depicting a gallows). Indeed there could be various creative extensions, requiring imaginative interpretive visualisation on the part of the addressee, of this stock phrase: the person who says 'My family tree has always been deciduous', or the person tracing their own ancestry who says that for many weeks of research they were 'barking up the wrong family tree'. And so on without limit. Naciscione's broad conclusion is that all such situated phrasal metaphorising is a reflex of, and an aid to, cognitive articulation and development.

Ken Nakagawa's essay on Wordsworth's 'Daffodils' is all about the poet's craft, and either structural or philological techniques of analysis and reading, rather than technology. Insofar as the poem reports an observer's stimulation – by witnessing 'a host of golden daffodils' – of reflection, thought, and memory on 'that inward eye', the poem would seem to speak of the irrelevance, or at least mere contingent impact, of technology. Humanly fashioned tools play not even an indirect part in 'Daffodils'; the speaker's key tool is the eye. And perhaps this applies more generally to the work of those designated 'nature poets'. Nakagawa's close attention to eye rhymes and grammatical parallels may be felt by some to be old-fashioned (and not merely 'unfashionable'). But certain considerations speak in its favour. For one thing, it is close to a dominant way of writing about poems in British secondary schools (and no doubt elsewhere). For another, it may manage to single out some of the material to which a reader actually, wittingly or otherwise, is responsive. Indeed, to be justified, it must so identify real sources of reader response. But proving such influence – proving, for example, that readers take note of the *gay/gazed* echo-rhyme, and that this recurrence reinforces (to those readers) ideas of delight – is a difficult matter. Perhaps easier to seek confirmation of are the larger movements, for example that which Nakagawa notes from – and later back to – the solitude or loneliness, and hinted melancholy, of the first and final stanzas, which envelop stanzas of dancing bliss. Chafing at the 'limits' that a structuralist analysis seems to impose, Nakagawa turns to a philological reading, which highlights 'dynamic movement' in the poem.

In 'Seeing the Sea: Deixis and the Perceptions of Melville's Reader', **Robert Cockcroft** focuses on the dizzying use of deixis at important narrative moments in *Moby-Dick*, where we, following our focalising narrator Ishmael, seem to be deliberately disoriented, perceptually and cognitively. Melville exploits linguistic resources which generally assist us in the process of reading – deixis and story schemata – in ways which give us the textual experience of being as lost and insignificant as any Ishmael hallucinating while on watch at the top of the masthead. As Ishmael memorably warns:

> But while this sleep, this dream is on ye, move your foot or hand an inch; slip your hold at all; and your identity comes back in horror. Over Descartian vortices you hover. And perhaps, at midday, in the fairest weather, with one half-throttled shriek you drop through that transparent air into the summer sea, no more to rise forever.
>
> (Chapter 35: 'The Masthead')

Anna Elizabeth Balocco's study is of 'transgressive' narratives, published in a Brazilian magazine: stories in which Brazilian lesbian women publicly affirm their sexual orientation. Balocco argues that these narratives function as a resource through which social meaning is attached to these women's private experiences, enabling them to structure their collective memory. At the same time, however, the point of view which *incorporates* these narratives into our own collective memories is fundamentally *male*: these women, who represent so-called 'chic lesbianism', remain within the scope of the male gaze and are easily eroticised as such. Thus the distinct patterning of discourses in these narratives doubly inscribes the informants as the Other of hegemonic discourses on *sex* and on *gender*. The main theoretical assumption of Balocco's paper is that social identities, across different dimensions, are discursively constructed. She claims that although storytellers challenge the boundaries of 'competent discourses' constituted to erase cultural, linguistic, ethnic, gender, or sexual differences, their narratives are contained within a dominant code, which defines a particular type of representation for homoerotic women.

In 'The Translator's Craft as a Cross-Cultural Discourse', **Mirjana Bonačić** emphasises the plurality of translational discourses derived from a single original text by exploring how different frames of reference are reflected in, or created by, the use of language during translation. The text taken for exemplification is Frost's 'Nothing Gold Can Stay', and the translations of this poem into Polish and Croatian. Bonačić makes a case for regarding translation as crucial contemporary 'work' (which runs counter to the homogenised, 'translation-less', world promised or threatened by some versions of globalism), going across and between languages, cultures, and viewpoints. Translation's work is part art, part technologically assisted creativity. In some ways the translator is a representative figure of the postmodern exile, always lonely and at home (like Heaney's persona, or, for that matter, Rushdie's).

Just how significantly differently might students apprehend a 'difficult' text if they encounter it in a modified format, where the written text is supplemented by comic-book-style illustrations? This is the question **Marika Schwaiger** explores, using two groups of German grammar-school students as her subjects, and Kafka's *Before the Law* (in text only and text-plus-illustrations formats) as the 'difficult' textual material. In addition Schwaiger asks such scandalous questions as: Do literary classics appear, to today's students, to be not worth reading, due to their bygone textuality? Do teachers need to contemplate 'a kind of compromise between yesterday's literature and today's students' reading habits or their perceptive faculties?' Can we not only bring our student-horses to the trough of literature, but actually get them to drink deep, if (and only if?) we substitute water with diet Coke? Schwaiger is well aware that her study invites further explorations. For example at the end of their reading, recipients of both the text and picture-text versions could be asked to produce their own drawings (of the Doorkeeper, for instance, or of the face of the enquirer). It might be instructive to see what work this produced – whether, for example, picture-text subjects' depictions tended to be slavish copies of the artwork previously presented to them, and whether the drawings of the text-only subjects might be judged to be more varied and imaginative than those of the other group. Schwaiger is not afraid to assert (in particular circumstances, of course) 'unimodality bad, multimodality good'. But hers is by no means a blanket endorsement of lit with pix; rather she closes by recommending 'a well-directed use of illustrations in specific situations' with young and inexperienced readers grappling with more abstract or symbolic writing.

Papers in Part III, **Changing Cultures of Report**, are united in being explorations of kinds of reporting and representation of others' words at different times and in different media – principally, contemporary newspapers, contemporary documentary television, and 18th-century fiction.

Geoff Hall revisits the issue of reported speech in newspaper stories. It has long been noted (especially in British tabloid newspapers but in the 'quality' broadsheets too) that quotations from people in the news are frequently an edited record of what was actually said or written, and are sometimes surprisingly inaccurate, or hypothetical. In view of the extent of this rhetorically driven 'creativity', some theorists have wondered how heavily we should focus on matters of 'fidelity of report' as a benchmark and in some discoursal situations (legal, political, book reviewing and criticism, and financial matters) a required standard. Hall reviews the 'going to war with Iraq' narrative and President Bush's speech to the United States Congress in which he identified Iraq, Iran, North Korea as 'an axis of evil', and alleged that all three countries were linked with weapons of mass destruction. What sort of link did he assert? Did these countries actually have such weapons and could they deploy them rapidly; or did they merely want them, and so were seeking them? As everyone can see, there are significant differences here. But as Hall shows, journalism is routinely a process of accumulation, cutting and pasting of other scribes' fragments, and that even in purportedly direct report of a major political speech, beamed around the world, not insignificant differences and reformulations emerge or are fostered, as the spinning requires. While Hall recognises that identification of key parameters affecting faithfulness of representation has helped to give a more nuanced picture, he suggests that there may still be room for a more wide-ranging model of communication, in which stylistics adopts a more elaborated linguistics of writing.

Joe Bray's '"Print Culture" and the Language of the 18th-Century Novel' reflects on the fluidity and slipperiness of the 'body' of the *Pamela* text, and its openness to readerly interpretations by Mr B. As Bray shows, Mr B repeatedly conflates Pamela and her texts, and is as infatuated by the one as much as the other, or by one because of the other. But the 'equivalence' (to use a term put under pressure in the Bonačić essay) of Pamela and the novel is by no means Mr B's exclusive folly, but rather is quite openly and deliberately intimated, in plot and detail, by Richardson: e. g., in the way Pamela 'stitches' various parts of her text 'about her body'. Bray challenges the assumption that digitised technology enables, in a way never before imaginable, the permeability of text to text, and of authorial property to readerly reinterpretation and alteration. He finds, in the use or uptake of Pamela/*Pamela*, Richardson's first novel or first heroine, ample 18th-century evidence of quite similar trends. Of the re-workings, the 'spinning', of the Pamela phenomenon (what he calls 'the Pamela media event') in the years surrounding its publication Bray sees a forerunner of contemporary technology-driven appropriations and decouplings of authorial intention from use or interpretation. Pamela/*Pamela* seems to have appeared in at least as many popular-cultural guises as Madonna or Princess Diana in our own day. As a result of the proliferation of published 'versions', irresolvable debates arose concerning *Pamela*'s destabilised 'meaning'; but Bray goes on to argue that uncertainties of interpretation and possibilities of misreading were actually inherent in the text from the outset, in its first edition.

Susan Hunston's 'Truth and Lies: The Construction of Factuality in a Television Documentary' is an analysis of a television documentary prompted by the publication of Binjamin Wilkomirski's *Fragments*, a memoir of childhood in the Nazi concentration camps. In the television documentary, two contradictory versions of an individual's life story are presented: version 1 tells of a young child who endured and survived the Holocaust death camps, and lived to write a moving, best-selling book about his experiences; version 2 tells of a man who merely 'imagined himself' into the experience of being a Holocaust victim and survivor, and wrote a bestseller out of that imagining. Crucially, the documentary about Wilkomirski/Grosjean presents these two versions in sequence without explicit narratorial guidance or a viewer's sense of narratorial inconsistency, incoherence, or dishonesty. Without explicit narratorial help, the reader infers that version 2 is true and corrective of the fabrications in version 1. Part 1 is reinterpreted by Part 2, Hunston suggests, and this in turn is possible because the status of the utterances and the images in the first part of the film are in fact epistemically indeterminate (between record or mere reconstruction, and between narratorial averral and mere attribution), and these indeterminacies are partially resolved by the (epistemically determinate) words and images in the second half of the film. Hunston's epistemic categories (record vs. reconstruction; attributed vs. averred) usefully help to articulate how film-makers' tellings of events can slip between truth and fiction.

In Part IV, **Corpus-Enabled Stylistics**, essays that discuss or demonstrate the uses of corpora in stylistic studies are gathered together.

Donald Hardy introduces and advocates use of his own text-analysis program, TEXTANT, which he suggests circumvents some familiar off-putting features of high-tech analytical programs. Even beginning students can make headway with TEXTANT, while more advanced users with particular needs can be accommodated by relatively easy modifications of the program. The essay is of interest, too, as a report on just how introductory graduate-level stylistics is taught in the English department of an American university 'having no linguistics department but having a diffuse collection of linguists and linguistics students across campus'. Hardy is sensibly aware that a text-analysis program can easily become an end in itself, disastrously detached from the 'Why?' of text analysis which prompted the development of the software in the first place. He is also keenly aware that the question why one might use software in text analysis cannot receive one privileged answer, but different answers in different circumstances. And of course certain kinds of text – a short poem by Wallace Stevens, say – perhaps do not merit use of a text analysis program at all, save indirectly (where patterns, frequencies, collocations, etc. in comparator corpora are used to highlight features that are normal or exceptional in the Stevens poem). But as Hardy notes, TEXTANT (and other programs such as TACT and Wordsmith Tools) are particularly useful in searches of large swathes of text (such as all of Flannery O'Connor's fiction) in ways that are humanly difficult: e. g., searches for particular words or phrases in an entire novel's dialogue or narrative, or in the dialogue of one particular character. These are small steps, and like corpus linguistics generally, may be felt to lure the analyst into a distortingly 'wordlist' or 'literalist' view both of language and of literary creativity; at the same time such searches and results create a way of viewing text-making, and therefore of thinking about it, that was not hitherto practically possible.

Michi Shiina's essay uses a thorough classification of vocative types, as found in a corpus of early modern English comedies, to show how the rich variety of vocatives is exploited to present human networks in their dramatic worlds. (Despite the radically different discourse studied, there are affinities with Balocco's essay, as both demonstrate the variety of textual dimensions by means of which individuals' identities are textually constructed, reflected, and even negotiated.) A particular concern here is the kinds and meanings of vocatives between husbands and wives among the gentry. Shiina notes that the woman in such a relationship 'is in a contradictory space' in that the power semantics would suggest she should use a deferential vocative while the solidarity semantics might prompt use of the opposite. A frequent solution is a formulation that combines premodifiers of intimacy or endearment with a headword that attends to formality or hierarchy, as when a wife addresses her husband as *(my) dear Mr. Strictland*. Is there also some degree of accommodation on the husband-to-wife side, where he says to her *my Dear* or *poor Madam*?

Masahiro Hori's corpus-based study of the two intertwined narratives of *Bleak House* (those of Esther, and of a heterodiegetic reporter for whom all the characters are denoted by third-person pronouns: hereafter abbreviated as EN and TN respectively) uncovers a number of contrasting collocational characteristics of these two narrators' voices. To begin with, Esther's non-dialogue narrative is significantly more repetitive, while the TN is significantly lexically richer, than its partner. Unsurprising perhaps, but nevertheless reflective of Dickens' skill. A variety of noted differences at the level of collocation are also intriguing. Among oxymoronic NP collocations, for example, Hori finds that Esther's more often combine an inherently semantically positive modifier with a semantically negative or undesirable headword (e. g. *good-natured vexation* and similar, are far more frequent than *disagreeable gallantry* and similar), while in the TN that weighting is reversed, so that *awful politeness*, *wicked relief*, are more frequent than phrases such as *harmonious impeachment*. Many have felt that Esther is uncritical and self-effacing to the point of reader-infuriating banality; the case for saying she is not must be strongest where she resorts to figures such as the oxymoron. But it is striking that even here, she appears less challenging than the TN: she inclines towards charity in her judgements of circumstances, even problematic ones (the vexation was *good-natured*), while TN in similar conditions inclines towards criticism, even where the circumstances are unproblematic.

The study of text has expanded rapidly over recent decades, and during this period (as we can attest from the papers presented here) a series of new theoretical influences and paradigms have come into play. As we suggested earlier, this collection reflects the challenges we face in the age of the new digital technology and multimedia: the hypertext, the World Wide Web, the internet, and the issues related to interactivity. What we have in this collection, therefore, is a range of different approaches to the analysis of style, text, and imagetext, but all concerned with the question of how literary or non-literary creativity relates to a culture's technological affordances.

We hope that the proposals and debates which are represented within these 16 papers will be of assistance as we adjust, under pressure from our changing cultures and technologies, our ways of reading and producing text. We have to start to understand, as stylisticians and discourse analysts, how multi-modal aspects of style and text design and composition add meanings to the craft of the writer. Perhaps we should begin thinking of a *digital stylistics*.

We cannot end this introduction without making special mention of the exceptional contribution to the editing and preparation of this book made by the series editor, Donald C. Freeman. When our own time, energies, and technical resources for preparing this volume were all spent, Don took over and piloted the project to its final condition, where papers were presentationally uniform at a professional standard of camera-readiness. Without Don's enormous contribution the book would have been at best a far inferior product, if it had appeared at all. All involved in this book, and the series that it launches, are greatly in his debt; but the present editors are especially so.

Michael Toolan
Carmen Rosa Caldas-Coulthard

Birmingham, April 2005

PART I

THE WRITER'S WEB

Anti-Laokoön:
Mixed and Merged Modes of Imagetext on the Web

George L. Dillon

Abstract

The new media facilitate the handling of text, image, and sound in digitised artworks in ever more ingenious and varied ways; all such multimodal integrations run wholly counter to the former high-modernist exclusion of words from visual images. Here I discuss three of the means by which relations between text and image (and sound) are being created in contemporary Web artworks: I term these textmontage, image-text chains, and dynamic textmontage. Central to the reader/viewer's processing of hypertext is the cross-modal link. By comparison with the source-to-target inferential bridge entailed in reading written text, when the link is from word to image or vice-versa, the search domain is considerably larger and the process of 'bridging' tends to make text-parts and image-parts exchangeable. Web artworks seem to foster two receptive shifts, with the physical/visual elements tending to be apprehended as more emblematic or metaphorical, and the textual/verbal elements as more a part of design and performance, than they would do elsewhere. One of the affordances of hypertext links, then, is to weave fragments together into complex signifying structures and to make us alert to how we are constantly shifting interpretive rules and frames to make sense of our world.

Key words: imagetext; dynamic textmontage; hypertext; Flash; links.

> It was painting on canvas that was, I think, a faithful rendering of a photo with a guy leaning against a pole smack in the middle, with the word 'wrong' at the bottom. This is meta-discourse; I had never seen photographic meta-discourse before. Not only did he use a dumb photo, he made a point of it by sticking a word on it, because of course words were forbidden in photography (Rosler 1998: 38).

In an interview with Benjamin Buchloh, the photographer and multimedia artist Martha Rosler describes the powerfully liberating effect of seeing some of John Baldessari's photographic work in 1968. The *of course* reflects the power that the High Modernist ban on mixing words and images most famously articulated in Clement Greenberg's 'Towards a Newer Laokoön' (Mitchell 1994: 35, 215ff.) had over artists in the mid-20th century. Much has been written subsequently about the breakdown of this Modernist stricture of High (or museum-gallery) Art by the Conceptualists and many other artists as well. The restoration of 'imagetext' to its rightful throne has been proclaimed by W. J. T. Mitchell, and recently, Simon Morley (2003) has written a history of 20th-century art as overthrowing the segregation of word and image, confusing conventional relations between them, and culminating in the practices of the new digital media which bring into sight 'the kind of universal language of which the avant-garde once dreamed, a language based on the fusion of words and images into a sign system that one enthusiast has called "iconographics"' (Morley 2003: 203). (The enthusiast is Nicholas Negroponte.) And Morley sees yet farther that 'eventually digitalization may well do away with verbal language altogether' (204) – which is no great loss, one supposes, for an art guy.

Despite his almost ecstatic embrace of the new digital technology – of the World Wide Web, interactivity, hypertext, Photoshop, and the whole shebang – Morley says little about actual pieces of work on line or about how particular 'fusions' are accomplished. This is most surprising to one coming from the language and literature side, where fusions of disparate things are frequently described and closely analysed. I agree with Morley that the new media facilitates the handling of text, image, and sound in ways that continue and extend the overthrow of Greenbergian separation and the mixing of word and image in novel ways. In this article, I will try to spell out some of those ways, and to begin thinking about the stylistics of digital imagetexts. In particular, I will describe three tactics that move toward equivalence and fusion of text and image (and sound): what I will call textmontage, the chaining of words and images as hypertext anchors, and the rendering of text as visual event through animation (dynamic textmontage).

A terminological note: I am using the term *montage* in the sense of photomontage or compositing, rather than in the cinematic sense of the juxtaposition of one sequence to the other. The line seems clear enough, but becomes blurry when the text and frame are no longer static, but animated, as is the case with dynamic textmontage. Also, by text I mean written words; hence the montaging of text is visual. This too becomes more complicated when the visual display is accompanied by audio sequences of speech, which are verbal and text-like in engaging us in processing language rather than images, but are not visually represented and merged. To make analysis even more complicated, the audio with some of the pieces we will look at is itself an audio montage of voices, sounds, and tunes.

1. Textmontage

Among the many ways that artist-writers have begun to, or resumed mixing image and text is a particularly merged style I am calling **textmontage**. Only the most rabid and extreme Modernist would insist that text and image never occur together, that all pieces be entitled Untitled, or 'Untitled, No. what-have-you' on walls with no legends or commentary, and with no exhibit catalogue or notes. There are certain standard fixed places for words and they are basically outside the frame. Things begin to be more seriously mixed when words can get inside the frame and become part of the visual design. Then we begin to see the words as shapes in relation to other shapes and we flip back and forth between reading and seeing, often frequently and quickly. The most common device is to simply write the words over an image, where the words constitute a connected message and can be read as a text. Victor Burgin did a whole series of these in the early 1980s with white text placed in generally vacant areas of black-and-white photographs. That too is not quite what I mean by textmontage, not even if the text were to seriously overwrite parts of the image (as is quite often done in far-out graphic design). You start to have textmontage when the words are integrated into the image usually with fading or transparency and soft edges. At the extreme end, text becomes visual form and design, as in the (nonelectronic) light sculptures in the new British Library, one of which is depicted here in Figure 1. These sculptures are made of two sheets of plexiglas with inscriptions appropriate to their disciplines painted or etched on the back sides. The sheets are sandwiched together to provide an image of a transparent page with writing on both sides and are lighted on the edge so that the writing glows much as it might on a computer display. This arrangement results in reflections of the writing which appear as 'ghosts' or shadows.

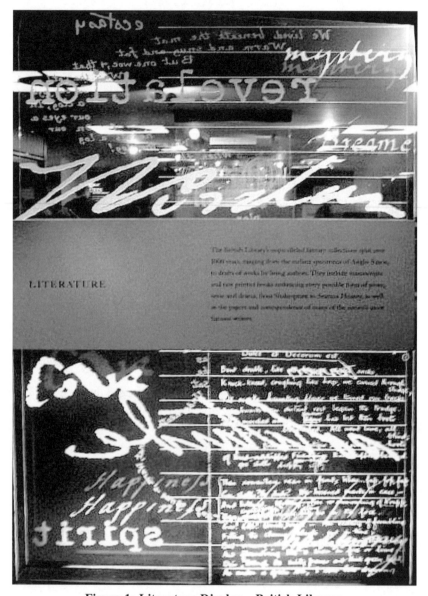

Figure 1: Literature Display – British Library

Talk about merging and integration of text and image is very nice, but it is also easy to see the relation as one of competition (as Foucault maintained in his little book on Magritte) – at least for real estate on the canvas, page, or screen, if not semiotic hegemony. In the following piece ('The Shadow') by Stef Zelynskyj, the text is viewed as through a spyglass (note changes of scale) in fragments and further fragmented by a tear that allows the landscape to show through. For me, this display rouses a ferocious urge to recover and complete the text, especially because it is almost possible to do that. The image thus sets off an alternating between viewing image and reading for text. It is not possible to do both at once: they are incompatible uses of the eyes, visual cortex, and so forth. I went to a collection of Jonson's poetry and place the text in unmutilated form beneath the image:

Figure 2: Stef Zelynskyj – 'The Shadow'

FOllow a shaddow, it still flies you;
Seeme to flye it, it will pursue:
So court a mistris, shee denyes you;

Let her alone, shee will court you.
Say, are not women truely, then,
Stil'd but the shaddowes of us men?
At morne, and even, shades are longest;
At noone, they are or short, or none:
So men at weakest, they are strongest,
But grant us perfect, they're not knowne.
Say, are not women truely, then
Stil'd but the shaddowes of us men?

Fully restored and presented front and centre, this little misogynistic
conceit, so typical of its period, seems unspeakable and not at all
funny today. The visual erosion and tattering may represent not so
much the effect of time as the loss of the cultural assumptions that
sustained it and made it clever.

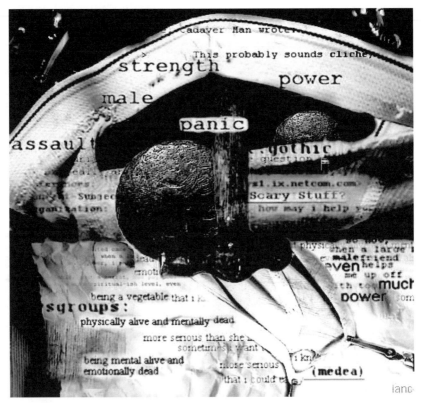

Figure 3: Ian Campbell – 'Male Cliché'

Figure 3 ('Male Cliché'), one of several digital montages by Ian Campbell, also fragments texts. In this case the texts are postings to USENET groups that were found by putting the key words 'male cliché' in a search engine. The snippets, rendered in several fonts but especially Courier-looking ones evoking text consoles, manage only phrases and simple clauses layered over the talismanic emblems of maleness (the ball peen hammers) and torn cotton briefs. Indeed, it is hard to imagine how much sustained text could fit on a screen with strong images. But what the image gives us are just fragments of gender stereotypes. Its timeliness may have passed; it is no longer exhibited on Campbell's website.

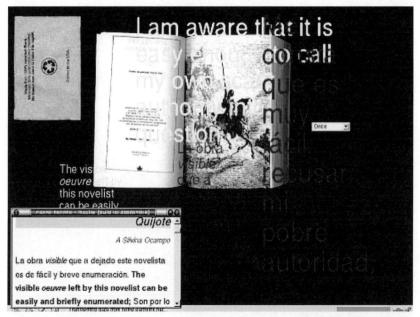

Figure 4: Eduardo Navas – Screen from 'The Quixote'

One site that manages to have a lot of text and pieces of text with images both ways is Eduardo Navas' 'The Quixote'. This edition of Borges' 'Pierre Menard, Author of the Quixote' wants to display two languages (those of translation and original) and to use sentences as panels superposed over a book image. The site divides the story into a series of such pages. On all of them, the flow of text is interrupted at the sentence, and the visual integrity of the text is reduced by making the 'pages' transparent (and the type very large). However, Navas also

George L. Dillon

presents the connected text (albeit alternating Spanish and English translation) in a pop-up window that can be positioned and scrolled and is in a sense outside the design frame (though depicted here in the lower left-hand corner of the main window – caution: this frame will be blocked by popup blockers, which are set by default to 'on' these days).

Figure 5: Geoff Broadway – 'Mirage'

Another solution to including extended stretches of text in a visual composition can be seen in Geoff Broadway's 'The Glass'. This is a series of six emblems ('totem poles', one of my students called them).

These emblems exist in .html and Flash forms, the latter providing support for a number of sound clips associated with regions of each of the six emblems. These clips are activated by mousing over the images, and there are some overlaps between regions so that occasionally two clips can be heard at once. With Figure 5 ('Mirage'), which deals with Western constructions of The Arab, are four such clips: associated with the riding horseman is the 'Lawrence of Arabia' theme song; another clip is of an Arab commenting (in English) on certain stereotypes; yet another is a clip from a newsreel reporting Israeli independence; and a fourth one is a segment of an ABC News broadcast covering the return of the American troops from Operation Desert Storm. One might hesitate to call this textmontage, since there is no text competing and blending with the images in the visual channel, but the sound and speech are still spatialised and a part of the composition by virtue of the hotspots that activate it. (The volume of the sound also appears to have a focal centre.)

As parts of these multimedia emblems, the words and images seem to resonate with allusiveness and to interanimate each other, as I. A. Richards used to say of words in poems. The visual contexts do draw out and heighten some connotations of the words, and the words do select certain aspects of the images over others. Ball peen hammers, for example, take on quite a different aspect in a metal-working shop. But these interlinked webs of association are not organised into statements and claims on the one hand, or representations of the world (or visual pattern and design) on the other. It can, however, convey a certain take on the world, a certain positioning with respect to things that may sometimes deserve to be called political or social critique, though it is often hard to state in discursive prose what that positioning is.[1]

It may be that textmontage will prove just a brief fad brought on by the new technology for compositing layers and altering their opacity, and that it will quickly come to seem jumbled both in conception and the viewing, rather than the trigger for bits of stimulating semiotic dexterity. Or, perhaps equally likely, it may be taken to convey a certain contemporary look and start turning up on posters, adverts, textbooks, and brochures, where it may only occasionally suggest the richness of connection that we associate with a good poem. But there does nonetheless seem to be much more to be explored in this vein.

2. Image-text chains and webs
Sooner or later, however, one come to the limits of what can be contained on a single page and it is necessary to employ hypertext

links to set pages in a sequence (or sequences). The image anchors of the links, which are often hot areas in the image rather than the entire image, may take you to another image, or a piece of text, and similarly with the text anchors. The effect is to make words and parts of images interchangeable as links. I offer as a first example Doll Yoko and Andi Freeman's 'Princess Zombie', a smallish site that resists the mediatising of Diana Spencer's unfortunate end. The site is made up of 14 full-screen images with hot spots (and sometimes a few words) and 10 pages of text (with underlined link anchors). The hot spots must be sought out with the mouse and we learn to find them on this site by touching facial features (among other things) such as eyes, lips, cheeks, and earrings. Indeed, eyes are everywhere on this site, sometimes composited over other things. They are thematic to be sure, but it is a little disconcerting to poke the cursor, which turns to a hand with extended finger, into the eyes of the observers and mourners. Many of the images are in fact photomontages with several layers of partially transparent images – associated impressions, of the funeral, as it were, since reduced opacity has long been linked to dematerialisation and hence to memory, dream, and apparition. Figure 6 is entirely typical:

Figure 6: Doll Yoko and Andi Freeman – Screen from 'Princess Zombie'

Within these half-seen, glimpsed, remembered scenes and impressions are one or two hotspots that trigger jumps: here the eye is one and the scrawled 'HELPLESS IN APAPTHY' is the other. In general, the visual parts of Doll Yoko's images that are hot are visually salient parts of the head, face, or hands. Also, she uses quite a number of sustained images which are often hot and lace the visual pages together almost as the hypertext cross references do. Neither images nor text are primary in 'Princess Zombie'. All are just signs linking to signs.

To browse the next site, the viewer has to be somewhat more inventive in finding and synthesising cues. '"Moles" is multi-media self-examination', Liz Miller says, calling it an autobiographical narrative, which is promising a lot for a site that opens with a black screen and seven thumbnail images which align themselves on the left to make up a table of contents. Each of these if touched fills the main window with a large version of itself partitioned into three sections. The central, slender section of each is the clickable part and activates reloading with a bit of narrative text appearing, usually over image and sometimes as a mouse-over with one of the moles.

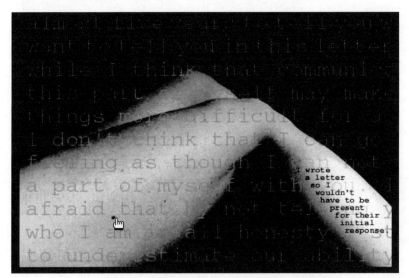

Figure 7: Liz Miller – Screen from 'Moles'

One of the seven strands has some 'refresh' auto-loading, but the general mode rewards engagements with the mouse in various ways: the effect is sometimes of sliding panels that the viewer must pull back to read the text behind them, sometimes of painting the screen with the mouse to trigger mouse-overs, and often of touching the moles with the cursor to trigger text or jump to the next screen. The bits of story are there, linked to the moles, waiting to be released.

The seven narrative segments advance a theme of growing up, leaving home, discovering attraction to women, wanting to and finally telling her parents in a letter of her lesbian identification. Figure 7 illustrates how this all works as technique and content.

The grey text-over in monospace type can be readily made out as the text of the letter she has been struggling to write. The cursor is touching a mole on her thigh and triggering the appearance of the text on the calf of the leg, which describes her having written the letter. This is text that is written upon and part of the body: experiences are recorded in the moles, the maculae; touching them causes narratives of the experiences to appear on the screen and on the body.

Figure 8: Caitlin Fisher – 'Vanessa' from 'These Waves of Girls'

A third example of the technique of textmontage is the large, prize-winning site 'These Waves of Girls' by Caitlin Fisher of York University.[2] 'These Waves of Girls' evokes the experiences inside and outside of school of the narrator Tracey, a 'bad cat' (as one teacher calls her), who experiments with other girls long before she begins to call herself lesbian.

It is highly hypertextual and densely cross-linked, and linked as well by repeated images, but since it does not tell one story but many, the hypertext does not disrupt the story-telling, though it does disrupt any master narrative of causation or development, there being on Fisher's view nothing anomalous or aberrant to explain. Indeed, cruelty and baffled desire are as much themes as kissings and touchings, but my female students inform me that this all is more or less in the realm of their experience. Most of the action described is as reassuringly ordinary: attending school, riding bicycles, going to camp, hanging out with friends, playing party games. Somehow, filtered through the interface, it is not boring or mundane but exciting and universal.

This transformation is largely the work of Fisher's visual language for memory. The images, which are a complete mix of digitally modified photographs, drawings, and manipulable flash images (such as ones with magnifying glasses, or which distort/ripple as you touch them with the cursor), number well over two hundred, and they are recycled at different sizes as well. Making the images of remembered childhood blurry, as Fisher does, follows a long standing tradition (found, for example, in Squier's piece), but in that tradition they are usually also grey (or sepia-toned), whereas Fisher punches up the saturation of the colours and rotates their palates in denaturalising ways. She also pushes some to the point of pixilation and the ghosts of excessive .jpg compression. She inverts palates and applies 'water-colour' and 'oil-painting' filters. She also crops many images so tightly that the effect is sometimes more of glimpsing than seeing. We have not the distance even to see things whole, much less to see them in perspective. Moreover, the general setup of the screen is a set of frames with a central viewing window and wide margin frames with a 'menu' style list of main topic links in the left margin frame which open in the central window. These frames also have a common or similar background images, thus providing a literal frame or context for the central window. This framing context is so strong that one may view a page and think it similar in theme and treatment to one that one has already seen when in fact it is identical to the one that one has already seen. And of course the recurrent images, in different scales and locations, also function as 'links' to the other pages where they occur. The bicycle drawing in Figure 8 is one such thread, and it is a hypertext link in an image-text chain as well. The material in 'These Waves of Girls' is presented as if remembered, or, at least, remembered by a graphic artist.

There are certainly differences of technique among the three works we have looked at, but strong common traits as well. All three net artists use images to represent memories and perceptions rather than to establish or document a public, historical world. As remembered rather than freshly seen, they come intertwined with language, also representing the remembered thoughts and events, and the triggers and paths of association crisscross the boundaries of text and image.

A hypertext link minimally suggests connection: a kind of equivalence – or continuation, development (relay), association, or perspective. But to grasp the connection, we have to bridge the source and target. This is of course true in writing as well, even when there is an explicit connective word or words used, but the connective word or link information points us in the intended direction and limits the search for possible connections. And whether the link is from word to image or vice versa, we still have to bridge them together; this bridging tends to make text-parts and image-parts exchangeable. The hot spots of hypertext anchors in text and in images are all regions on a surface, and regions which do not have any inherent bounds other than those set by the writer. Image-text links re-establish the readability of the visual world, at least in places, and the seeability of words, to which we can add the hearability of words and images: we can make literally speaking pictures. These correspondences do not extend as a code outside of the world of the particular work, but we can use various heuristics in finding them, both in the concrete sense of finding the hot spots in images and in the more abstract sense of finding a basis for a link. One such is the heuristic of touching, which I think is always simmering beneath the index-finger icon that signifies 'you are in a linked region'. When we touch someone's eyes, we expect to see; when we touch their ears, to hear, and their mouth, to speak. It is a kind of probing, releasing touch, as when we read the body through massage, probe for pain, or touch gingerly, not knowing what may pop out.[3] I don't mean that the semiotic modes themselves are fused – they are still distinct and multiple, but effect of the free and rapid movement from text to image to text to sound, etc. is to create the effect of a super-semiotic system where there is no competition and no gulf of incomprehensibility between reading, seeing, and hearing, between diagrammatic abstraction and photographic realism, maps and memoirs, news broadcasts and chronologies, theme songs and native dances. No one of these is authorial or authoritative, all must answer the question: what is **that** doing here?

3. Dynamic textmontage

Thus far, we have been thinking of text as an element in a static visual composition; one of the most attractive affordances of Macromedia Flash, however, has proved to be its easy animation of lines and blocks of text; a second attraction has been the easy syncing of sound with scripted animation, and the ability to play concurrent tracks on any platform and browser. Flash has become the online multimedia medium par excellence: in the first four issues of *Ctheory Multimedia,* for example, the great majority employ Macromedia Flash or Shockwave. The great popularity of this software can be seen also in the 'Congruence' branch of *The Cauldron and Net* and in the winners and honourable mentions of recent net.art competitions.

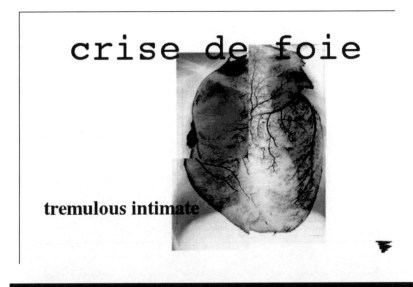

Figure 9: Miranda and Neumark – Screen from 'Machine Organs'

Issue 2 of *Ctheory Multimedia* contains Maria Miranda and Norie Neumark's 'Machine Organs' where words and phrases write over the images of computer-organs accompanied by distinctly 'bioform' sounds and a montage of voices, whispers, and noises – lest, as it were, that we in our rush to virtual life in virtual space forget 'the meat'. Figure 9 is a screen capture of one moment in the animation of the 'Heart Pump Machine' – this pseudo-organ combines the heart and liver to figure the computer as constantly working and as the seat of emotions. There are three other 'organs': digestion (the computer as 'hungry for information'), breath, and x-ray vision. The work is thus a visual-textual-aural metaphor identifying the computer's vital processes in terms of 'our own'. One might say that technically we have gone beyond 'textmontage' in this case since we have added another medium: sound clips of voices saying the words that over-write the image are not 'text', which is verbal-visual, any more, but verbal-auditory, and this verbal-auditory is accompanied by gurgles, burps, sighs, gasps, pops, and sucking. These sounds are not synced to the words or images – that is to say they are an independent channel, as it were – but I am not sure that sounds can share the stage on an equal footing with words and images because there is a very long tradition of treating sounds as background and supportive rather than bearing a primary theme (opera and other vocal music excepted). The effect of the sounds here, however, is very much to merge, associate, and evoke proximity to animate things; this effect is strongly enhanced by the sounds and voices themselves overlaying each other in a sound montage.

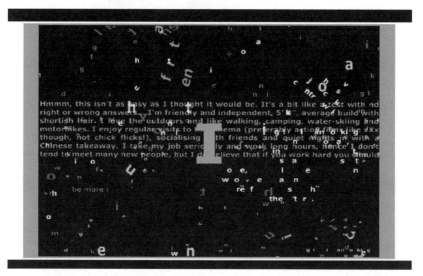

Figure 10: Jess Loseby – Screen from 'Textual Tango'

My second example of this new mélange of media is Jess Loseby's 'Textual Tango' (snapshot in Figure 10), which repaints the screen over and over with two texts of personal ads and lines from others. One speaker is represented in red, one in green, but as the flow of text continues, other texts enter, disintegrate, and drift or fade away, only to be replaced with others asserting the desire to 'find someone'. This cascade mounts to two climaxes of speed and abundance synced to a voice (Sting?) singing 'Roxanne', a song originally written by Sting and performed by him and The Police, but featured recently in the film *Moulin Rouge* with Ewan McGregor and Nicole Kidman. The singer is a man who loves a prostitute and is promising her she need not go into the street any more – a stern if not perhaps entirely excessive comment on 'the discourse of personal ads'.

In Figure 10, we see a moment approaching the climax of the piece, where letters and words and phrases from other disintegrated personal adverts float about like autumn leaves in the wind. One of the two basic adverts is visible, but over it is being written the words of deep demand, one word at a time. Here the words and letters both float and appear with dominating insistence (large and red) in centre screen; in other moments, the lines fly in from off-frame, giving screens like Figure 11.

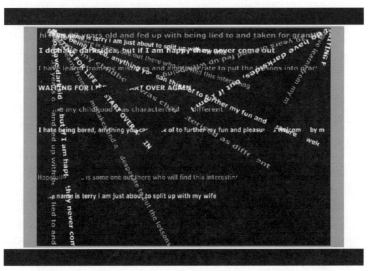

Figure 11: Jess Loseby – Screen from 'Textual Tango'

Here again it might be argued that we do not have text being montaged into a visual space, for they are the only visual elements in a black space and they do not hold a stable position. We approach visual poetry ('vizpo', Poems That Move), though the site is a critique of the discourse of personal adverts, the words are all citational (or parodic), and the rhythms of the piece are of their appearance, movement, and disappearance.

Although 'Textual Tango' uses a very restricted palette and no image, it does engross the eye with rhythmic movement. Even more austere is the style of Young-hae Chang Heavy Industries (Marc Voge and Young-hae Chang) which scrolls very large text (most often white against black) very rapidly (like a reading tachistoscope) and closely synced to a piece of classic jazz, not only by beat but by emotional contours as well. YHCHI 'do voices' and evoke scenarios with an élan that matches Joyce's, parodying the epic narrator in Ezra Pound's first two Cantos, bar girls and businessmen, a subway attendant in Seoul who taught Derrida the key of deconstruction, and Kim-il Sung. In recent work, YHCHI have begun using songs, the words of which frequently offer oblique or ironic contrasts to the lines of text scrolling up the screen. For example, the Kim-il Sung piece ('Cunnilingus in North Korea') delivers a message from the Dear Leader to South Koreans (and presumably *tout le monde* since it is in English) extolling the superiority of North Korean sexual experience over that available under capitalism (itself a wonderfully daft parody of hard ideological sell) while the audio track has Nina Simone singing 'C-line Woman', a blues song celebrating a sexually powerful woman ('wiggle, wiggle, turn like a cat, / wink at a man and he wink back'). The technique has points of similarity with 'Textual Tango', but YHCHI's 'remixes' have a special tendency toward cross-cultural montage, as if the multiple coordinated modes of Flash afford opportunities for displaying and celebrating fluency in numerous quite disparate cultural idioms – the artistic response, YHCHI might say, to globalisation. Fortunately, when viewing these works, one is already on the Web, and typing into Google a line or two from an unfamiliar song (such as, to me, 'C-line Woman', 'Ramona', or 'Arirang') will tap the collective online wisdom of the globe, which on such points is considerable.[4]

4. Conclusion

Combining a very rapid scrolling tempo with multiple channels and with culturally unfamiliar material pushes our capacities to process what we see/hear to the extreme (and Flash cannot be paused or rewound, only replayed). To read it at all requires one's utmost, focused, and sustained attention – well, sustained for three to five minutes at least, which on the Web, that most distracting of places, is a very long time. Clearly the contemporary Web enlarges the possibilities for mixing text and image far beyond what Greenberg might have imagined: dynamic textmontage represents the point of furthest distance from the classical single-channel Modernist painting presented in a museum – say the Rothko room – for absorption and serene contemplation. Walter Benjamin realised that Dada – and even more, cinema – challenged this ideal image of 'the aesthetic' in favour of one that re-enacted the shocks of modern city life under conditions of distraction (1966: §§14 and 15). Paradoxically, however, these Flash works reward the concentration of some of their viewers with an almost rapturous absorption. Others report migraine headaches.

I do not mean to suggest that these last pieces are the fullest realisation of multimodal Web writing. They mark one extreme, and while they may elicit concentration in their viewers, they are not strong as objects of contemplation. Shockwave and Flash sites are scripted and will run with little or no viewer input, casting the viewer back in the role of spectator. But this software only affords 'bombardment mode'; it does not force it on the artist, and it is also possible to make sites where the viewer chooses the pace and direction of movement: Broadway's set of six emblems is done in Director and Miller's 'Moles' in Flash, and these intend a reflective engagement with the viewer.

If we ask what engages the mind and eye in the pages and sites discussed here and makes them more than text-with-illustration, we can extract one or two traits: in these pages, the physical and visual tend to move in the direction of emblem and metaphor rather than providing anchors to a literal, concrete world, and the textual and verbal shift from being pieces of speech acts to elements of design and performance – each, one might say, by attraction to the other. These disparate media and semiotic modes are yoked together with montage, hypertext, or Flash into multimodal conceits which suggest the perfect equivalence that Dr. Donne says we glimpsed in the person of Elizabeth Drury:

> We understood
> Her by her sight; her pure and eloquent blood
> Spoke in her cheeks, and so distinctly wrought
> That one might almost say her body thought.

Endnotes

[1] I am commenting here on Broadway's M.Phil. thesis, which defends the claim that the mode of 'The Glass' is realism.

[2] 'These Waves of Girls' won the Electronic Literature Award in 2001 (with a purse of $10,000).

[3] Caitlin Fisher's 'These Waves of Girls' uses Java-like applets in Flash to make the cursor-finger trouble reflections and palp a woman's breast.

[4] Another brief piece in this vein is Thomas Swiss's (and Skye Giordano's) 'Genius'.

References

Benjamin, Walter. [1936] 1966. 'The Work of Art in the Age of Mechanical Reproduction' in Arendt, Hannah (ed.) *Illuminations*. New York: Schocken: 217-51.

Foucault, Michel. [1973] 1983. *This is Not a Pipe* (tr. James Harkness). Berkeley: University of California Press.

Mitchell, W. J. T. 1994. *Picture Theory*. Chicago: University of Chicago Press.

Morley, Simon. 2003. *Writing on the Wall: Word and Image in Modern Art*. Berkeley: University of California Press.

Rosler, Martha. 1998. *Positions in the Life World* (ed. Catherine de Zegher). Cambridge, MA: The MIT Press.

URLs for pages discussed

Note: The illustrations are greyscale reproductions of screen captures. The reader is urged to consult the original versions online.

Broadway, Geoff. 'The Glass'. http://www.intentional.co.uk/glass/index.htm.

Campbell, Ian. 'Male Cliché'. http://courses.washington.edu/hypertxt/cgi-bin/book/wordsinimages/ianc_male.jpg.

Doll, Yoko, and Andi Freeman. 'Princess Zombie'. http://dollyoko.thing.net//zombie/.

Fisher, Caitlin. 'These Waves of Girls'. http://www.yorku.ca/caitlin/waves/.

Loseby, Jess. 'Textual Tango'. http://www.rssgallery.com/textualtango.htm.

Miller, Liz. 'Moles'. http://helios.hampshire.edu/~elmIA/moles/.

Miranda, Maria, and Norie Newmark. 'Machine Organs'. http://ctheory.library. cornell.edu/art/11/.

Navas, Eduardo. 'Q Story'. http://home.earthlink.net/~navasse/Qstory/once.html.

Swiss, Thomas, and Skye Giordano. 'Genius'. *Drunken Boat*, 2. http://www. drunkenboat.com/db2/s-g/s-g.html.

Young Hae Chang Heavy Industries. 'Cunnilingus in North Korea'. http://www. yhchang.com/CUNNILINGUS_IN_NORTH_KOREA.html.

Zelynskyj, Stef. 'The Shadow'. http://courses.washington.edu/hypertxt/cgi-bin/book/wordsinimages/szelynsky.jpg.

Personal Web Pages and the Semiotic Construction of Academic Identities

Carmen Rosa Caldas-Coulthard

Abstract

In 2002, The University of Birmingham started to standardise staff Web pages. For the institutionalised world of universities, the creativity of the personal should be in principle rejected since the corporate image has to take precedence over the individual. However, what is happening in the virtual world is that the domain of the private, even among members of institutions, is taking over, and personal Web pages, created by individuals from all walks of life, present to the world discourses of the self. New forms of virtual identities are therefore created daily.

In this chapter, I examine the effect of culture and gender on the discursive strategies used by Web page writers to present themselves in terms of:

1. the narrativisation of their lives – what kinds of life events are given prominence;
2. the multimodal choices – what kinds of pictures, colours, spaces, scenarios help to create a particular character.

I also discuss the implications of this kind of one-sided interaction for discourse analysis – the Web page addresser sends a message not to an implied audience but to anybody out there in the world who happens to open her or his page. The strategies used to address an unspecified audience are a question that we need to pursue in the new virtual world of the Internet.

My interest here is in looking specifically at how participants in this new genre recontextualise, in the public sphere, a fictionalised representation of themselves. Through what seems to be a light and inconsequential 'message in a bottle' to the world, social activity is presented, evaluated and possibly new norms of behaviour are being created.

Key words: discourse; narrative; multimodality; virtual identities.

1. Introduction

Visual communication is central to the information society and to the practices of Late Modernity. Pictures, photos, illustrations are everywhere – they permeate our academic work, everyday lives, and activities. It is common nowadays to refer to brand images, corporate images, national images, and self-images. These are interwoven with our professional and personal identities, and they are signposts to lifestyles, cultures, and societies.

In his seminal book *Ways of Seeing*, John Berger (1972: 7) points out that:

> Seeing comes before words – the child looks and recognizes before it can speak. But there is also another sense in which seeing comes before words. It is seeing which established our place in the surrounding world. We explain that world with words, but words can never undo the fact that we are surrounded by it. The relation between what we see and what we know is never settled. The way we see things is affected by what we know or what we believe.
>
> To look is an act of choice.

Scollon & Scollon (2003b) suggest that humanity has undergone at least four 'ages' in its development: the *oral*, the *literate*, the *imagistic,* and currently, the *information* age. For them, oral societies were constructed through oral narratives; literate societies, through the standardisation of genres and documentation (essays, plans, forms, scripts, charts, tables, etc.); while the still-current imagistic society constructs itself through the moving picture – the camera, the analogue and the digital video. The information society, by contrast, is constructed through the digital pathway that makes its meaning through the combination of many semiotic resources. We take this for granted. Meaning-making is dependent on the interplay of different resources, and these surround us in our everyday life. New technologies, especially the Internet and the World Wide Web, are pushing forward, almost daily, new communication strategies and people interact through these new resources.

According to NUA (a resource for Internet statistics run by *INQUIRA,* NUA internet surveys – http://www/nua.com/surveys), an exact estimation of how many people are online throughout the world is not possible. However, they say, there are many surveys that use different measurement parameters and from observing many of the published surveys over the last two years, they claim that up to September 2002, approximately 605.6 million people had online access worldwide.

Just one year later, Global Reach (Global Internet Statistics by Language – www.glreach.com) gives us the following results:

**Online Language Populations Total: 649 Million
(March 2003)**

Language	Percentage
Dutch	1.9
Russian	2.7
Portuguese	2.8
French	3.3
Italian	3.6
Korean	4.2
German	6.5
Spanish	8.1
Japanese	10.3
Chinese	11.9
English	35.2

The sheer numbers of people using virtual communication and the affordances of the new media are producing a visual revolution, in which everything from the structure of books to the layout of pages, distribution of images such as photographs, illustrations or digital backgrounds, and the use of typography and colour are brought to bear on conveying specific meanings. Representation, modality and multimodality therefore enter into the very constitution of things since an object's or idea's meaning is shaped by the very process of representing it by way of language or images or other semiotic resources.

Representation for Hall (1997: 61) is the process by which members of a culture use signs to produce meaning – 'things, objects, people or events do not have in themselves any fixed, final or true meaning. It is us, in society, who makes things mean, who signify'.

Representation, as a cultural process, establishes individual and collective identities, and symbolic systems provide possible answers to the questions: who am I? what could I be? who do I want to be? (Woodward 1997: 14).

Modality is the concept used by communication specialists to talk about different modes or codes of communication – speaking, writing, using images, gestures, sounds, colour, drawings, etc. to communicate a specific message.

Multimodality (Kress & van Leeuwen 2001: 20), the concept used by semioticians and discourse analysts, on the other hand, is 'the use of several semiotic modes in the design of a semiotic product or event'. Modes are resources for making meaning. The same meaning, in any cultural domain, can be expressed in different semiotic modes – (music can encode action, images can encode emotion). We would miss out important aspects of a film without considering the role of music in the ongoing narrative, for example, or of a magazine without interpreting its pictures and illustrations. Therefore, for Kress and van Leeuwen, the particular ways that modes are combined (they may, for instance, reinforce or complement each other) will determined the ways we receive and interpret a message. The authors claim that all semiotic products and events are communicative since they undergo processes of articulation, interpretation, and ultimately, use and action.

An important point to make is that *all messages are multimodal* since all messages make use of multiple modes. Web pages are archetypal examples of multimodal messages. Web authors use many semiotic resources in their pages to communicate their identities – the language used, the photos, the colours,[1] the objects chosen and displayed, all signify symbolically different aspects of their identities.

Multimodal analysis therefore is crucial for understanding and interpreting the world. Our tendency so far as linguists, however, has been to privilege written and spoken texts above all other modes, and to consider objects, actions, and people as simply making up 'the environment in which the text comes to life', as Halliday (1978: 25) suggests.

The internet and the World Wide Web have changed our views dramatically. As Kress & van Leeuwen (2001) have pointed out, the desire for crossing boundaries inspired 20th-century semioticians to develop new theoretical frameworks that are applicable to all semiotic modes.

In this chapter, therefore, I will examine academics' personal Web pages in order to consider the multimodal discursive strategies used by Web page creators to present themselves in terms of:

1. the narrativisation of their lives;

2. the multimodal choices that help to create a particular identity.

I will also want to point out the implications of this kind of one-sided interaction for discourse analysis – the Web-page addresser sends a message not to an implied audience but to anybody out there in the world who happens to open her or his page. The strategies used to address an unspecified audience are a question that we need to pursue in the new virtual world of the Web.

My interest here is in looking specifically at how participants in this new genre recontextualise (Bernstein 1981), in the public sphere, a fictionalised representation of themselves. Through what seems to be a light and inconsequential 'message in a bottle' to the world, social activity is presented, evaluated, and possibly new norms of behaviour are being created.

2. Personal Web pages – the personal in the public sphere – real or fictional story telling?

On a day of internet surfing, I came across a page, http://www.cs.bham.ac.uk/~axs/#who, by one of the members of the University of Birmingham staff, a computational scientist named Aaron. At first sight, this was an academic page, giving the internet surfer information about the professor's career, his publications, courses given, etc. However, there was a link to family issues, which I pursued. This hyperlink seduced me in many ways, especially for the force of the narration. For many minutes, I followed attentively the story being told. This was the 'real', not fictional, story of a young man who died of cancer, Ben, retold by his father, the professor. I saw Ben's wedding photos, then the events of his illness, and finally, the events surrounding his death at 34 years of age.

Many different semiotic resources were posted on this Web page – photos of different occasions of the family life, a map of the cemetery where Ben was buried, the speech delivered by his young wife during his funeral, a poem read by a friend, etc. I was very touched by the telling, so much so that I wrote to Aaron, who then wrote back to me and sent my message to Ben's wife, who then wrote back to me. There has never been any face-to-face interaction with the participants of this virtual exchange. This experience prompted me to look more closely at the question of personalisation of the public space of the

University. My data for this paper are therefore restricted to academic Web pages, especially those of the University of Birmingham – pages of teaching staff, postgraduate students, and some technicians.

Academic pages should be in principle public statements, but as Aaron's page demonstrates, academics tend to use the public site to include their private sphere in this kind of communication. Hence, my interest in investigating more the question of how the personal intrudes in the public world of academia and the multimodal resources used by 'webbers' to achieve their goals. (According to a new report from www.nua.com - Internet Surveys by Category, by January 2000, 19 million U. S. internet users, or 29 percent of the total number of users, have personalised Web pages, and 88 percent of users believe that personalisation is the best way for companies to learn about consumers.)

The University of Birmingham index of individual Web pages linked to departments listed, in April 2002, a total of 425 of which only 23 belonged to female academics. This seems surprising since I would expect that many more women were actively involved in communicating virtually. Unfortunately, this is not the case. Not surprisingly, scientists, especially engineers, produce the majority of pages. The arts academics tend to be much more parsimonious in their production.

Before I start examining some examples of Web pages, I want to consider briefly the question of computer mediation as communication and the question of recontextualisation.

3. Computer mediation as communication, narration, and the construction of identities

Over the past ten years, as Rodney Jones (2002) has pointed out, many areas of investigation, especially in sociology, anthropology, linguistics, cultural and communication studies became interested in Computer-Mediated Communication (CMC). The internet and the World Wide Web are producing new forms of interaction, both in the business and personal spheres as well as new forms of social organisation. New discursive practices have therefore been developed. Jones points out that different professionals like linguists and communication scholars concentrate on linguistic features (registers and genres), sociologists and anthropologists are interested in the development of online 'communities and cultures', while psychologists focus on the cognitive aspects of computer-mediated communication. Jones continues (2002: 3) that although there are many perspectives on CMC,

> the kinds of data that are gathered to answer these varied questions are remarkably limited. Nearly all of the studies look for answers to their questions in the words typed on the screen. Data typically take the form of downloaded 'logs' of computer chat sessions or corpora of emails or Usenet postings, and analysis is generally confined to those words. Interactions are assumed to exist in a kind of virtual vacuum, identities are hardly ever linked to the lives of the people producing the words, and communities and cultures are generally seen to stop at the screen's edge.

The main problem with looking at computer-mediated communication in this way, he suggests, is that it ignores the importance of online behaviour as well as the importance of semiotic meanings.

Another problem with such studies, Jones (2002: 3) suggests, is that they tend to focus on the *mediational means* (Scollon 1998) 'at the expense of looking at the kinds of actions that are taken, leading them into a kind of technological determinism in which actions are interpreted only as "effects" of the media'. For mediational discourse analysts (Wertsch 1991; Scollon 1998, 2001; Scollon & Scollon 2003a, 2003b), the main focus of interest is on the complex and indirect connections between discourse and action – they propose the notion that social identities and practices are not only realised in texts since what goes on in social interaction is much more complex:

> A *mediated action* is defined as a social action taken with or through a mediational means (a cultural tool). All social actions are construed as mediated actions, it being definitional that 'social' *means* socially mediated. The principal mediational means (or cultural tool) of interest is language or discourse, but the concept includes all objects in the material world including other social actors. Within MDA [Mediated Discourse Analysis] there is no action (agency) without some mediational means (i.e., the semiotic/material means of communicating the action) and there is no mediational means without a social actor (agency). (Scollon & Scollon 2003b: http://www.
> gutenbergdump.net, valid in April 2002[2])

If action is ignored in CMC then, researchers are examining culture *in the cultural tools* (Wertsch 1991) instead of examining culture through its relationships with action, agents, and tools.

The problem with the concentration purely on 'mediational means', as Jones (2002) demonstrates very well in his research on Chinese learners of English using *ICQ,* a chat and instant messaging software, is that often what is sought by users of *ICQ* and other interfaces of this type is not 'communication' at all, but rather 'connectivity', 'social presence', or 'play'. My computer conversations with Aaron exemplify this point. We were connected somehow.

In order to overcome these limitations, I want to propose, based on Jones' research, another way of approaching my Web pages, one which focuses not just on the texts people produce when they are sitting in front of their screens, but on the multimodal resources used to construct identities which the new media now make possible. These identities are inevitably connected to the world outside the computer screen.

By representing themselves in particular ways, a narrator 'gives off', to use Goffman's terms (1959), personal clues about the social role performances he or she is making and this representation indexes these invisible psychological or social cultural states.

Of this vast brave new world, I will concentrate on the question of how identities are presented through multimodal aspects. These are the questions:

- Are my webbers constructed as 'characters' or 'idealisations' differing from the actual person behind the keyboard? (For example, the 2003 case of an American GI who, pretending to be 19 years old, engaged through a chat room with a supposed 19-year-old English girl – he was 30 years old and she was 12 years old. He was then prosecuted for a criminal offence.)
- Alternatively, are they 'hybrid extensions' of their offline identities?

For the most part, I want to claim, online identities are not purely reflections of offline identities or complete reconstructions, but recontextualisations, convenient hybrids of both processes whose uses often have as much to do with what is happening in the offline social life of users as their online social life.

3.1. Webbers' identities and the question of recontextualisation
The discourse of personal Web pages is a discourse about social practices which takes place outside the context of that practice and

within the context of another one – the virtual context. The process of including one social practice into another is a *recontextualisation*, or

> ...a sequence of communicative activities which make the social practices explicit to a greater or lesser degree. Social practices are things that people do, with greater or lesser degree of freedom, fixed by custom or prescription, or some mixture of these two. (van Leeuwen 1993: 30)

Texts and images are representations of given practices, not the practices themselves. As soon as one writes or speaks about any social practice, one is already recontextualising. The moment we recontextualise, we are transforming and creating other practices.

Web pages are recontextualisations that not only represent social practices, they also have to explain and legitimate – in other words, they have to make explicit the 'why' of their representations.

In the corporate world of today's universities, there is a pressure on academics to communicate values, to advertise and 'sell' themselves. They have to recontextualise their self-identities in order to do this.

Giddens (1991) says that in postmodern societies self-identity becomes a reflexive project – an effort that we constantly work and reflect on. We produce and revise a set of biographical stories – the telling of who we are, and how we came to be where we are now.

> Self-identity, then, is not a set of traits or observable characteristics. It is a person's own reflexive understanding of their biography. Self-identity has continuity – that is, it cannot easily be completely changed at will – but that continuity is only a product of the person's reflexive beliefs about their own biography. (Giddens 1991: 53)

> A person's identity is not to be found in behaviour, nor – important though this is – in the reactions of others, but in the capacity *to keep a particular narrative going*. The individual's biography, if she is to maintain regular interaction with others in the day-to-day world, cannot be wholly fictive. It must continually integrate events which occur in the external world, and sort them into the ongoing 'story' about the self. (Giddens 1991: 54)

For Giddens, then, the self is not something we are born with and it is not fixed. The self is reflexively made, constructed by the individual (Gauntlett 2002):

> What to do, how to act, whom to be?

> These are focal questions for everyone living in circumstances of late modernity – the ones which on some level or another, all of us answer, either discursively or through day-to-day social behaviour. (Giddens 1991:70)

However, as Lemke (http://www-personal.umich.edu/~jaylemke) points out, identity construction is also a verbal and non-verbal performance (of attitudes, beliefs, and values). People participate in activities through interactions and practices, and this participation, he argues,

> constitutes and shapes a) identity choice, b) identity display, and c) identity construction. Identity is thus a positioning of self or other in a system of meaning-relations and in a network of material practices, including a system of power relations..., and discourse in general serves to construct identity and positioning with respect to this system of meanings.

What webbers do when they create their personal pages is to choose a set of self-characteristics that are important for them (life moments and achievements, relations, places and moments) and construe a persona. From the multitude of identities that academic users have available to them, I will discuss next two main kinds of identity formation in virtual recontextualisations: narrators and characters.

3.2. Narrators as extensions of self and as characters

For the psychologist Kohut (1971), according to Barry O'Connor (in www.selfpsychology.com), a sense of 'self' is

> a fundamental aspect of our life experience, and integrated with the totality of our life. It not only encompasses who and what 'I am', at critical stages of our growth, but in addition it is the totality of the inner workings of our true-self. One could say, that within the development experience of the human, which I would argue lasts our entire lives. There are certain 'way points' that need to be arrived at in terms of realizing 'self-potential'. Significant others are an essential aspect of our self development.

> This of course commences at the very earliest stages of our existence with the critical relationship with our mother, and with this the influence of our father on both mother and ourselves. This is further complicated in the modern environment with the diminishment of the nuclear family, and the re-designation of what comprises a family, with or without societal support.

The principal description of the 'self', in my data, follows the pure and minimal forms of identity representation:

- I exist.
- Here I am.
- My name is so and so.
- I come from such a place.
- This is my family.

- These are my things.
- These are my interests.

Consider these examples (given the space constraints, I will illustrate with only a few pages):

Welcome to the

Who Am I?

I am just a normal (?) British bloke who happens to be called Rob Branston, but I have nothing to do with the famous Branston Pickle. Now I have that sorted out and just on the off chance that the odd person is continuing to have a look, I will tell the rest of you a bit more about me. I am a 24-year-old Economist, researching for a PhD in Industrial Economics at the University of Birmingham in the UK. I am approximately 6 feet 4¼ inches tall (195cm to my metric orientated friends), have short brown hair and green/hazel coloured eyes. If you really want you can see some pictures of me, but I warn you that I am not at my finest!!

At the moment I am looking for a job, so I have been spending a great deal of my spare time working on a page containing an academic orientated CV and information about PhD. I have also made a more 'city' orientated CV as I am not sure what my future direction will be. If you like what you read, why not send me an email? I have also been spending a lot of time updating, expanding and enhancing the suite of pages I created for *L'institute* – Institute for Industrial Development Policy and the **pages** for *L'institute* – Ferrara Graduate School in Industrial Economics. As my friend Don Fazio says, I've got some work to do now, so we'll continue this chat a bit later ....

Webpage 1

How is Rob Branston construing his 'self'? The answer to the question 'Who am I' in this case, is linked, interdiscursively, with material goods of a given society – you need to be at least Anglo-Saxon, to recognise the illustration (Branston pickle) and understand the semiotic value and pun of the naming approximation. Rob Branston then becomes

> just a **normal British** bloke who happens to be called Branston.

The representation of the pickle bottle is crucial for determining not only the self-identity (normal) but also the national one (British).

Some other examples from the data reaffirm **place of origin** as an important aspect of their identities. The webbers are 'outsiders' and need to assert their foreignness:

> I am a **Venezuelan** plant biologist.
>
> I **hail** from a **serene** town Kovilpatti the 'matchless town of matches' in Tamil Nadu.

Naming is a very important form of identification and webbers tend to make sure their names are foregrounded, like these examples:

> According to the Keirsey Temperament Sorter I've got a ENTP (Extraverted iNtuitive Thinking Perceiving) personality type – this means I'm an Inventor – who am I to argue?
>
> **I've an unusual surname - <u>Pryke</u>** and so I've set up a web page listing other <u>Prykes</u> on the net.
>
> **My name is Alberto** and I'm Italian. I'm an Aerospace Engineer and for the time being I'm working as Research Associate at the School of Electronic and Electrical Engineering of the University of Birmingham. If you are interested in knowing something more about me (for professional reasons only please, I'm the happy husband of a wonderful young lady...) you can download my Curriculum Vitae...
>
> One thing that **I would like to make clear is my surname**, is it Cirre or Cirre-Torres? Well, in Spain we use 2 surnames, the 1st is the surname of your father and the 2nd of your mother. When I came here, I wrote my 2 surnames linked by a hyphen, so my 1st surname is Cirre and the 2nd is Torres.

For some webbers the use of the language of 'affect' (Martin 2000) is a strategy used to identify their selves:

> I started writing this page during one lonely, homesick September night, between a Volterra integro-differential equation and a multi-domain boundary element approximation. Warmed only by a strong Italian coffee, with Elton John filling the dark of my room, I was dreaming my dreams of far planets and unknown realms, the depth of the ocean, the mystical power of ancient oriental traditions.
>
> This page is nothing but the pale shadow of my thoughts of that night, but if even only one among you will find in it a reason to look further into the sky and into himself, then this is one of the most important things I could ever do.

This kind of representation, in fact, reaffirms stereotypical constructions of Latin people – emotional, perhaps 'out of control' – the warm 'Italian coffee, the homesickness, the darkness of the room' construe the identity of the lonely student in a cold and foreign place.

Others identify themselves through humour generally using self-deprecation:

> Welcome to Derek's Home Page. I'm Derek Carter, and at present I'm a third year PhD student studying in the Department of Electronics and Electrical Engineering at The University of Birmingham. **Yes I'm yet another of those boring engineers**, and yes I do spend most of my time in front of computer terminals. My field of research is parallel heterogeneous computer architectures, sounds very impressive doesn't it!

This negative appraisal (Martin 2000) is legitimised through a cartoonesque representation of self:

Webpage 2

Kohut (1971) refers to *self-object experiences*, experiences (usually with other people) that nourish the self and which define the experience of the self and self-esteem. Significant others, like family relations, are an essential aspect of our self-development. That is why so many family relations are presented in Web pages – the self of the webber is being represented through self-objects that reinforce her or his own performances.

Photographs showing the webber within the family context are therefore extremely common in my examples. Marriage photos or simple stills of family groups recontextualise the webber as not only a member of a group but also as *belonging* to a group. Not only parents, siblings, partners, but even pets are introduced as parts of the self, as the example below shows:

INFORMATION YOU REALLY WANTED TO KNOW ABOUT ME!!

This is us on our BIG Day!!

Hi! My name is Cathy Lowe, and up until 24th June 1995, I was known as Cathy Smart. I am 28 Years Old and married to Tony. We live in Birmingham and have done so for the last 5 years, well I say we, Tony has lived in Birmingham all his life, I moved all the way from Solihull (for my sins) in 1992. I am a very lazy individual, much to my husband's dismay, but I occasionally get off my backside to go Swimming and the odd Step Aerobics Class. I enjoy pottering around in the garden, especially since we had our Garden Pond re-built. I also enjoy reading, once I'm into a good book I'm oblivious to everything around me, even my husband!! We are both also Dog Lovers and up until a two years ago we had a BEAUTIFUL Alsatian called RADAR, unfortunately we had to have him put to sleep as he was very ill, he was only 8 years old.

Here he is

Webpage 3

Physical appearance and embodiment seem to be one of the other ways webbers recontextualise themselves – all my examples present either a photo or an illustration of 'self', especially of the 'face'. Laurie, below, shows us a sort of 'passport photo' of himself, but he self-evaluates his own appearance when he says, revealingly, at the end of the page: 'By the way, I have had a haircut'.

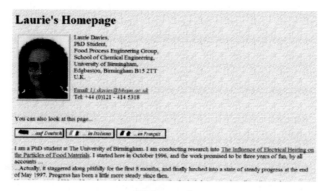

Webpage 4

What makes the 'self' a supposedly 'real self' in such situations is not necessarily contingent on the realm of 'facts' or 'personal information', but rather on the opportunities for users to create the 'real selves' they thought they 'should be' or 'could be', anchored in the semiotic representations chosen, either verbal or non-verbal.

What is interesting about participants' conception of their 'online' selves is that the complexity and multiplicity of these selves are seen as features that actually make them 'more real' rather than 'less real'. Computer-mediated interaction for these participants, because of the choices made, seems to be something which did not fragment their sense of their 'real selves', but expanded it.

We have to see then, as Jones suggests, cyberspace, not as the site of 'cyber society' (Jones 2002), but regard it more as what Scollon (1998) calls a *site of engagement*, a 'field' upon which multiple actions, identities, and communities can be enacted.

The second identity type of construction I want to concentrate on is character.

3.3. Character

Many of the concepts developed in narrative theory are not specific to language. I want to point out here that the way narrators construct characters (and consequently their life stories) is by the choice of how they recontextualise themselves, in particular spaces, in particular settings (like in a literary text). The spaces are created through the representation of locations and objects. The dimension of the 'activity' being engaged in (what participants are doing when recontextualised) is also very important – some characters are recontextualised as moving in spaces, others as static and in particular positions.

By using especially the multimodal resource of photographs, narrators construct through their choices of how to present themselves, a particular version of the self, creating scenarios, spaces, and attributes. The visual landscape is part of this characterisation. By interpreting the way the narrators construe themselves via image, we recreate a narrative of their lives – what they do, where they do it, who they position themselves as in the social practices around them.

Photos are memorable – they represent a neat slice of time, not a flow. Susan Sontag (1999) suggests that photos furnish evidence, a more accurate relation to visible reality than other mimetic objects. Coleman (1998: 57) adds that

> Photographs however do not show how things look. What a photograph shows us is how a particular thing or person could be seen or could be made to look at a specific moment in a specific context, by a specific photographer employing specific tools.

Photos are the most plausible and straightforward representations of identity – part of our identity is an awareness of ourselves, as we would want others to see us. The very artificiality of the pose (smiling or not, looking at the camera or not) demonstrates the gap between the way we are and the way we would like to appear as Barthes (2000) suggests in his *Camera Lucida*. Certainly, the smiling face is an attempt not only to produce a positive evaluation from gazers, but also to interact with them.

However, albeit being faithful to the way we 'look', we have to remember that, as Kress & van Leeuwen (2001) point out, in some domains certain visuals are 'truer' than others. The authors call this the *coding orientation* and this has to do with modality. Modality, here, in the linguistic and semiotic sense, as Scollon & Scollon (2003b, www.gutenbergdump.net) explain, is the word that

> linguists and logicians use to talk about alternate realities. 'Irrealis' (not real) contrasts with 'realis' (real). *Ought* contrasts with *is, was, will be*. *Realis* is something 'real', 'definite', 'perceived by the person speaking'. *Irrealis* is 'imagined', 'unreal', 'indefinite', 'unknown' or 'unknowable'. The linguistic and logical point of the distinction between realis and irrealis is that there *is no external truth or reality* that is being referenced. It is the mode of representation which is telling us what the producer of the language or image wants us to believe.

Images can make the same distinctions in modality. They can represent a person, a thing, or a space according to a scale of 'it might look like this' to 'it looks like this'. This is done through choices of colour, hue, distance, focus, and vectors. However, a photograph tends to make us believe that what we see is *the reality* in this sense. Visual resources tend to be more 'realis' orientated than texts, which are more easily 'irrealis' orientated, as Scollon & Scollon suggest (2003b, www.gutenbergdump.net).

My argument here, when examining the photos used by webbers, is that in fact, although these photos purport to be 'realis' representations of self, what authors do is to construct, through choices in modality, a 'characterisation' of the self in terms of the ways their identities are being displayed. The interesting point about the photographs below is that although these Web owners are academics and the photos are placed in academic Web pages, the visual/virtual landscapes chosen in a sense construe specific characters and the discourses that surround them – the discourse of action, the discourse of adventure. The modalities chosen, especially colour (in the original pages, blues, reds, greens), produce 'irrealis' effects. What we have here are therefore projections of ideal selves: the sportsman, the association with a particular musician, are facets of hybrid 'private' identities that also happen to be public (and academic). The examples below illustrate these points:

 **Me, on my way to work!**

Webpage 5

<u>Mark Erickson's</u> Grateful Dead Page

Mark's Tape Trade List

Webpage 6

4. Recontextualisation of interaction

I want briefly to look now at recontextualisations of verbal interactions.

According to Jones (2002), the vast majority of people who engage in computer-mediated communication regard it as an extension (McLuhan 1994) of their 'real-life' social interactions rather than as separate from them. Therefore, Jones concludes, the effects of CMC are to 'ground them more firmly within their existing material communities and circumstances' (Jones 2002: 5). Several of the participants in his research, in fact, were quite adamant in rejecting the traditional dichotomy of 'actual' and 'virtual' reality, insisting that computer-mediated communication is as 'real' as anything else is ('as real as a telephone call').

Contrary to my initial belief that Web page messages were sent to unknown addressees, Web narrators in fact try to facilitate the exchange of information among colleagues and peers and the sense of social 'connectivity'. Narrators are therefore agents acting upon the world – they send messages to particular (not well-defined) people, hoping to influence them in some way or other.

When asked about the recipients of their Web pages, one of the writers I contacted replied:

> I don't have a clear idea, but I would include, in no significant order: colleagues in the school, research students and undergraduates in the school; colleagues in other universities around the world; potential collaborators in many places, several types, in several disciplines; potential research students, people who may be able to learn something from my research or contribute to it by commenting or criticising; journalists who contact me to find out about artificial intelligence or cognitive science; school teachers; school leavers exploring the school's web site and wanting to know what's here; people around the university interested in management issues; people who have heard me give presentations and would like to see the slides (usually extended versions); people who may be interested in a book I wrote in 1978, which went out of print and is now free of charge online....

This is the testimony of another webber:

> At first there was no audience, actually, but one has appeared for many of the things there...[T]he idea was to make a brief visual essay using photos we had to organize our own reflections about our pasts and see if that would help us find connections...I have told a few students about them (the different pages) as I try to introduce myself as broadly as possible to them thinking there's no

way they could understand the academic slices of my life w/o knowing
something of the rest. But I don't like to ramble on in a seminar about how I
wrangled horses as a teenager, so if it's on the net I just say, 'go take a look'
and get on with the subject. So I guess you could say that much of it, maybe
most of it is this: I make little essays, highly personal, about things I or we
think about or have done, put them on the net so our own kids and family and
a few friends can see them.

…what's on my websites is the stuff that isn't in my formal academic vita but
which is essential to understand what's in the vita.

Incidentally, these pages are now found by search engines and visited by who
knows who. I average about 60,000 visits a year.

This shows that the message is addressed to targets, and not virtual
beings, out there in cyberspace. An interesting aspect of these
interactions however, is their spoken conversational features. Most of
the pages examined here have greetings, openings, closings,
apologies, and the address to a 'you'. Consider for example:

- Hi, I am (name)…. How are you my friends all over the
  world?
- Hello.
- Welcome!
- Hi, thanks for visiting this page!
- Want to know more about me? Well, then…come and browse
  through then….
- Hi, have you found something?
- Welcome everybody. I'm sorry it's taken such a long time, but
  here at last are the beginnings of my web page, with pictures
  showing highlights of the Big Day.
- Thank you for stumbling upon my humble website. I hope you
  find something of interest while you're here.
- Do not forget to come back. See you next time.
- Hope you're happy. Be nice to animals. And although this site
  hasn't got much, you never know.
- That's all, folks.

In Late Modernity, the need to communicate/talk (although through
virtual media) continues to be part of people's lives, even if people are
stuck in their houses in front of their computers. This is not very

different from old times, when people use to visit each other and chat on verandas, at least in warm countries like my own.

One of the opening messages of Paul McIlvenny's page (http://ntpaul.sprog.auc.dk) summarises extremely well the interdependency between the interactants in this virtual communication:

You browse, therefore I am.

Through pseudo-interactions webbers seem to continue traditions of diary or biography genres where people tell 'whoever is out there' about their personal experiences, their relationships. The informal aspect seems to diminish the distance between writer and reader – you are there, I do not know who you are. But somehow, like me and Aaron, *you browse and I exist*. That is why, I think, there are so many 'hi, hellos, goodbyes', opening and closings in virtual interactions. The material page is the mediational means for social action.

5. Final remarks

The University of Birmingham has now managed to standardise Web pages to make them compatible with the corporate image of the University. A corporate team produced a set of guidelines so that webbers should maintain the same institutional 'image'. The photos should look the same, nothing that is 'personal' should be inserted into the pages. This is the discourse of the institution trying once again to standardise, paradoxically, presentations that have to do with people's lives and identities. By doing this, the institution tries once more to exert control over its members.

However, from the examples discussed above, it seems that new creative formats resist corporate discourses. Self-presentation has to do with what we are, whom we deal with, and the choices we make in life. People, as Lemke (2002) suggests, choose the ways they want to display themselves and construct their identities. Identity construction is a complex phenomenon and people project in public spaces, idealisations of what they 'think' they are. The multitude of formats, photographs, and colour choice point to the hybrid formation of identity. The online construction is an extension of the offline persona. And institutions cannot control these representations. There will always be a way out of the institutionalised corporate 'image'.

To conclude, I want to emphasise the importance of the study of multimodality in the new communicative genres. Web pages combine language, image, and graphics into a single integrated text's structure. They are therefore:

- **interdiscursive**: 'positioned within multiple, overlapping and even conflicting discourses' (Scollon & Scollon 2003b, www.gutenbergdump.net) – the discourses of the family, the institution, and emotion;
- **intertextual**: they have links with other mass media, especially with classical and modern narratives of all sorts – books, films, comic strips, paintings, among others;
- **dialogical**: a means through which different kinds of 'conversations' can be established.

Web pages are also *sites of engagement*. In some ways, as Deborah Tannen (2002, cited in Jones 2002: 9) points out, 'Asking linguists to pay less attention to texts is like asking astronomers to stop looking up so much'. It is, however, only through breaking down the traditional hierarchical separation of different modes of representation and focusing more onto the *social actions, social identities,* and *social practices* that we will achieve a true understanding of the society we live in – and virtuality is here to stay. In the virtual world we live in, there is no more looking back.

Endnotes

[1]All the Web pages used in this chapter were in colour. Unfortunately, the illustrations in this book can only be reproduced in black and white.

[2]One of the essential features of Web pages is their ephemerality. The authors alter and delete items and even whole pages, as you will find if you attempt to follow this reference, Scollon & Scollon (2003b, www.gutenbergdump.net). This page no longer exists.

References

Barthes, Roland. 2000. 'Camera Lucida: Reflections on Photography' in Thomas (2000): 54-62.
Berger, John. 1972. *Ways of Seeing*. London: BBC and Penguin Books.
Bernstein, Basil. 1981. 'Codes, Modalities and the Process of Cultural Reproductions: A Model' in *Language and Society* 10: 327-63.
Caldas-Coulthard, Carmen Rosa. 2002. 'Cross-cultural Representation of "Otherness" in Media Discourse' in Weiss & Wodak (2002): 272-296.

Caldas-Coulthard, Carmen Rosa, and Theo van Leeuwen. 2001. 'Baby's First Toys and the Discursive Construction of Childhood' in Wodak, Ruth (ed.) *Critical Discourse Analysis in Post Modern Societies*. Special issue of *Folia Linguistica* 35(1-2): 157-182.

___. 2002. 'Stunning, Shimmering, Iridescent: Toys as the Representation of Gendered Social Actors' in Litosseleti, Lia, and Jane Sunderland (eds) *Gender Identity and Discourse Analysis*. Amsterdam: John Benjamins: 91-110.

Caldas-Coulthard, Carmen Rosa, and Malcolm Coulthard (eds). 1996. *Texts and Practices: Readings in Critical Discourse Analysis*. London: Routledge.

Coleman, Allan D. 1998. *Depth of Field: Essays on Photography, Mass Media and Lens Culture*. Albuquerque: University of New Mexico Press.

Evans, Jessica, and Stuart Hall (eds). 1999. *Visual Culture: The Reader*. London: Sage.

Gauntlett, David. 2002. *Media, Gender and Identity: An Introduction*. London: Routledge. Extracts available at www.theory.org.uk.

Giddens, Anthony. 1991. *Modernity and Self-Identity*. Cambridge: Polity Press.

Goffman, Erving. 1959. *The Presentation of the Self in Everyday Life*. New York; Doubleday.

Hall, Stuart (ed.). 1997. *Representation: Cultural Representations and Signifying Practices*. London: Sage and The Open University.

Halliday, M. A. K. 1978. *Language as Social Semiotic*. London: Arnold.

Jones, Rodney H. 2001. 'Beyond the Screen – A Participatory Study of Computer Mediated Communication among Hong Kong Youth'. Paper presented at the annual meeting of the American Anthropological Association (Nov. 28-Dec. 2, 2001).

___. 2002. 'The Problem of Context in Computer Mediated Communication'. Paper presented at the Georgetown Roundtable on Language and Linguistics (Georgetown University, March 7-9, 2002).

Kohut, Heinz. 1959. 'Introspection, Empathy and Psychoanalysis: An Examination of the Relationship Between Modes of Observation and Theory' in *Journal of the American Psychoanalytic Association* 7: 459-83.

___. 1971. *The Analysis of the Self*. New York: International Universities Press.

Kress, Gunther, and Theo van Leeuwen. 1996. *Reading Images: The Grammar of Visual Design*. London: Routledge.

___. 2001. *Multimodal Discourse: The Modes and Media of Contemporary Communication*. London: Arnold.

Lemke, Jay L. 2002. http://academic.brooklyn.cuny.edu/education/jlemke/papers/polcart.htm.

___. 2003. 'Texts and Discourses in the Technologies of Social Organization' in Weiss & Wodak (2002): 130-49.

Martin, James. 2000. 'Beyond Exchange: Appraisal Systems in English' in Hunston, Susan, and Geoff Thompson (eds) *Evaluation in Text*. Oxford: Oxford University Press: 142-75.

McLuhan, Marshall. 1994. *Understanding Media: The Extensions of Man.* Cambridge, MA: The MIT Press.

Scollon, Ron. 1998. *Mediated Discourse as Social Interaction: A Study of News Discourse.* London: Longman.

__. 2001. *Mediated Discourse: The Nexus of Practice.* London: Routledge.

Scollon, Ron, and Suzie Wong Scollon. 2003a. *Discourses in Place: Language in the Material World.* London: Routledge.

__. 2003b. *Globalization: The Multimodal Shaping of Public Discourse.* http://www.gutenbergdump.net.

Sontag, Susan. 1999. 'The Image-World' in Evans & Hall (1999): 80-94.

__. 2000. 'In Plato's Cave' in Thomas (2000): 40-53.

Tannen, Deborah. 2002. Personal conversation with Rodney Jones. March 9.

Thomas, Julia (ed.). 2000. *Reading Images.* Basingstoke: Palgrave.

van Leeuwen, Theo. 1993. 'Recontextualisation of Social Practice'. Unpublished manuscript.

Weiss, Gilbert, and Ruth Wodak (eds). 2002. *Critical Discourse Analysis: Theory and Interdisciplinarity.* Basingstoke: Palgrave.

Wertsch, James V. 1991. *Voices of the Mind: A Sociocultural Approach to Mediated Action.* Cambridge, MA: Harvard University Press.

Woodward, Kathryn. 1997. 'Identity and Difference' in Woodward, Kathryn (ed.) *Culture, Media and Identities.* London: Sage: 10-22.

Hypertext, Prosthetics, and the Netocracy: Posthumanism and Jeanette Wintersons *The PowerBook*

Ulf Cronquist

Abstract

Our technological age is posthumanist. As far as identity and self may go, we can now look in the rear-view mirror for essentialist notions of sex and social constructions of gender. In our time there emerges a new being: the Netocrat. In posthumanism we are beyond (ir)rational differences: we are all cyborgs, for better or worse, part for whole. The final barrier against posthumanism and cybernetics, where resistance is futile, is the notion that biological life must be protected from technology. In this paper, against this background, I analyse Jeanette Winterson's Internet novel *The PowerBook*, particularly its ideology of freedom in cyberspace. The multi-voiced narrator offers the reader 'freedom for just one night'. But what is this freedom *of* or *from*? Or *inside*? The implication that the body of a biological entity or social construction can escape temporarily into a posthumanist world is interesting, but calls for some examination as regards layered hypertextuality, extensive prosthetics, and a positional Netocracy. I therefore examine Winterson's text through current theoretical works by N. Kathleen Hayles, Donna Haraway, Mark Poster, Caren Kaplan, among others. Winterson's narrator is the author of her own polyphonic body; s/he is not born a machine, s/he is in the process of becoming one; s/he is not born a cyborg but in the process of becoming a posthumanist Netocrat. I investigate here what affordances and constraints define this design.

Key words: posthumanism; hypertext; prosthetics; gender/cyborg; Netizen/Netocracy.

Jeanette Winterson's *The PowerBook* is an 'Internet novel', a product of our technological age that is currently being defined, where the multivoiced narrator repeatedly offers the reader '*Freedom for just one night*' (Winterson 2001: 3). S/he says: this 'is an invented world. You can be free for just one night' (Winterson 2001: 4). You can relax, undress, take off *your body,* and start a new story about your self in the 'long lines of laptop DNA' (Winterson 2001: 4). This temporary escape offered initially is relative to the past: somewhere in the 60s we began taking off our clothes but we did not yet take off our bodies; we began creating new stories in our minds, not yet using laptop DNA but perhaps other mind-expanding substances like the vinyl of 'Lucy in the Sky with Diamonds'. Thus, some steps ahead, we are now being prompted to undress and separate our body from our mind to escape virtually, leave the flesh and its clumsy biology somewhere else – to become digitally forwarded subjectivities.

But is the escape – even if it is just for one night – really an escape from the body? Does freedom in cyberspace afford the 'absence' of the body? How do we really consider information and technology in relation to a virtually vanishing materiality – when at the same time our branded laptops are being assembled by grossly underpaid workers in Asian sweatshops (cf. Robbins 2002)? What happens in language and literature when the humanist subject is no longer being written on the body, when we are already cyborgs?

I investigate here what happens to ourselves as cyborgs, and similarly bodily posthumanist aspects in Jeanette Winterson's *The PowerBook*. First, I comment on the construction of *hypertext* and how we understand it in relation to previous fragmented literary forms. Second, I consider – with references to Michel Foucault's anti-humanism (e.g. Foucault 1970) and Judith Butler's theory of queer performativity (Butler 1990, 2000) – how the Cartesian subject became deconstructed in a process that foreshadows today's liminal posthuman subject. Thus I analyse posthumanism and its *prosthetics* in relation to postmodernism, poststructuralism, and deconstruction. Third, I look into the problematic concepts of *Netocracy* and *Netizen* in our webbed era of globalisation – what it means that the information age is built on exclusive and expensive platforms that deny access to many individuals. I then finish with a section (reconnecting to the Cartesian subject) on what the Information Age has been doing with the cognitive (post)/human body.

1. Text and hypertext

What really constitutes a hypertext is not yet decided. But the term 'hypertext' describes highlighted text on a computer screen that we click on with a computer mouse in order to reveal another chunk of text, another link on our laptop screen; or, we associate it with any kind of fragmented text that urges us to make links to other and yet other fragments, like recurring metaphors or motifs, in a material paper-book reading process. Thus the whole of the Web is of course one big indefinite hypertext, prefigured by our typical Modernist or Postmodernist experimental, fragmented texts that offer never-ending readings (like Joyce's *Finnegans Wake,* or Pynchon's *Gravity's Rainbow*), where we find interrelated events and parallel worlds side by side in an unbounded continuum. There is a dividing line, however, between poststructural theories of the 'floating signifier', which are relatively dated in assuming that text is always *printed* – although we could say that theorists like Barthes, Deleuze and Derrida foreshadow the electronic hypertext, a media-specific analysis will reveal details of how the electronic hypertext takes shape. N. Katherine Hayles offers fascinating insights into this subject in her article 'Flickering Connectivities' (Hayles 2000). She begins by stressing that Vannevar Bush, generally credited with having invented the term 'hypertext', is not talking about hypertext as electronic but as mechanical (Bush 1945).[1] Hayles makes an outline for a general definition where hypertext is characterised by possible multiple ways of reading, some kind of linking mechanism, and the relation of textual chunks. Since a dictionary, for example, offers a multitude of readings with linking mechanisms and chunks of text, it can be classified as a hypertext.

Hayles, who calls for a medium-specific analysis, outlines the characteristics of electronic hypertexts especially with reference to the notion of the cyborg, cognitive environments, analogous sameness, and digital coding. One of the overriding aspects she discusses is the difference between the flatness of the printed text and the depth of the electronic text that operates in three dimensions. There is an inevitably dynamic action involved when using a computer screen – and the time aspect: it takes less time to click with your mouse, compared to looking up a footnote at the end of a book or leafing through a dictionary. Jay Bolter (1991) claims that hypertext makes many of the difficult, abstract, postmodern, deconstructive ideas (cf. e. g. Barthes, Derrida, Deleuze) an everyday experience. Thus, our understanding of the relations between printed fragmentary text and electronic hypertext is a key issue.

As Hayles points out, some texts today, for example Don DeLillo's *Underworld* (1997), imitate electronic hypertexts (Hayles 2000). At a first glance, this is also exactly what Winterson's *The PowerBook* does. In the table of contents that initially addresses the reader's eyes, there are computer key-words like OPEN HARD DRIVE, NEW DOCUMENT, VIEW AS ICON, EMPTY TRASH, and QUIT, SAVE. On the inside of the cover there is a picture of a Macintosh PowerBook laptop with the key sentence 'Freedom just for one night' coming towards the reader on the screen. On the back inside there is the same laptop screen saying: 'You can change the story. You are the story.' The paratextual effect is somewhat banal since freedom and storytelling are, of course, not dependent on virtual space technology.

Also if one begins to read the novel expecting to find new and innovative writing that utilises or problematises electronic hypertext one might be disappointed. The chapters read like chapters in any Modernist or Postmodernist fragmented text. It is only *the frame* of narration that asserts that the characters in the novel live in an electronic age. *The PowerBook* turns out to be a printed text that mimes hypertext – the novel never radically questions its ontological status as a printed text that *mimetically* represents reality.

2. Prosthetics and the body

As regards the humanist and posthumanist subject, the line of thought to follow is from the Cartesian *cogito* to 20th-century theorisation: postmodernist images of the self; poststructuralist displacement; feminist questioning of the biological subject (sex/gender); queer theory that destabilises any notion of some kind of ahistorical matrix for the subject. And today: cyberpunk in its modal subjectivities, our limbs extending into digital space.

Put in another way: we have now yielded to the universal relativity of cultural constructions – we accept that we speak from moveable pragmatic platforms where we all are constructivists (constructing our bodies). In *Simians, Cyborgs and Women* (1991), Donna Haraway makes us focus our attention again and again on the category of 'Nature' being non-existent outside language and history. Similarly, Judith Butler's queer/gender theories make clear that rather than getting stuck with the opposition sex/gender, we should be aware that there is no ahistorical platform that produces gender and identity: on the contrary, anything or *anybody* is possible through the constructedness of non-referential performativity. And posthumanly put, before Butler, Foucault prophesied that 'man would be erased, like a face drawn in sand at the edge of the sea' (Foucault 1970: 387).

But at the same time as poststructural deconstructive thought urges us to put the biological body into parenthesis, there is of course also a struggle going on *for* our bodies, especially so among the hard sciences and scientists. Prozac is designed to keep us happy and productive; Viagra is produced to keep us happy and procreative. The final frontier when it comes to our bodies has to do with hard computer science, of course: how we will connect our virtual bodies in cyberspace. Today our post-poststructural identities can literally, virtually, float in relatively uncontrolled chains of signification, and each individual example of mankind can now become, very palpably, that space which is not space, a part of the text and hypertext that is non-referential text or hypertext. There is nothing except text, hypertext, hypertext, text, except nothing is there. But is this really for everybody's body?

Stone writes about how she fell in love with her prosthesis (Stone 1995). In *The PowerBook,* Winterson does not extend her body in any such innovative way. The love story in the novel, like a soft-core Hollywood movie, has two endings, one happy and one tragic. Her metaphor for the fragmented stories that might or might not reach a reader is the familiar one of a message in a bottle (Winterson 2001: 83). Sex is freedom is Utopia which can 'never happen beyond bed' (Winterson 2001: 175). Death and love, love and death: it is the same quest for the Holy Grail. And we even find it: 'Lancelot fails...because he can't distinguish between love's symbol and what it represents' (Winterson 2001: 188). We find Winterson turning lead into gold: the Holy Signifier turning into signified Grail.

3. Netocracy and its Netizens
If we are the new knights of the round table we also need to consider the concept of the Netizen, and the possible future of a Netocracy. There is an on-going public discussion as regards the electronic age and the Internet: what it is doing to people, also the power of people – and for some: possibilities of empowerment. This problematic area concerns the general question what it means that certain people get more space and freedom through digital communication while others, in some places in the world, will not even make one phone call during their lifetimes. Mobile citizenship is for those who can afford it. That is, although radical forums exist on the Internet, and radical groups and individuals can benefit from fast electronic communications, to

organise resistance against global capitalism – there may be much more at stake. As Manuel Castells points out, political democracy in nation-states is threatened not only by globalisation of economic activities – but movements of resistance are also organised and growing into powerful (and difficult-to-control) networks (Castells 1997). The oppositional forces both undermine our 20th-century sense of political democracy from their different positions: as technologically determined forces clash there is a fundamental crisis for us all as to how we can perceive our 'world citizenships' and if we can all become Netizens.

As poststructuralism and queer/gender theory take us beyond the moment of the (Cartesian) humanist subject, so the present process of technological posthumanism takes us beyond the very idea of the rights of man. As Mark Poster stresses: 'New democratizing principles must take into account the cultural construction of the human-machine interface...we may build new political structures outside the nation-state only in collaboration with machines' (Poster 2002: 99). Some individuals see this developing area of prosthetics as quite unproblematic, as if the basic point were that we have now left not only sexual but also economic repression behind: here is our very liberated brand new world with a very liberated social class: the Netocracy. Bard and Söderqvist claim that after capitalism comes Netocracy, consisting of people with great talents for the manipulation of media, people who will control the new economy and the governments – at the expense of those who lack skills in using the latest technology (Bard & Söderqvist 2002). This is a challenging vision in many ways of what comes after capitalism. Will global networking in the future (that is already here) only consist of a rich, technologically skilful part of the world's population?

In *The PowerBook* there is really no dimension that historicises man's usage of machines; there is a lack of materiality in the critical sense. At worst 'freedom for just one night' is an imaginary and regressively ahistorical trip to Capri, a romantic island where a romantic couple can develop their romantic relationship. 'The air is like a kiss' (Winterson 2001: 93) as the narrator lies on the bed in a hotel room with her laptop. The narrator looks at the computer and wonders what changes the world – what world? Which world? Whose? Her answer is an ideal virtual reality: 'It used to be that the real and the invented were parallel lives that never met. Then we discovered that space is curved, and in curved space parallel lines always meet' (Winterson 2001: 94).

Space. And space again, in Winterson's (virtual) reality.

But where is the body?

4. If information wipes out the body?

We are now in an age where we move from the familiar trope of the modernist bourgeois traveler through postmodern displacement to the mobility of the interactive posthuman. But who is paying the price for this – and where are we then, floating a-topically in cyberspace? Are we out-of-the-body-experiencing this era of globalisation? Caren Kaplan, who has investigated postmodern and posthuman questions of travel (Kaplan 1996), now asks the question, how can we 'theorize the locatedness of travel in an era of globalization?' (Kaplan 2002: 34) In the here and now of displacement of corporeality, she points out:

> Cyberspace may appear to be the ultimate vacation from the Puritan work ethic and from grounded industries of liberal modernity, but a closer look reveals location and materiality in the mobility and disembodied discursive practices of new information technologies. (Kaplan 2002: 34)

In other wor(l)ds, we have to consider if information can lose its real virtual body. Can there be *jouissance* in cyberspace – without embodiment? Generally the answer must be no.

Donna Haraway warns us of the limitless possibilities for the subject in the new technologies and claims that there is a risk of 'unregulated gluttony; all perspective gives way to infinitely mobile vision' (Haraway 1991: 189). Haraway calls for a reconfigured socialist feminist praxis of limited location and situated knowledge, even 'when the other is our own machine' (Haraway 1991: 189-90). Similarly, Hayles (1999: 5) is concerned with the discourse of glib techno-ecstasy and sees into the future of a dialectic embodiment:

> If my nightmare is a culture inhabited by posthumans who regard their bodies as fashion accessories rather than the ground of being, my dream is a version of the posthuman that embraces the possibilities of information technologies without being seduced by fantasies of unlimited power and disembodied immortality, that recognizes and celebrates finitude as a condition of human being, and that understands human life is embedded in a material world of great complexity, one on which we depend for our continued survival.

There is also always already a harsh materiality that prefigures our electronic age of affluent economic digitality. Globalisation hurts, as we know. The underpaid workers who assemble high-tech electronic equipment suffer – their bodies are real and they are far from the sublime trading of binary signs that is now building a New Empire. The whole world now turning digits on the stock market and the value of production is even more incommensurably separated from material corporeality than before – this may be the exact meaning of the term globalisation. To quote Julian Stallabrass: 'clean, mobile cyberspace forms can never show the material suffering behind a row of financial figures, for this has been stripped away a long time ago in the very collection of data' (Stallabrass 1995: 9).

We are now like Mary Shelley's scientist. Have we yet to see the monster?

We are now like Plato with a laptop: our displaced images are transforming into pure forms. Is this the end of the thing itself? Or is it the beginning of a New Republic?

But, to quote Kaplan, '[s]imply stating distaste for a life as a bundle of data is not very effective' (Kaplan 2002: 37). New media offers possibilities for the construction of new planetary political subjects, i.e. netizens who will be multiple, dispersed, and virtual (Poster 2002: 103; cf. Lévy 1997).

However, Winterson's novel is always already *branded*: it is a PowerBook by Macintosh. Sold, advertised, produced: a daydream nation logo (cf. Klein 1999). The browser she uses for her PowerBook is Netscape. This is indeed monstrous.

And maybe this is Utopia. Winterson says:

> QUIT.
> REALLY QUIT?
> RESTART.
> SAVE/DELETE FILE.
> Or
> QUIT-DELETE

the-information-body-that-lost-its-body. As Hayles (1999) underlines repeatedly: human consciousness is not disembodied, human consciousness cannot be downloaded into the empty shell of a computer. In that sense, Winterson's Utopia denies access to the body and therefore her novel denies access to freedom – even if it is *just for one night*. Thus, freedom in cyberspace does not afford absence of body.

Endnotes

[1]Vannevar Bush is credited with having first described 'hypertext' in 1945, but based on microfilm. It was, however, Ted Nelson who coined the term, in a paper he presented at a national conference of the Association for Computing Machinery in 1965. See www.xanadu.net and http://ted.hyperland.com/.

References

Bard, Alexander and Jan Söderqvist. 2002. *Netocracy: The New Power Elite and Life after Capitalism*. London: Reuters.

Bolter, Jay. 1991. *Writing Space: The Computer, Hypertext, and the History of Writing*. Hillsdale, NJ: Lawrence Erlbaum Associates.

Bush, Vannevar. 1945. 'As We May Think' in *The Atlantic Monthly* 176:101-08.

Butler, Judith. 1990. *Gender Trouble*. New York: Taylor & Francis.

___. 2000. *Antigone's Claim*. New York: Columbia University Press.

Castells, Manuel. 1997. *The Power of Identity*. Oxford: Blackwell.

Foucault, Michel. 1970. *The Order of Things*. London: Tavistock.

Haraway, Donna. 1991. *Simians, Cyborgs and Women: The Reinvention of Nature*. New York: Routledge.

Hayles, N. Katherine. 1999. *How We Became Posthumans: Virtual Bodies in Cybernetics, Literature and Informatics*. Chicago: University of Chicago Press.

___. 2000. 'Flickering Connectivities in Shelley Jackson's Patchwork Girl: The Importance of Media-Specific Analysis'. Online at: http://jefferson.village. virginia.edu/pmc.contents.all.html. (consulted 22.02.2002).

Kaplan, Caren. 1996. *Questions of Travel: Postmodern Poetics of Displacement*. Durham, NC: Duke University Press.

___. 2002 'Transporting the Subject: Technologies of Mobility and Location in an Era of Globalization' in *PMLA* 117(1): 32-41.

Klein, Naomi. 1999. *No Logo: Taking Aim at the Brand Bullies*. New York: Picador.

Lévy, Pierre. 1997. *Collective Intelligence*. New York: Plenum.

Poster, Mark. 2002. 'Digital Networks and Citizenship' in *PMLA* 117(1): 98-109.

Robbins, Bruce. 2002. 'The Sweatshop Sublime' in *PMLA* 117(1): 84-97.

Stallabrass, Julian. 1995. 'Empowering Technology: The Exploration of Cyberspace' in *New Left Review* 211: 3-32.

Stone, Allucquere Rosanne. 1995. *The War of Desire and Technology at the Close of the Mechanical Age*. Cambridge, MA: The MIT Press.

Winterson, Jeanette. 2001. *The PowerBook*. London: Vintage.

http//ted.hyperland.com/ (consulted 22.02.2002).

www.xanadu.net (consulted 22.02.2002).

The Influence of Hypertext on Genre: Exploring Online Book Reviews

Rosario Caballero

Abstract

The aim of this paper is twofold. On the one hand, it aims to shed light on the influence of electronic technology and media (World Wide Web and hypertext) on a particular genre, through the analysis of a small corpus of 80 book reviews taken from online sources. Attention is focused on the use made by an established genre of hypertext technology and its implications for the evolution and diversification of this particular type of discourse activity. On the other hand, this analysis draws attention to the problems involved in regarding the book review as a recognisable genre rather than a group of writing practices that might be regarded as genres in their own right. The use of hypertext technology highlights divergences already existing in these practices and propels them into new life. A particularly revealing aspect in this regard is the system of links used by the online reviews in the corpus, which are discussed in relation to two central parameters of genre – audience and communicative purpose – and are found to play a similarly significant rhetorical goal in hyperdiscourse interaction.

Key words: hypertext; electronic genre(s); link rhetoric; genre variation and evolution.

1. Introduction

Computer Mediated Communication (henceforth, CMC) and its prototypical hypertextual artifacts have deserved the attention of scholars from different fields of research due to their quantitative and qualitative impact on discourse interaction. Computers and electronic webs have opened up access to information and communication by breaking out spatial and temporal constraints, to the extent that they are often praised as having 'democratized, distributed, and interlinked knowledge, teaching, learning, and expertise on a massive scale' (Sussex & White 1996: 202). At the same time, our traditional concept of text is being superseded by *hypertext*, a flexible, non-linear, and intrinsically intertextual artifact made up by internally linked chunks of information of various sorts which are, at the same time, externally linked to other similar chunks. As a result, texts are becoming the virtual rather than physical supports for a hybrid mixture of language, images, and sound. In short, the new technologies are affecting the ways knowledge may be both constructed and transmitted, and are leading to a redefinition of literacy, which now involves handling different semiotic codes as well as having some kind of technical expertise.

These questions have deserved the attention of genre scholars, who have explored the impact of CMC and the virtual contexts in which it takes place on what they call *cybergenres*, that is, genres emerging first as a replication of already existing ones but evolving along newly created parameters (Crowston & Williams 1997; Shepherd & Watters 1998). This is the case of well-established genres such as personal and business letters which have given way to the less formal e-mail, of personal narratives now turned into Web pages, and of the discursive event known as e-chat.

As also happens with conventional genres, the rationale of cybergenres rests upon several factors, among which rhetorical purpose and intended audience are particularly determining. Indeed, the impact of technology on these – and, hence, on the final result – appears to be more salient in virtual contexts than in conventional, written ones. When analysing cybertexts we must not only bear in mind the purposes inherent to their generic affiliation, but also the broader-in-scope goal(s) of the Web or virtual context where these appear. Thus, although their acknowledged aim is to provide easy and quick access to a vast amount of information in an organised way, many websites and pages must also meet a number of commercial demands which often impinge upon the textual artifacts posted in them (consider, for instance, the large amount of advertising in most texts in the electronic webs available). The concept of audience or discourse community – now *virtual community* – has also changed: it has broadened in scope and, as a result, the boundaries delimiting one audience from another have become blurred. In fact, any computer user or cybernaut may potentially become a member of the different audiences at which cybertexts are targeted within the macro 'hypercommunity' favoured by the Net. A third factor affecting cybergenres concerns technical and implementation issues, that is, the different linking options in hypertextual artifacts.

A frequently discussed question – inextricably linked to those outlined above – concerns the technology's promise of an egalitarian share of the new communication space, and the resulting emergence of a true democratic cyber-community free from gender, power, race, or political barriers. However, this remains largely an idealistic picture. On the one hand, although access to information may be theoretically free, its technical dependency makes it available for users within the Western world rather than those from less technically developed societies. At the same time, the different webs in cyberspace are not only becoming more institutionally and commercially driven, but make use of a technological jargon which may also work as an excluding rather than including factor for many new users.

This paper brings in all these issues, framing them in the description of the electronic version of such a recognisable genre and text type as the book review. Attention is focused on the use made by the genre of hypertext technology, and the implications of this use for the evolution and diversification of this particular type of discourse activity. The following questions make up the backbone of the discussion:

  • Does the application of hypertext technology illustrate generic factors such as goal(s), intertextual relations with other texts, audience construction; or, rather, does hypertext involve a rationale of its own?
  • Do topological changes affect our (formal and/or content) knowledge of genre? In other words, how does hypertext enable participation in the genre?

The paper is organised as follows: after a brief reflection on theoretical and methodological questions, I provide an analysis of the links in 80 book reviews from different online publications in order to see which generic factors are most susceptible to being affected by the new medium and technology. This is followed by a discussion of the implications of hypertext for the genre under exploration.

2. Theoretical and methodological preliminaries

The starting assumption in the present discussion is that genre – in any of its versions, electronic or otherwise – is a social and semiotic construct instantiated by standardised communicative acts that result from the interaction of writers and readers in given contexts through recognisable textual artifacts. This definition pivots on three essential traits of genre. The first trait concerns its cognitive dimension, since it is our knowledge of genres that enables us to recognise and participate in them. Second, genres are self-generating in the sense that by interacting with others through a given genre we are actually *enacting* it according to a set of prototypical guidelines learnt from use. Finally, as Berkenkotter & Huckin (1995: 24) point out, 'to be fully effective [...] genres must be flexible and dynamic, capable of modification according to the rhetorical exigencies of the situation'.

The intrinsically dynamic nature of genres acquires larger proportions in electronic or virtual environments due to several factors. The first of these is the dynamic nature of the concept of audience which, as pointed out earlier, is especially salient in cyberspace where it appears broader in scope and somewhat hybrid in the sense that everybody may potentially become a member of a virtual community or audience at any time by a click of the mouse. Dynamism is also affected by the convergence of several communicative purposes in electronic texts, that is, the particular purposes of the genre, those of the online publication, and the global aim of the mass medium itself. Finally, we must also take into account the intrinsically dynamic nature of the electronic medium, which, in Maingueneau's (1998: 68) words is affecting the 'dématérialisation des supports physiques des énoncés'.

This *dematerialisation* of textuality is the result of the linking system characterising hypertexts. Links are the connections between different textual chunks or informational nodes enabling users to move within a text (internal links) or go from that text to other texts posted in hyperspace (external links). For the purposes of this paper, the interest of links rests upon three aspects. First, links may expand the text's topics by linking *topical* key words with other texts dealing with similar issues. Links may also provide readers/users with different reading options according to their own interests and, in this sense, have a bearing on text organisation. Finally, links may open discourse spaces where writers and readers can engage in generic activity faster and more actively than in traditional print practices. In other words, the link system of online texts is what actually enables the interactive and collaborative textual activity promised by hypertext and electronic discourse. Hypertext allows the constructed or imagined reader and the implied author to be less constructed and implied, and not only favours quasi-simultaneous interaction, but may also foster a reshaping of genre activity as it takes place.

In order to explore the effect of hypertext on generic activity I built a corpus of 80 book reviews selected at random from four online journals, namely, *Architectural Record* (architecture), *Scientific American* (general or popular science), *Psyche* (neuroscience), and *Kairos* (applied linguistics), all of them posted in the World Wide Web (henceforth, Web). The analysis of the reviews in the corpus focused on how links appear within the rhetorical structure of the genre on the assumption that it is this structure that seems to be most affected by hypertext. The links were analysed according to three parameters, namely their destination route, their text-structural position, and the communicative purpose underlying them – the former related to the topical dimension of links, and the latter two more rhetorically driven.

As described in Motta-Roth (1998), book reviews are relatively short texts characterised by the communicative goals of describing and, especially, evaluating new publications on a given field to a given audience. These goals are reflected in their textual structure, which rests upon three basic textual sequences devoted to different aspects of the book under review. Thus, books are first introduced by Titles, Leads, and an Introduction sequence where we may find information about the topic covered by the book, its author and intended audience, and the ways in which the work under evaluation may be related to other books within the same field and/or dealing with similar topic(s). The book is described in some detail in the Description part, where we may find a general outline of the book contents, a brief summary of its chapters, or a more in-depth description of a particularly outstanding chapter or section. Finally, book reviews usually incorporate a Closing Evaluation section recommending the book or disqualifying it, and those in academic publications may also provide a reference list at the end.

With this prototypical structure in mind, I explored the number and characteristics of the links in the texts of the corpus. Concerning quantification, the reviews with the largest number of links come from *Kairos* (417 links) and *Scientific American* (102 links), followed by those from *Psyche* (37 links) and *Architectural Record* (29). Nevertheless, the real differences among the reviews appear to be determined by qualitative issues such as the destination of the links and the communicative purpose suggested by this route (both also determining the insertion of links within the reviews' structure). The rhetoric of links in the book reviews in the corpus is described in the following section.

3. The rhetoric of links in electronic book reviews

The book reviews analysed yielded four broad types of links according to destination or linking route and rhetorical purpose, which I labelled as *commercial* links, *situational* links, *informational* links, and *hypertextual* links. The distribution of links in the texts appears to be motivated by both route and rhetorical purpose. A schematised view of the types of links in the reviews analysed is provided in Table 1 below.

Table 1 Types of Links

TYPE OF LINK	LINKS TO	TOT. LINKS	MAGAZINES	% PER PUB
Commercial Links Purpose: facilitate book purchase	• Publishing co. or bookstore	7.5%	Sc. American Kairos Arch. Record Psyche	66% 16% 11% 7%
Situational links Purpose A: provide additional information Purpose B: open discourse spaces (interaction)	• Reviewer's inst. • Author's inst. • Reviewer's e-address • Author's e-address • Publication (review response)	26.4%	Kairos Arch. Record Psyche Sc. American	72% 13% 13% 2%
Informational links Purpose A: promote critical reading Purpose B: online tutorials (topic and Web literacy)	• Related Web pubs. • Education sites • Orgs. (public) • Companies (pvt) • Related pubs. • 'Cool' stuff	27.5%	Kairos Sc. American Psyche Arch. Record	45.3% 43.5% 8.7% 2.5%
Hyptertextual links	• Table of contents • Book sections (chaps, summaries) • Glossary • Quotes from book, related works • Expand reviewer's argument	38.6%	Kairos	100%

Commercial links appear to be oriented towards facilitating the acquisition or purchase of the book under assessment. Here the four publications show some differences: whereas all reviews in *Scientific American* are linked to a well-known online bookstore, those in the other three journals are linked to various publishing companies related to the academic world. Moreover, while the links in *Scientific American* and *Architectural Record* can be found at the beginning of the review (in what appears to be the online reference card of the book), *Psyche* always incorporates them in the reference section at the end of the reviews, and the few provided in *Kairos* are interspersed throughout the reviews.

A second class comprises *situational* links, which may be further classified into two types. On the one hand, we have those links that provide additional information about the reviewers or the authors of the books at issue, and often direct readers/users to their place of work (usually, an academic institution) or Web pages. Apart from satisfying the curiosity of readers, the information about reviewers may also respond to the need of validating their status as evaluators or referees. Accordingly, these links usually appear at the very beginning of the review. A second set involves links to the e-mail addresses of reviewers and authors, as well as review-response links enabling readers/users to send their own comments to the magazine publishing the reviews. Both types in this group may be discussed as opening discourse spaces where authors and audiences can interact (e. g. praise the work, counter-argue some of the claims sustained, add further comments, and so forth). Especially interesting in this respect are links to the e-mail of the author(s), as is the case of some reviews in *Kairos*. These insert such links in the tables of contents of the books under assessment, which not only enables readers to quickly spot the author of every section in the book, but also offers them the possibility to contact them as they go along the text. In contrast, review-response links are always placed at the very end of the review or at the bar-side option menu, which suggests that interaction is postponed until the whole review has been read.

A third class concerns *informational* links, which may also be grouped into two sub-classes. The first class involves links to papers or other reviews related to either the review proper or to the book under evaluation. Although their main purpose seems to be to provide readers with different views on the book (either backing up the reviewer's claims or contrasting different positions), they may also be discussed as helping promote critical reading practices. These links would thus play a role somewhat similar to that of references in an academic paper. A second class includes links to (a) education sites, (b) organisation sites, (c) private companies' sites, (d) related magazines or journals, and (e) what appears as 'cool stuff', usually dealing with hypertext technologies and sites. All of them seem to fulfil an explanatory or tutorial function: they are related to the topic discussed in the book, and provide either background information on it or expand pre-existing knowledge. In this respect, the links may also be discussed as aimed at promoting two different (yet sometimes related) kinds of literacy: *topic literacy* (in the traditional sense of the term), and *Web literacy*, the latter being the purpose of all the links to hypertext stuff in the various websites. Furthermore, irrespective of the different aims, all the links actually point to one of the acknowledged (and most celebrated) traits of the electronic medium: that of being a macro intertext and knowledge repository. The point of insertion of both types within the rhetorical structure of reviews seems to corroborate the purposes suggested above. Thus, all the links to related texts usually appear at the reference section of the reviews as also happens with links promoting Web literacy (e. g. in *Kairos*). On the other hand, links related to expanding knowledge on the topic appear in the Introduction part, and are one of the characteristic features of the reviews from *Scientific American*.

A final set involves *hypertextual* links. In principle, these are structurally or text-oriented: they act as cues for the organisation of the text, the whole structure usually being provided in an opening screen or frame from which all the other nodes can be accessed. The diverse reading routes thus signposted are devised by the author of the review who, in this sense, foregrounds certain textual aspects/parts at the expense of others according to his/her specific interests. However, in true hypertextual fashion they are also ultimately reader-oriented inasmuch as they also allow readers to build diverse reading paths according to their own choices and liking. The insertion of these links usually responds to the agendas of a number of magazines/journals that aim at promoting hypertext literacy by putting it to work. Yet, this may also put off readers since some of the texts are really difficult to follow and may not meet the audience's previous textual expectations or default knowledge of the generic conventions of the texts.

The only journal exhibiting an extensive display of such links is *Kairos*. The distribution of hypertextual links in the 20-text sample from this journal is schematised below:

Table 2 Routes of hypertextual links

Hypertextual Links (*Kairos*)	Number of Links
Table of contents	5
Sections of book (chapters, summaries)	137
Glossary	7
Quotes from book (or related works)	8
Nodes expanding reviewer's argument	69

Of these five types of hypertextual links, the first four seem to respond to the descriptive goal of the genre. Thus, the links that take readers/users to the table of contents and to the different sections of the books at issue may be seen as the electronic counterparts of the textual sequence devoted to outlining the book and/or highlighting some of its parts in the genre's print version. On the other hand, the links that lead to glossaries and quotes provide further description when needed, even if these may also be used by reviewers to back up their arguments, as also happens with print texts, especially academic ones. Additionally, these links also help readers/users avoid scrolling when reading online texts. In this regard, together with helping reviewers overcome the spatial constraints characterising print texts, such links also contribute to the hypertextual flavour of the reviews incorporating them. Nevertheless, it should be noted that since description and evaluation are sometimes difficult to distinguish (e. g. highlighting parts of a book involves both description and evaluation), some of the links in the first four categories may also be regarded as responding to some kind of evaluative concern. In contrast, the fifth type of link is essentially argumentative – that is, it appears to be used for further expanding the reviewers' commentary without interrupting the general development of the review.

However, despite their higher hypertextual *feel*, not all the reviews in *Kairos* are equally hypertextual or provide the same kind of information. Thus, we may further distinguish between three types of reviews according to a hypertextuality cline. In the first place, we have reviews that look like normal print texts even if somewhat more schematic and, therefore, can be read as such. These are actually a reduced version of a print review, the links usually expanding the information thus summarised in a number of ways, especially the reviewer's argumentative line and personal comments.

Second, we find reviews that display a fairly patterned reading route in a first screen or frame by means of well-ordered links with explicit names. Here the links follow a review pattern although the reader is always free to access the different parts of the texts as s/he likes best. The last group concerns reviews which do not cue readers as to where they should start or how to follow their line of description and argument. These represent the most disturbing type, and illustrate the hypertextual assumption that 'literacy – in all its varied forms – keeps us in motion' (Alexander 2000). They often combine visual and verbal information which, in certain cases, keeps changing until the user clicks on one of the icons or cue words – often turning the reading of the reviews into a playful activity.

4. Implications of hypertext in genre

In general, link quantification seems to corroborate the Web's acknowledged purpose of being a huge textual and informational repository where everything is easily accessible: papers, public and private information, bookstores, and so forth. This is illustrated by links leading to educational and public sites maintained by universities, governments, and various organisations, as well as by links to other papers posted in the Web. These sites and papers are usually related to the topic of the review which they help expand in a substantial way.

Links are, nevertheless, seldom motivated by a single purpose, as is also the case of any textual sequence in conventional, written texts which usually illustrates a combination of communicative goals. In other words, many of the links that apparently fulfil the descriptive concerns of reviews may also be discussed as responding to other needs and constraints, some of them related to the genre's evaluative purpose, and others pointing to some of the less informational aims of the Web. The links leading to publishing companies and bookstores are especially interesting in this respect, and particularly significant – and noticeable – in those magazines with no other (or very few) links to non-commercial sites. For instance, all the reviews published by *Scientific American* in 2001 show a single link taking the audience to a popular online bookstore, in clear contrast with those of 2000 which, although always providing access to that store, also link the reviews with different sites providing information of another kind. In this respect, although the assessment in reviews in general does not necessarily aim at the audience's purchase of the book (i. e. it may be borrowed from a library), the links to online bookstores suggest a commercial purpose rather than a solely informative one.

All other links in the electronic reviews under focus are related to the more specific evaluative concern of the genre to a greater or lesser extent. For instance, the links that provide additional information about reviewers also warrant their status and authority as reviewers, and the links leading to related papers on the Web may also help evaluation by promoting critical reading practices. In principle, these would be more reader oriented since it is the forming of the audience's opinions that seems to be at work here. Finally, the kind of evaluation implicit in the links referred to as *situation links* relates to the whole situation created by the review genre. Here readers and authors are provided with interaction spaces where the latter can put forward their views and opinions on a given book and topic, and the former can respond to those (agreeing with or contesting them). The only links with a clearly evaluative role are those concerned with expanding the reviewer's argument, yet appear somewhat disguised within descriptive stretches. These often appear inserted within the main body of the review (i. e. as description develops) or as menu options at the very end. In other words, the reviews appear as essentially descriptive at first sight, and only after clicking certain words may audiences access the reviewer's opinions and judgements on the book.

Two basic questions arise from this brief discussion of the motives underlying the rhetoric of links in electronic books reviews: How do readers participate in the genre? Does the electronic version of the texts meet their generic expectations? Of course, answering these questions asks for a research different from the one presented here (that is, a more user-centred exploration). However, we may still draw a hypothetical picture of how the reader is constructed by the different magazines, as is suggested by the way links appear in online book reviews (all of them consciously devised by their authors) and the reading paths and interaction options enabled by them.

In this connection, assumptions about the non-expert nature of the intended audience of publications such as *Scientific American* are reflected in the links of reviews from this magazine. All of them help extend the topic of the book under review by taking readers to related texts in different websites sustained by well-known organisations (e.g. NASA, medical associations, etc.). These *topically driven* links provide information in a way print reviews cannot, and, in this sense, compensate for their spatial constraints. The texts may be therefore seen as motivated by an informative and pedagogical purpose similar to that of the links' destination sites, to the extent that many reviews may well be regarded as online tutorials in their own right. In clear contrast, specialised publications such as *Psyche* or *Architectural Record* do not provide their expert audiences with extra information. Rather, they appear to use the Web to speed up access to the different magazine issues. Nevertheless, the links in their respective texts may also be described as opening discourse spaces for academic discussion which go beyond the possibilities of their print counterparts. Finally, as also happens with *Scientific American*, the links do not affect the rhetorical structure of the reviews. Therefore, audiences do not need to be technically expert, or to make use of their knowledge of the genre in order to deal with the texts and the topics developed in them. In other words, although topics may be expanded endlessly by following the links leading to other texts in the Web, readers/users may ignore these and read the reviews as if they were conventional print ones.

Kairos offers a radically different picture. The acknowledged aim of the journal is to promote hypertextual writing and reading practices, bridge the gap between different semiotic modes, and, according to the journal's website (http://english.ttu.edu/kairos), 'support the voices of those too often marginalized in the academy, especially graduate students and adjunct and other part-time faculty'. This agenda, openly acknowledged by the journal itself in its website and illustrated by the texts posted in the magazine, also presupposes a specific kind of audience, which may be hypertextually literate or can gradually become so by engaging with the texts in the journal. Most of these are true exponents of hypertextual practices, and hence can be either reconstructed by readers/users from their initial representation of the genre – which, in this sense, gears their clicking sequence – or constructed anew as they choose.

In short, the four publications under analysis illustrate how texts may be hypertextually implemented and adjusted to an electronic environment according to the goals intrinsic to their generic ascription as well as to the idiosyncrasy of both the publications and media disseminating them. Their different use of hypertext technology may also provide insights into the general workings of the genre. In the first place, it prompts discussion as to whether genre variation in the case of book reviews is solely determined by field or discipline variables, as suggested by scholars dealing with the print version of the genre (see, for instance, Motta-Roth's work [1998]). Indeed, the texts in the corpus suggest that variation is also affected by audience and goal factors. This may be illustrated by the links in electronic reviews which, although they appear to leave their prototypical structure unaffected, also reveal that the genre is susceptible to evolving into different textual practices in time. As previously discussed, the two extremes would be represented by *Scientific American* and *Kairos*, the former evolving into a sort of online tutorial and, thus, foregrounding the descriptive side of the genre versus its evaluative role, and the latter playing up the evaluative component of reviewing practices while also providing argumentation floors for the two sides involved.

On the other hand, linking practices in electronic texts also foreground the multidimensional and intrinsically dynamic nature of genres by revealing the existence of several communicative purposes within the same textual artifact in the first place. If this is important when dealing with written texts due to their often heterogeneous nature, it is a must in approaching online texts. Second, they not only allow readers/users to actively engage with the genre, but favour a more dynamic concept of audience or discourse community. Finally, they challenge the concept of rhetorical structure as a unitary and prototypical textual pattern, favouring instead *flexible* textual artifacts that can be collaboratively constructed anew by both writers and users/readers. The starting – and crucial – premise in researching CMC and the different genres articulating it is, then, a concept of genre rationale that rests upon a plurality of goals, audiences and rhetorical structures. Regarding these three aspects as composites rather than singular concepts is a necessary prerequisite if we want to successfully explore the possibilities afforded by electronic texts, and how different agendas, expectations, and interests may determine generic variation and evolution.

5. Conclusions

Online genres have a dual relationship with their medium of transmission: if on the one hand hypertextual links help overcome the typical space constraints of such a short genre as the book review, the medium's own idiosyncrasies mix with those of the genre itself, affecting its variation and further evolution towards new forms. This is more evident in those genre practices that share the websites' purpose and intended audience, and, accordingly, are more adaptable to it (the book reviews in *Scientific American* being a case in point). The evolution and possible emergence of genres must therefore be seen as a continuum, but one highly favoured by technological and media issues.

References

Alexander, Jonathan. 2000. Review of *The Emerging Cyberculture: Literacy, Paradigm, and Paradox* ed. Stephanie Gibson and Ollie Oviedo (Cresskill, NJ: Hampton Press, 2000) in *Kairos* 6(1). Online at http://english.ttu.edu/kairos/6.1/reviews/alexander/ (consulted 14.10.2001).

Berkenkotter, Carol, and Thomas Huckin. 1995. *Genre Knowledge in Disciplinary Communication*. Hillsdale, NJ: Lawrence Erlbaum Associates.

Crowston, Kevin, and Marie Williams. 1997. 'Reproduced and Emergent Genres of Communication on the World-Wide Web' in *Proceedings of the 30th Annual Hawaii International Conference on System Sciences*. Maui (Hawaii): 30-39.

Maingueneau, Dominique. 1998. *Analyser les textes de communication*. Paris: Dunod.

Motta-Roth, Désirée. 1998. 'Discourse Analysis and Academic Book Reviews: A Study of Text and Disciplinary Cultures' in Fortanet, Inmaculada, et al. (eds) *Genre Studies in English for Academic Purposes*. Castelló, Spain: Universitat Jaume I. Servei de Publicacions: 29-58.

Shepherd, Michael, and Carolyn Watters. 1998. 'The Evolution of Cybergenres' in *Proceedings of the 31st Annual Hawaii International Conference on System Sciences*. Maui (Hawaii): 97-109.

Sussex, Roland, and Peter White. 1996. 'Electronic Networking' in *Annual Review of Applied Linguistics* 16: 200-25.

PART II

TEXTUAL AND TECHNOLOGICAL
TRANSITIONS

Visual Representation of Phraseological Metaphor in Discourse: A Cognitive Approach

Anita Naciscione

Abstract

This paper deals with the creative aspects of textual and visual saturation in a multimodal discourse. It explores the benefits of the cognitive approach to the stylistic aspects of language in use and focuses on perception and comprehension of the textual and the visual. The perception of an image, whether it is lexical or phraseological, is a cognitive process, which creates a mental picture in one's imagination, a kind of visualisation in one's mind's eye. A visual representation of the image serves to create a new mode of narrative, which is both visual and textual. Comprehension and interpretation rely on the ties between the visual and the verbal, as well as the knowledge of the sociocultural background and the symbolic implications. The visual representation of instantial stylistic use of phraseological units has a semantic function: it enhances and interprets the image, creates a new meaning and sustains figurative thought.

Key words: phraseological unit; instantial stylistic use; extended phraseological metaphor; visual representation; stylistic awareness.

In this article I am concerned with some aspects of metaphorical thought representation and the creative use of phraseological metaphor in verbal and visual discourse. I rely on the achievements of cognitive linguistics, which have made successive contributions to the understanding of metaphor and thought, and the explorations of metaphor as a major mode of conceptual organisation. Studies by cognitive scholars in the 1980s and the 1990s have established metaphor as both a figure of thought and a linguistic entity (see Lakoff & Johnson 1980; Paprotté & Dirven 1985; Lakoff 1986; Lakoff & Turner 1989; Gibbs 1990; Gibbs [1994] 1999; Steen 1992; Steen 1994; Kövecses 2002 and many others). Cognitive study has added a new dimension to discourse analysis and narrative comprehension (see Emmott [1997] 1999; Freeman 2000; Burke 2003). The use of metaphor has been recognised as part and parcel of cognition, a revealing cognitive mechanism. I fully agree with Steen (1994: 3; 2002: 386) that metaphors need to be investigated from the cognitive linguistic point of view, not only that of literary criticism, as it has been the case traditionally. Cognitive linguistics has emerged as a modern form of semantics (see Steen 1994: 8). In semantic research it is crucial to see what happens to metaphorical meaning and follow its change and development in discourse, including visual representation.

My aim is to explore the linguistic meaning of metaphor, especially its semantic aspects: the instantiation and development of meaning in discourse, the emergence of new associations or their chains, resulting in the creation of successive sub-images, coupled with the visual development of metaphorical meaning. Metaphor identification, comprehension, and appreciation become more challenging and also more interesting when metaphor is represented by a phraseological unit[1] (PU), not separate words. Gibbs notes that, contrary to the traditional view that idioms, clichés, and proverbs are frozen semantic units or dead metaphors, the evidence from cognitive linguistics and psycholinguistics indicates that many of these conventional expressions reflect metaphoric thought that is very much alive and part of everyday conceptual systems (Gibbs [1994] 1999: 436).

Let me turn to an example of verbal and visual extension of phraseological meaning as represented in Mark Twain's humorous sketch 'A Burlesque Biography'. The meaning of the PU *a family tree* is based on a common metaphorical mapping. In its base form[2] the PU is a conventional phraseological metaphor, available to users of English. First the PU appears in core use,[3] that is, in its most common form and meaning. As the example shows there is no change in phraseological meaning in the text; the figurative thought is neither developed nor sustained:

a family tree[4]

Then for the next two hundred years **the family tree** shows a succession of soldiers – noble, high-spirited fellows, who always went into battle singing, right behind the army, and always went out a-whooping, right ahead of it.

Mark Twain, A Burlesque Biography, p. 178.

In cognitive psychology the image is generally viewed as a mental representation, as a picture in the head. As Steen has pointed out, when processing metaphors, readers are able to construct at least three different kinds of mental representations: a linguistic representation of the meaning of a metaphor, a conceptual representation of the referential content, and communicative representation of the message it is attempting to convey (Steen 1994: 168).

In discourse a phraseological image may be extended over longer stretches of text, as it is in this sketch. The next paragraph contains instantial stylistic use.[5] A creative expression of a new idea is achieved by an instantiation of an extended metaphor. The metaphorical meaning is sustained, creating sub-images, which become part of the associative metaphorical network sustained on the basis of the image of the PU:

This is a scathing rebuke to old dead Froissart's poor witticism that **our family tree** never had but one limb to it, and that that one stuck out at right angles, and bore fruit winter and summer.

Twain, A Burlesque Biography, p. 178.

If the PU *a family tree* is in core use, it has only one meaning – a scheme of one's genealogical succession of ancestry. The base metaphor[6] stems from similarity and affinity of the two objects, i. e. both have a trunk and branches. In the given context only one branch or 'limb' is singled out, the only one which 'stuck out at right angles, and bore fruit winter and summer'. The latter metaphorical extension is actually an allusion to another PU – *a family (fruit) tree.*[7]

Discourse comprehension and analysis imply identification of instantial metaphorical meaning, which arises in a particular instance of a unique stylistic application of a PU and results in significant changes in its form and meaning determined by the thought expressed. The instantial use of phraseological metaphor is one of the ways to reflect a novel turn of thought in discourse. The words 'poor witticism' act as a cue, prompting and supporting the metaphorical network.

Through instantial use the PU *a family tree* acquires the meaning of 'a gallows' and turns into a contextual euphemism, resulting in the euphemisation of the text. In this sketch the meaning of 'a gallows' becomes the semantic centre of the sketch. This meaning covers practically the whole sketch (Twain 1961: 178-82), thus sustaining metaphorical thought.

The image of the family tree has been extended and we see it in our mind's eye: we imagine it by forming a mental image. It is what I would call mental visualisation. Actually we have to visualise each time when we perceive or think of an image. We visualise figurative meaning in our thoughts, as thought and imagination go together, creating a mental picture, even if there is no visual representation in the text.

In the sketch the extended metaphor of the family tree is followed by a pictorial illustration. The visual lends a new dimension: it further develops and reinforces the image, which the figurative meaning has evoked.

Twain, *A Burlesque Biography*, p. 178.

It is not an illustration of the base form of the PU as it can be found in a dictionary entry; it is a case of creative visualisation. The visual is, as it were, a continuation of the verbal text. The possibilities of novel extensions of metaphor in text have been pointed out by many cognitive linguists (see Lakoff 1986: 218-19). However, the visual offers new opportunities. The visual representation of instantial meaning enhances, develops, and sustains thought and language. The textual information is supported by the pictorial perception.

The drawing helps to bring out one of the metaphorical meanings of the second component of the PU *tree* (which is a polysemous word), namely, 'a gallows' (*Webster's New Universal Unabridged Dictionary* [1983] 1989: 1945). Another dictionary formulates this meaning as follows: 'a device used to hang a person, has one upright post and a projecting crosspiece' (*New Webster's Dictionary* 1988: 1642). By punning on the two meanings of the component *tree* Twain extends the image of the base metaphor. The semantic role of visual representations lies in sustaining and developing figurative thought. The illustration speaks a visual language of its own, accentuated by the caption *our family tree*, which acquires the effect of a coda. Thus, the understanding of some metaphors requires an extended and attentive focus processing (Steen 1994: 245). For full understanding of metaphor in use both the verbal and visual comprehension are important together with conceptual knowledge.

The PU *a family tree* is further extended in the sketch, creating a metaphorical chain, which calls for a sustained mental vision in one's mind's eye:

> I will remark here, in passing, that certain ancestors of mine are so thoroughly well-known in history by their *aliases*, that I have not felt it to be worth while to dwell upon them, or even mention them in the order of their birth. Among these may be mentioned Richard Brinsley Twain, *alias* Guy Fawkes; John Wentworth Twain, *alias* Sixteen-string Jack; William Hogarth Twain, *alias* Jack Sheppard; Ananias Twain, *alias* Baron Münchausen; John George Twain, *alias* Captain Kydd; and then there are George Francis Twain, Tom Pepper, Nebuchadnezzar, and Baalam's Ass – they all belong to our family, but to a branch of it somewhat distinctly removed from the honorable direct line – in fact a collateral branch, whose members chiefly differ from the ancient stock in that, in order to acquire the notoriety we have always yearned and hungered for, they have got into a low way of going to jail instead of getting hanged.
>
> Twain, *A Burlesque Biography*, p. 182.

With the sub-image of 'a collateral branch' that is 'distinctly removed from the honorable direct line', Twain establishes a semantic and stylistic tie with the base metaphor of the PU. Semantic and stylistic cohesion and coherence are made possible because PUs are stable cohesive word combinations with a figurative meaning. The extended phraseological metaphor is sustained across five pages. The sub-image conveys a new instantial euphemistic meaning. However, only at the very end of the paragraph does the non-euphemistic meaning 'hanged' appear as a sudden revelation of the plain and bitter truth, disclosing the meaning of the instantial metaphor – 'a gallows', which remains in the centre of events described in the sketch. The final paragraph contains a reiteration of the non-euphemistic 'hanged':

My own history would really seem so tame contrasted with that of my
ancestors, that it is simply wisdom to leave it unwritten until I am hanged.

Twain, *A Burlesque Biography*, p. 182.

The sketch reveals how the base metaphor of the PU *a family tree*
undergoes instantial semantic and stylistic changes in discourse: it is
extended across the whole sketch to sustain figurative thought. The
extended metaphor is also linked with other stylistic features – pun
and euphemism. In cognitive processes 'figures of thought do not
exist in isolation from one another' (Gibbs [1994] 1999: 449), and
hence in language tropes are combined, they interact with each other.
The individual tropes do not work independently; they are
functionally related to each other to provide not only figurative
coherence to the text that cannot be explained merely in logical or
causal terms (Gibbs [1994] 1999: 454), but also semantic and stylistic
cohesion. In discourse the language is alive, new meanings are created
and sustained. It is essential to develop an understanding of the
discoursal dimensions of phraseological metaphor, including visual
discourse. This example brings out the role of visual representation in
the extension of the image of a metaphorical PU in discourse.
Illustrations open up a possibility for creating a visual impact. The
extended phraseological metaphor is enhanced and developed by a
pictorial illustration of the instantial image. This example shows that
extended phraseological metaphor reflects extended figurative
thought.

Another way to assist mental visualisation of figurative thought is the
instantial use of PUs in stage remarks in plays. Instantial use reveals
information about the attitude, which the character has to convey more
accurately. Here it has a paralinguistic function: it gives precise
instructions for the actor or actress how to enact the scene. For
instance, George Bernard Shaw is known for his meticulous stage
remarks in which he frequently resorts to stylistic use:

to give someone the cold shoulder

He sits down next to the Newly Born who pouts and turns a very
cold right **shoulder to him**, a demonstration utterly lost on him.

George Bernard Shaw, *Back to Methuselah*.

The interaction of tropes is not only a phenomenon to be observed in
discourse but also in the base form of PUs, which brings out the
complexity of phraseological meaning.[8] This PU has both

metaphorical and metonymic features in the semantic structure of its base form. A new meaning is additionally created in text. This way instantial use offers a new vision, which is different from core use. The non-verbal enactment is another mode of the presentation of message and the visualisation of thought.

A merger of verbal and non-verbal communication is a feature of the discoursal use of PUs. 'How elements in visual and verbal modes interact on the page is a central issue in multi-modal texts' (Goodman 1996: 69), that is, in texts which use features from more than one semiotic mode of communication simultaneously. It is revealing to follow the ways in which visual and verbal representation can interact within a text, reinforcing the message or creating additional meanings (see Goodman 1996: 38). As a rule, a pictorial illustration follows the stretch of text or appears in the middle of it. Yet it may also precede the text, as is the case in 'The Thurber Carnival', bringing the literal meaning to the fore:

an old bird

> *Question.* After a severe storm we found this old male raven in the study of my father, the Hon. George Morton Bodwell, for many years head of the Latin Department at Tufts, sitting on a bust of Livy which was a gift to him from the class of '92. All <u>the old bird</u> will say is "Grawk!"

> *Answer.* <u>I am handicapped by an uncertainty</u> as to <u>who says "Grawk", the raven or your father. It just happens that "Arrk" is what ravens say. I have never known a raven that said anything but "Arrk."</u>

James Thurber, *The Pet Department.*

An old bird is a metaphorical PU used to denote someone who is too experienced and shrewd to be taken in. The picture of a bird and the question addressed to the Pet Department are non-figurative; they both feature an old raven sitting on a bust in the direct sense of the word. However, the answer involves parallel perception, and the reader is simultaneously aware of figurative thought and the literal meaning. Phraseological pun is a way to stretch imagination and reflect experience beyond the possibilities offered by a PU in core use. Moreover, the pun has turned visual: the pictorial representation becomes part of the process of change and development of thought in discourse.

Change and development of phraseological meaning is not merely a feature of literary discourse, but also a mode of figuration that is common in various types of newspaper texts which easily combine verbal and visual representation. Let me examine the PU *to put one's best foot forward*, which appears in the headline of a news item ***The Queen puts her best (bare) foot forward*** in *The* [London] *Times* (22 April 1999, p. 1). The headline is instantial use due to the insertion of the epithet *bare* which is put in brackets. This is very unusual as the base form never contains any brackets. The brackets become a semantic technique. Moreover, the instantial component *bare* brings out the literal meaning of the component *foot*, which results in

phraseological pun as part of the process of semantic change in the instantiation of the phraseological metaphor. The pun is enhanced by a big photograph of Queen Elizabeth with one of her shoes off (with one bare foot).

To put one's best foot forward is a polysemous PU. One of the meanings is 'to make the best possible showing'.[9] When the Queen celebrated her 73rd birthday in Korea she had to remove her white court shoes, entering a traditional house in her stockinged feet to observe the local customs. The literal meaning of *shoes* is spread throughout the news item: the Queen is kicking them off and wriggling her feet back into them again.

The phraseological pun permeates the text, creating a visual narrative and contributing to its coherence and cohesion.

The last paragraph mentions 'the Queen's momentary scowl at being wrong-footed', that is, at being put in an unexpected or difficult situation (*Collins Cobuild English Dictionary for Advanced Learners* [1987] 2001: 1816). One aspect (having no shoes on) stands for the Queen's general feeling at being put at a disadvantage. This is a metonymic link effected by associations of contiguity. The successive change from one figurative mode to another – metaphor–pun–visual pun–metonymy – reveals the complex interaction of different tropes (see Gibbs [1994] 1999: 434-54).

The pun is further visualised in a cartoon placed at the end of the news item.

"*I think we should get her a pair of shoes*"

The caption 'I think we should get her a pair of shoes' is non-metaphorical;[10] however, in this context the cartoon reinforces the visual pun. This sequence constitutes a kind of narrative strategy, which reflects the development of figurative thought and a continual return to literal meanings in the realisation of a PU-based pun. The PU is sustained verbally and visually throughout the news item.

Phraseological metaphors may be sustained and visualised not only in news items and articles of a general type but also in serious specialist articles, as, for instance, a financial article 'Send Your Money Home' in *Time* (29 September 1997, p. 44) dealing with interest rates, stocks, and mortgages. The semantic focus of the article is the conceptual metaphor *home*. The idea of home as a desired place to live in is manifest in the use of three phraseological units, which have one common component *home*, occurring within the limits of a short article. The first lines read as follows:

> **Your home has always been your castle**, and is used to double as a piggy bank, until a classic late-'80s bust crushed the notion of housing as an investment.
>
> *Time*, 29 September 1997, p. 44.

The article actually deals with the nonfigurative meaning of *home*, discussing the existing homes and home prices, and the idea of a house as an investment. The article ends with another PU with the component *home*, creating a frame construction and acting as a coda:

> A house as an investment is a pitch that hasn't opened many doors lately. But today, **home isn't just where the heart is**; it's where the smart money is too.
>
> *Time*, 29 September 1997, p. 44.

The base form of the PU *home is where the heart is* has a positive meaning: your true home is in the place you love most.[11] In the text the PU is used in the opposite meaning. The PU is extended by a parallel construction, which conveys the message of the article: a house is a good investment now.

The visual focus of the article is a graphic: the drawing of a house placed in the middle of the article, containing information on home prices in various states in the USA. As the article is financial, the house is drawn in austere lines, not like a dream house in home adverts. The graphic gives the necessary financial information to persuade the reader of the sound investment, yet it reveals creative thinking.

Home $weet Home
Areas with the biggest jump
in median home prices

	1997 price	% change from '96
Gainesville, Fla.	$99,000	12.5%
Lansing/E. Lansing, Mich.	92,800	10.7
Kalamazoo, Mich.	102,000	10.5
Fort Lauderdale, Fla.	121,800	9.6
Lincoln, Neb.	94,500	9.2
Phoenix, Ariz.	113,200	9.1
Austin/San Marcos, Texas	118,200	8.6
Portland, Ore.	151,100	8.4
Columbus, Ohio	117,300	8.1
Grand Rapids, Mich.	94,000	7.8

Source: National Association of Realtors   TIME Graphic by Steve Hart

The graphic is of stylistic and cognitive interest. Usually phraseological puns have one or several components, which are used in their literal meaning(s). In this case the pun is created through an associative link between *a home* and *a house*. The graphic has an unusual headline, '**Home $weet Home**', which is a case of instantial use of a popular PU. The sweetness of home (the dream of a house of your own) is enhanced by a visual representation of the dollar sign $, which is always seen as a symbol of wealth and money. The symbolic meaning is incorporated in the semantic structure of the PU: it becomes part of the meaning of the PU in the given instantiation.

For the identification of the instantial graphic implications it is also important to know the cultural background: the use and the symbolic meaning of the currency sign. Graphic properties are generally used to represent the extra-linguistic world in an accurate manner (see Goodman 1996: 184). The visual effect works together with the verbal in the creation of a visual pun.

The use of a symbol is one of the visualisation techniques. The graphic representation is inextricably linked with the content of the article. The symbol $ has a semantic function. The visual creation stretches the usual system of typography and affects the relation between the visual and the verbal. The use of the dollar symbol has a special visual effect that adds a new visual and semantic dimension to the text, a dimension which is not available in standard writing.

Cognitive linguistics has shown that one conceptual metaphor may be expressed in many variations of linguistic organisation (see Dirven 1985; Steen 1994: 7). This magazine article has made use of three metaphorical PUs containing the component *home* and a visual representation to reflect the semantic development of the conceptual metaphor *home*. Visual comprehension is facilitated by the metaphorical context.

In conclusion, this paper deals with the creative aspect of textual and visual representation of figurative thought. Extended phraseological metaphor is one of the figurative modes whereby people conceptualise their experience. It provides for the development and sustainability of metaphorical thought and language in discourse. Visual representation helps to disambiguate instantial stylistic use. The cognitive approach promotes the comprehension and interpretation of phraseological metaphor in verbal and visual discourse. Mental visualisation of instantial stylistic use is part of cognitive performance, enhanced by a visual representation of the extended image. The visual reinforces mental representations, and sustains and develops the message expressed by the PU, lending a visual dimension to the text. Extended metaphor calls for greater stylistic awareness, which involves a conscious perception and understanding of significant changes in form and meaning, associative links and their networks, stylistic cohesive ties, and the creation of a new meaning in discourse. As thought develops, phraseological metaphor develops, too. Extended phraseological metaphor reflects extended figurative thought.

Endnotes

[1] The phraseological unit is a stable, cohesive combination of words with a fully or partially figurative meaning. For my understanding of the basic terms in phraseology see Naciscione 2001.

[2] *The base form* of a PU is the form to which other forms can be related and with which they can be compared. It is the dictionary form and meaning, recorded as the head form. The base form is stored in the long-term memory of the language user as a language unit, which is accessed when a discourse situation calls for it.

[3]*Core use* is the use of the PU in its most common form and meaning. In core use the PU does not acquire any additional stylistic features in discourse and does not exceed the boundaries of one sentence.

[4]I have indicated the forms of PUs for emphasis: base forms are marked **bold and underlined**; instantial elements are spaced and underlined; replaced elements are underlined double and spaced; cues are marked with a dotted line.

[5]*Instantial stylistic use* is a particular instance of a unique stylistic application of a PU in discourse resulting in significant changes in its form and meaning determined by the context.

[6]The *base metaphor* is the metaphor that is part of the image of the PU in its base form.

[7]*A family (fruit) tree* – a fruit tree bearing different varieties of the same fruit grafted on to it (Kirkpatrick [1983] 1987: 455).

[8]The semantic structure of phraseological meaning frequently includes a number of tropes. For the formation of phraseological meaning and types of phraseological abstraction see Melerovich 1982; Dobrovolsky 1998; Naciscione 2001.

[9]See *Webster's New Universal Unabridged Dictionary* [1983] 1989: 713.

[10]It is significant to explore the aspects of human cognition which are grounded in everyday bodily and perceptual experiences that form the nonmetaphorical part of thought and language (Gibbs [1994] 1999: 79).

[11]See *Cambridge International Dictionary of Idioms* 1998: 195.

References

Burke, Michael. 2003. 'Literature as Parable' in Gavins, Joanna, and Gerard Steen (eds) *Cognitive Poetics in Practice*. London: Routledge: 115-28.

Cambridge International Dictionary of Idioms. 1998. Cambridge: Cambridge University Press.

Collins Cobuild English Dictionary for Advanced Learners. [1987] 2001. Glasgow: Harper Collins Publishers.

Dirven, René. 1985. 'Metaphor as a Basic Means for Extending Lexicon' in Paprotté & Dirven (1985): vii-xix.

Dobrovolsky, Dmitrij O. 1998. 'Vnutrennyaya forma idiom i problema tolkovaniya' in *Izvestiya AN. Seriya literaturi i yazika* 57(1): 36-44.

Emmott, Catherine. [1997] 1999. *Narrative Comprehension: A Discourse Perspective.* Oxford: Oxford University Press.

Freeman, Margaret H. 2000. 'Poetry and the Scope of Metaphor: Toward a Cognitive Theory of Literature' in Barcelona, Antonio (ed.) *Metaphor and Metonymy at the Crossroads: A Cognitive Perspective.* Berlin: Mouton de Gruyter: 253-81.

Gibbs, Raymond W. Jr. 1990. 'The Process of Understanding Literary Metaphor' in *Journal of Literary Semantics* 19: 65-79.

__. [1994] 1999. *The Poetics of Mind: Figurative Thought, Language and Understanding.* Cambridge: Cambridge University Press.

Goodman, Sharon. 1996. 'Visual English' in Goodman, Sharon, and David Graddol (eds) *Redesigning English: New Texts, New Identities*. London: Routledge: 38-72.

Kirkpatrick, E. M. (ed.). [1983] 1987. *Chambers 20th Century Dictionary*. Edinburgh: Chambers.

Kövecses, Zoltán. 2002. *Metaphor*. Oxford: Oxford University Press.

Lakoff, George. 1986. 'A Figure of Thought' in *Metaphor and Symbolic Activity* 1: 215-25.

Lakoff, George, and Mark Johnson. 1980. *Metaphors We Live By*. Chicago: University of Chicago Press.

Lakoff, George, and Mark Turner. 1989. *More than Cool Reason: A Field Guide to Poetic Metaphor*. Chicago: University of Chicago Press.

Melerovich, Alina M. 1982. 'Semanticheskaya struktura frazeologicheskih yedinits v sovremennom russkom yazike kak lingvisticheskaya problema'. Doctoral habilitation dissertation. Leningrad: Leningrad University.

Naciscione, Anita. 2001. *Phraseological Units in Discourse: Towards Applied Stylistics*. Riga: Latvian Academy of Culture.

New Webster's Dictionary. 1988. New Delhi: Allied Publishers.

Paprotté, Wolf, and René Dirven (eds). 1985. *The Ubiquity of Metaphor: Metaphor in Language and Thought*. Amsterdam: John Benjamins.

Steen, Gerard. 1992. 'Literary and Nonliterary Aspect of Metaphor' in *Poetics Today* 13: 687-704.

__. 1994. *Understanding Metaphor in Literature*. London: Longman.

__. 2002. 'Identifying Metaphor in Language: A Cognitive Approach' in *Style* 36(3): 386-407.

Twain, Mark. 1961. *The Complete Humorous Sketches and Tales of Mark Twain*. New York: Hanover House.

Webster's New Universal Unabridged Dictionary. [1983] 1989. New York: Dorset & Baber.

A Structural Analysis of Wordsworth's 'Daffodils'

Ken Nakagawa

Abstract

Roman Jakobson's analytical approach can help us realise what we might otherwise ignore or fail to notice with regard to the meaning of a poem. A Jakobsonian approach to Wordsworth's 'Daffodils' reveals that the poem has the following structure: (1) The centre of the poem is literally in the centre; (2) from a descriptive viewpoint, we can observe parallelism in ll. 1-8 and ll. 17-24, whereas no parallel expressions are found between ll. 9 and 16; (3) as for the object of the poet's description, the poet depicts external and natural elements in ll. 1-14; in contrast, he describes internal and spiritual objects in ll. 15-24; and (4) turning to the poet's attitude to Nature, we find an observation stage in ll. 1-12, a gazing stage in ll. 13-18, and finally a stage of contemplation and union with Nature in ll. 19-24. This structural analysis, however, results in a static observation. In order to make up for this deficiency and investigate the dynamic movement of the poem, I employ a philological reading and examine the poem stanza by stanza.

Keywords: Jakobsonian structural analysis; componential analysis; juxtaposition; mirror-image relation; poet's craft.

1. Introduction

The purpose of this paper is a structural analysis of William Wordsworth's 'Daffodils'. In the first part (§2), I will adopt a Jakobsonian approach to the poem. The models I refer to are Jakobson (1962, 1970a, 1970b). Using the so-called 'binary opposition' I will analyse 'Daffodils' from four perspectives: (1) anterior [stanzas] against posterior [stanzas]; (2) outer against inner; (3) odd against even; and (4) centre against margins.

It is said that structural analysis is fated to be static. In the second part (§§3-7), in order to compensate for this defect, I will employ a traditional, philological reading. I will look at the poem stanza by stanza, paying special attention to the result of the observation from the fourth perspective. In so doing we will be able to see a far more dynamic movement of 'Daffodils' emerge. The following topics will be discussed: (5) variation of subject and object; (6) the craft of Wordsworth's syntax; (7) organic and cohesive function of 'golden'; (8) mirror-image relation of sounds; and (9) distribution of 'dance'.

2. Jakobsonian reading

2.1. Anterior against posterior

For the text of the poem and its rhyme scheme, refer to Figure 1 on p. 88. The linguistic aspects that connect the first stanza with the second and organise them into a group are the following:

First, each anterior stanza contains an *as*-phrase and the object of the preposition *as* is modified by a relative pronoun *that*, respectively.

Second, we can observe a parallel structure between ll. 3 to 6 in the first stanza and ll. 11 to 12 in the second stanza. The former is an SVOC pattern: 'I saw a crowd, / A host, of golden daffodils ... / Fluttering and dancing in the breeze' and the latter is an OVSC pattern: 'Ten thousand saw I ... / Tossing their heads in sprightly dance', which derives from an underlying SVOC structure.

In the posterior stanzas, on the other hand, we can see an echo rhyme, which is lacking in the anterior. In the third stanza, the rhyme word 'gay' in l. 15 echoes in 'gazed – and gazed –' in l. 17 (/gei/ /geizd/ /geizd/). This echo rhyme helps to create the picture of a poet who is watching intently at the daffodils with great delight. The feeling of delight, that is, 'gay' (/gei/), which means 'cheerful and excited', is literally included in the act of 'gazing' (/geiziŋ/).

Similarly, in the fourth stanza we observe an echo rhyme in l. 19, 'On my couch I lie' (/ai/ /ai/ /ai/), which constitute an internal rhyme, and 'lie' (/lai/) then rhymes with its rhyme-pair 'eye' (/ai/) in l. 21.

2.2. Outer against inner

Let us turn to those elements which characterise a binary opposition between outer and inner stanzas. We can take note of five elements.

First, the word 'daffodils' appears in the outer stanzas: in ll. 4 and 24. It does not appear in the inner stanzas.

Second, words which express *solitariness* appear in the outer stanzas: 'lonely' in the first line and 'solitude' in l. 22, whereas no such words appear in the inner stanzas. Words suggesting *melancholy* appear in the outer stanzas as well: 'lonely' (just mentioned) and 'In vacant or in pensive mood' in l. 20. In contrast, what appears in the inner stanzas is nothing else but the 'dancing daffodils in sprightly dance' and 'the sparkling waves' and 'a poet who can not but be gay' and 'a jocund company'.

Third, the conjunction 'when' appears only in the outer stanzas: that is to say, in l. 3 of the first stanza and in l. 19 of the last stanza.

Fourth, negative lexical items appear only in the inner stanzas: '<u>never</u>-ending' in l. 9 and 'could <u>not</u> but' in l. 15, and '<u>little</u>' in l. 17. There are no negatives in the outer stanzas.

Lastly, in the outer stanzas, the rhyme-pair *b*: 'hi<u>lls</u>', 'daffod<u>ils</u>' in ll. 2 and 4 circularly evokes *l*: 'fi<u>lls</u>', 'daffod<u>ils</u>' in the fourth stanza. Similarly, in the inner stanzas, the rhyme-pair *e*: the 'ei' sound in 'w<u>ay</u>' and 'b<u>ay</u>' gives rise to *g*: 'th<u>ey</u>' and 'g<u>ay</u>' in the third stanza.

2.3. Odd against even

Features characterising this third type of grouping are scarce. First, the odd stanzas begin with grammatical subjects, whereas the even stanzas do not. However, in each even stanza 'They' begins the third line.

Second, possessive cases of pronouns do not appear in the odd stanzas, but only in the even stanzas. To be exact, '<u>their</u> heads' in l. 12, '<u>my</u> couch' in l. 19, and '<u>my</u> heart' in l. 23.

Third and last, in the odd stanzas, imperfect masculine rhymes appear: *cc*, in ll. 5 and 6 of the first stanza, and *hh*, in ll. 14 and 16 of the third stanza. The remaining are all perfect masculine rhymes.

2.4. Centre against margins

This poem unifies itself every two lines from the standpoint of meaning and punctuation. When we observe each pair of lines in the poem's centre minutely, we find no parallelism (ll. 9, 10; 11, 12; 13, 14; and 15, 16). On the contrary, parallel juxtaposed expressions are realised in the margins (highlighted in Figure 1): 'vales' and 'hills' and 'on high' and 'o'er vales and hills' (ll. 1, 2); 'a crowd', 'A host' (3, 4); 'Beside the lake', 'beneath the trees' and 'Fluttering' and 'dancing' (5, 6); 'shine' and 'twinkle' (7, 8); 'gazed –' and 'gazed –' (ll. 17, 18); 'In vacant' or 'in pensive' (19, 20); 'that inward eye', 'the bliss of solitude' (21, 22); and 'with pleasure fills', and 'dances with the daffodils' (23, 24). All these expressions reveal strong parallelism. Contrary to this, there is no parallelism at all between ll. 9 and 16.

Figure 1 Centre against margins

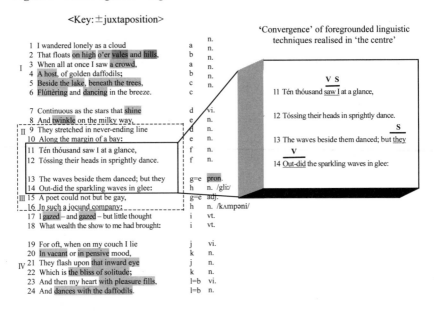

It follows that what I call 'the centre' (ll. 9-16) shows a remarkable contrast to its surroundings in that the centre shows no juxtaposition opposed to that found in the margins.

Let us examine the punctuation, especially the use of colons and semicolons, which help to split the stanzas into quatrain-like units. There is a semicolon at the end of the fourth line of Stanza I; in Stanza II there is a colon at the end of the fourth line. In Stanza III there is a colon at the end of the second, the fourth, and the sixth lines; and then in Stanza IV there is a semicolon in the fourth line. This would seem to constitute a strong coherence in the first four lines of each stanza as units. If we seek the most cohesive four lines between ll. 9 and 16, we must focus on ll. 11-14 despite the existence of a break between the second and third stanzas. As for elements that connect l. 11 to l. 14, we can point out that, phonologically, the /gl/ sound of rhyme word '*gl*ance' in l. 11 forms a strong framework with that of '*gl*ee' in l. 14; and the /sp/ consonant cluster and /l/ duplication found in '*sp*right*l*y' in l. 12 and '*sp*ark*l*ing' in l. 14 show sound equivalence. Grammatically, the possessive pronoun 'their' in l. 12 continues to the objective case 'them' in l. 13; and rhetorically, the last word of the second stanza, 'dance', is followed by 'danced' in l. 13 by means of anadiplosis and polyptoton. We may call these four lines the 'centre of the poem' with good reason.

First, the only instance of SV inversion in this poem is observed in l. 11 ('saw I').

Second, it is in ll. 6, 11 and 12 that the basic rhythm of this poem, i.e. iambic tetrameter, is altered. 'Flúttèrìng' is a dactyl, 'Tén thóusànd' is a spondee, 'Tóssìng', a trochee, and two of these alterations are found in consecutive lines of the centre.

Third, apart from the change of rhythm, a bold enjambment of 'they / Out-did' occurs from l. 13 to l. 14.

Fourth, 'they' is a unique word in that it is the only pronoun among the rhyme words.

Fifth, 'Out-did' is morphologically conspicuous because it has a hyphen, whereas the other 22 verbs in this poem do not.

Last, strictly speaking, as mentioned above, 'glee' in l. 14 does not constitute a complete masculine rhyme with its rhyme pair 'company' in l. 16. This rhyme is imperfect because /gliː/ has a long vowel and /kʌmpəni/ has a short one.

It is enough to point out the linguistic facts which make the 'centre' conspicuous against the margins.

To summarise this fourth perspective, these four lines constitute a 'convergence' (Riffaterre 1959: 172 [cited in Fowler 1966: 21]) of phonological, structural, grammatical, and rhetorical markedness in this poem. These four lines in which such 'foregrounded' linguistic properties converge play a role in what in music is called 'modulation'. They cause the poem to modulate from 'external' description into 'internal' description.

3. Philological reading

In the first part, we have examined formal and static aspects realised in the poem. Now, in the second part, based particularly on the result obtained in the fourth grouping, 'Centre against margins', I will look at the movement in the poem stanza by stanza basically from a fifth perspective, variation of subject and object, and illustrate some of the linguistic techniques of Wordsworth.

As is well known, this poem begins with the first person pronoun 'I'. The poet is identified with a cloud floating high above in the sky, which foreshadows his complete union and identification with Nature accomplished at the last stage of the poem. A lonely poet meets with a group of daffodils. The epithet 'golden' in l. 4 is considerably important, and we cannot ignore the significance of the emendation from 'dancing' in the 1807 edition to 'golden' in the 1815 edition. I will refer to this point later.

4. The craft of Wordsworth's syntax

The SVOC structure in ll. 3 to 6, which I mentioned in the first part, is noteworthy. At the end of l. 3, Wordsworth uses 'a crowd', and then at the beginning of the fourth line, he changes it to 'A host' appositionally. Let us have a closer look at the appositional change, and appreciate the craft of Wordsworth's syntax.

Figure 2 The craft of Wordsworth's syntax

S	V	order, harmony	O	C	
I	saw	−	a crowd	fluttering	→shine
			of golden daffodils		
		+	a host	dancing	→twinkle

According to the brilliant observation by Durrant (1969: 21-23; 1970: 129-31), the shift of the poet's description is that from 'a fluttering crowd' to 'a dancing host' which suggests 'order and harmony'. In other words, parallel phrases – 'crowd', 'host'; 'Fluttering', 'dancing' – form strong semantic links respectively.

Componential analysis for each pair of synonyms will make the point clearer:

crowd = <a large number>, <–order>, <–harmony>;
host = <a large number>, <+order>, <+harmony>
flutter = <move>, <–order>, <–harmony>;
dance = <move>, <+order>, <+harmony>

With the help of these distinctive features of <±order, ±harmony>, we can easily recognise the marked difference between the two noun phrases. Here Durrant catches the overt and succinct semantic change from 'a fluttering crowd' which has neither <order> nor <harmony> to 'a dancing host' which has both <order> and <harmony>. In my opinion, the same is true of 'shine' and 'twinkle' in ll. 7 and 8 because the former implies <-order, -harmony>; and the latter suggests <+order, +harmony>.

Now let us move on to the second stanza. The 'golden daffodils' which have been described as an object of the verb 'saw' now appear as a subject of the verb 'stretched' in l. 9 – though in the form of the pronoun 'They'. 'They' are identified with the stars in the Milky Way, just as, in the first stanza, 'I', the poet, was identified with a cloud in the sky. The description of daffodils in the second stanza and that of the first stanza have equivalence in respect of the multitude of number. The description in the second stanza is expanded dramatically by using a simile of tens of thousands of stars in the galaxy – a magnificent cosmic image. What makes this giant leap of association possible is the above-mentioned epithet 'golden' in 'golden daffodils' in l. 4 of the first stanza. It signifies <brightness of the colour> of the flowers, which is identical with that of 'stars'. Therefore the dramatic expansion of the image works smoothly.

At the beginning of l. 11, 'a crowd, / A host, of golden daffodils' in ll. 3 and 4 is now transformed to 'Ten thousand'. The headword 'daffodils' is hidden in the multitude. When we come across the expression 'in never-ending line' in l. 9, together with the whole cosmic image of endless numbers of stars, we feel the magnitude of the number itself is strengthened and enhanced into what might be called <spatial boundlessness>.

Incidentally, up to l. 12, either 'I' or 'daffodils' has been the subject of the lines, but at the beginning of the third stanza, 'The waves' takes up the position of subject as if to change the stream of description. The 'waves' are only presupposed by proximity or adjacency relation with

'Beside the lake' in l. 5 and 'Along the margin of a bay' in l. 10. It has not been expressed explicitly. The 'waves' here cause the poet to do 'comparative thinking'. So the poet asks himself a question: 'Which is superior, the dancing waves or the dancing daffodils?' (The dancing movements of both, of course, are caused by the 'breeze' at the end of l. 6.)

It is noteworthy that comparative thinking occurs in what I call 'the centre of the poem' in the word 'Out-did' (cited in *OED* under 'outdo' and defined as 'To be superior to'). The dancing of the 'daffodils' is definitely superior to that of the 'waves'. Why? Because, as the epithet 'sparkling' implies, the dancing of the waves is fleeting and transitory. On the other hand, the dancing of the daffodils is sufficiently permanent to be compared to the stars in the galaxy which have appeared without fail in the night sky since the creation of the universe. The dance by the daffodils is by far the superior because it has <order> and <harmony> and <eternity>.

In l. 15 an objective subject 'poet', not a subjective 'I', appears as the subject, which, till then, has been expressed by the first person pronoun 'I'. And in l. 17, the verb 'saw' changes to the double 'gazed – and gazed –' which has the semantic features <see> + <concentration>. Can we say that now the poet comes to the stage of gazing, which follows the stage of observation? No. The gazing stage has already begun at the latter part of the centre (ll. 13 and 14), because the above-mentioned 'Out-did' has already appeared there. To be more precise, 'Out-did' means 'to be superior to' and so is suggestive of comparative thinking. Thinking comparatively pre-supposes gazing. And gazing makes it possible to recognise the difference between two objects as a result of the comparative thinking.

At the end of l. 17 the verb 'to think' appears for the first time as 'thought', following the verbs of motion and perception used in the former part of the poem. But it is totally negated through the use of 'little'. Given Wordsworth's state of ecstasy, this use of 'little' is quite understandable and quite natural. Is it possible for someone to think when experiencing sheer joy?

5. Organic and cohesive function of 'golden'

Here we need to mention 'wealth' in the last line of this stanza. It is closely related to the other connotation of the epithet 'golden' stated before. Let us review the two meanings of 'golden' represented in

Figure 3. One semantic feature, <bright colour>, is related to 'stars', 'shine', 'twinkle', 'sparkling' and then 'flash' in the last stanza. The other semantic feature, <high value>, is closely related to 'wealth' here in l. 18. The adjective, 'golden', in fact, constitutes a starting point for this organic verbal network. The 'dancing' in the original version would not have performed such a cohesive function as 'golden' does. It should also be noted that the second stanza was added at the same time when original 'dancing' was replaced by 'golden' in 1815.

Figure 3 Organic function of 'golden'

□ = <bright colour> ▨ = <high value>

I
1 I wandered lonely as a cloud
2 That floats on high o'er vales and hills,
3 When all at once I saw a crowd,
4 A host, of golden daffodils;
5 Beside the lake, beneath the trees,
6 Fluttering and dancing in the breeze.

II
7 Continuous as the stars that shine
8 And twinkle on the milky way,
9 They stretched in never-ending line
10 Along the margin of a bay:
11 Ten thousand saw I at a glance,
12 Tossing their heads in sprightly dance.

III
13 The waves beside them danced; but they
14 Out-did the sparkling waves in glee:
15 A poet could not but be gay,
16 In such a jocund company:
17 I gazed – and gazed – but little thought
18 What wealth the show to me had brought:

IV
19 For oft, when on my couch I lie
20 In vacant or in pensive mood,
21 They flash upon that inward eye
22 Which is the bliss of solitude;
23 And then my heart with pleasure fills,
24 And dances with the daffodils.

6. Mirror-image relation of sounds

Now let us examine the sound structure between the last word of the third stanza and the first two words of the fourth stanza:

'… brought: / For oft …'

First of all, we need to remember, 'the conjunction "for" introduces new information, but suggests that the reason is given as an afterthought' (Swan 1995: 72). With that observation in mind, let us look at Figure 4-1.

Figure 4-1 Mirror-image of 'brought: / For oft' (i)

Stanza III	Stanza IV
(1) /brɔːt	fɔː ɔːft/
(2) /brɔːt	fɔː ɔːft/
(3) /brɔːt	fɔː ɔːft/

The vertical line in Figure 4-1 divides stanzas III and IV. Firstly, the long vowel /ɔː/ is common to the three words, as is illustrated by (1). Secondly, let us suppose a mirror is placed between 'For' and 'oft'. Then, as the opposing arrows in the Figure indicate, the initial consonant of the word 'For', /f/, reflects part of the third word 'oft', that is /f/, showing a mirror-image relation (/fɔː/↔/ɔːf/), which is depicted by (2). Thirdly, further scrutiny reveals that the final sound of the first word, /t/, plus the sound of the second word, /fɔː/, vs. the sound of the third word, /ɔːft/, are also in a mirror-image relationship (/tfɔː/↔/ɔːft/), as is shown by (3) (cf. Austin's idea of 'concentricity' [1984: 84]).

Figure 4-2 Mirror-image of 'brought: / For oft' (ii)

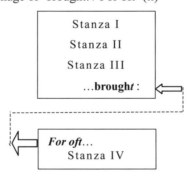

Therefore, seen from the viewpoints of phonology and semantics as indicated in Figure 4-2, this mirror-image sound structure helps the fourth stanza reflect the third stanza, just as a mirror reflects its object. Here we can see the poet's craft: form matches meaning.

Now back to the main argument. At the beginning of Stanza IV, the poet's inner feeling is clearly described: 'In vacant or in pensive mood'. In such a mood, what has been captured as an object of 'I saw', 'saw I', and 'I gazed – and gazed –' emerges as a subject, that is to say, 'They' in l. 21. And 'they' actively work on 'that inward eye / Which is the bliss of solitude', namely 'imagination'. But the subject itself is still a pronoun and is not manifested. We have to wait until the very end of the poem for the pronoun to change to 'daffodils' again. Furthermore 'I' and 'A poet', which so far appear as the subject of each action, suddenly disappear in l. 23, and this time, near the end of the poem, the emotional 'heart' (not the intellectual mind), which has been a main agent appreciating the pleasant dancing of the daffodils, becomes the subject. The poet hides himself in a possessive pronoun, 'my' in l. 23. His 'heart fills with pleasure' and 'dances with the daffodils'.

7. Distribution of 'dance'

Before concluding, I would like to highlight the word 'dance', which is a keyword of this poem realising <order> and <harmony>. The word 'dance' is distributed equally once in each stanza with its form slightly changed morphophonologically. The distribution is as follows: 'dancing' in l. 6, 'dance' in l. 12, 'danced' in l. 13, and 'dances' in the last line. Moreover, two of them appear in the centre. When the daffodils in the outer world dance, then correspondingly the heart dances. There is a dance all through the undercurrent of the poem's meaning.

8. Conclusion

In the first part, we applied a Jakobsonian approach and, then, in the second part, a philological reading, to the structure of 'Daffodils'. As a result we posited the following structure illustrated in Figure 5.

Figure 5 Structure of 'Daffodils'

Stanza	I		II		III		IV
Line	1 2 3 4 5 6	7 8 9 10	11 12	13 14	15 16 17 18		19 20 21 22 23 24
(1)	MARGIN			CENTRE		MARGIN	
(2)	+ juxtaposition		– juxtaposition			+ juxtaposition	
(3)	external, natural				internal, spiritual		
(4)	observation				gazing		contemplation, union

Summarising, I would like to reiterate the following four structural points which underpin this paper:

- Point (1): The centre of the poem is literally in the centre;

- Point (2): From a descriptive viewpoint, we can observe juxtaposition in ll. 1-8 and ll. 17-24, whereas no juxtaposed expressions are found between ll. 9-16;

- Point (3): As for the object of the poet's description, the poet depicts external and natural objects in ll. 1-14; in contrast, he describes internal and spiritual entities in ll. 15-24; and

- Point (4): Turning to the poet's attitude towards Nature, we find an observation stage in ll. 1-12, a gazing stage between ll. 13-18, and finally a stage of contemplation and union with Nature from l. 19 to the last.

References

All quotations are from Wordsworth, William. 1969. *The Poetical Works of William Wordsworth*, Vol. 2 (ed. Ernest de Selincourt, rev. H. Darbishire). Oxford: Clarendon Press. All italics and underlines are mine.

Austin, Timothy R. 1984. *Language Crafted.* Bloomington: Indiana University Press.

Durrant, Geoffrey. 1969. *William Wordsworth.* Cambridge: Cambridge University Press.

__. 1970. *Wordsworth and the Great System.* Cambridge: Cambridge University Press.

Fowler, Roger (ed.). 1966. *Essays on Style and Language.* London: Routledge & Kegan Paul.

Jakobson, Roman. 1960. 'Closing Statement: Linguistics and Poetics' in Sebeok, Thomas A. (ed.) *Style in Language.* Cambridge, MA: The MIT Press.

__. 1962. (with Claude Lévi-Strauss) '"Les Chats" de Charles Baudelaire' in *L'Homme* 2: 5-21. English tr. by Katie Furness-Lane in Lane (1970): 202-26.

__. 1970a. 'On the Verbal Art of William Blake and Other Poet-Painters' in *Linguistic Inquiry* 1: 3-23.

__. 1970b. (with Lawrence Jones) *Shakespeare's Verbal Art in 'Th'Expence of Spirit'.* The Hague: Mouton.

Lane, Michael (ed.). 1970. *Structuralism: A Reader.* London: Jonathan Cape.

Riffaterre, Michael. 1959. 'Criteria for Style Analysis' in *Word* 15: 154-74.

Swan, Michael. 1995. *Practical English Usage.* Oxford: Oxford University Press.

Seeing the Sea:
Deixis and the Perceptions of Melville's Reader

Robert Cockcroft

Abstract

This essay uses the concepts of deixis and schema theory to investigate how in *Moby-Dick*, Melville deliberately disorients the perceptions and cognition of his readers. Writing at a time of tension between the older epic and religious values echoed in Ahab's quest, and the rise of American industrialism and materialism, Melville reflects this in the tension between Ahab's warped religiosity and his repressed humanity – a quality shared with people as diverse as Ishmael and Queequeg, which in Melville's view stands to gain from the shift towards a more this-worldly perspective. But this opposition is never simple: humanity's pillaging of nature in the cause of material progress can seem as demonic as Ahab's more metaphysical obsession. Detailed study of a particular chapter shows how the writing constantly superimposes one deictic frame of reference, or one schematic *script* or *scene* upon another, changing the direction and determinants of the reader's engagement with the story, in line with that of its narrator. Ishmael's perception of the industrial process of 'trying out' whale blubber to whale oil is opposed to his perspective and responsibilities as helmsman, until in a moment of drowsiness he cannot, literally, tell whether he is coming or going.

Key words: affordance; cognition; deixis; scene.

1. Melville's world

In the marine world of Herman Melville's *Moby-Dick*, the author systematically familiarises his reader with two orders of things: with whales and whaling, and within that larger scheme, with the particular history of Ahab, his ship the *Pequod*, and the White Whale. However we conceive the genre of this work – fiction, epic, tragedy, or all three – it is shaped throughout by the technical, economic and political affordances of 19th-century America. Its original readers, of course, inhabited that world themselves, or, as with Melville's earliest English readers, saw in it the unrestrained development of tendencies apparent in their own society.

It is fitting that *Moby-Dick* was published in 1851, the year of the Great Exhibition, with its celebration of British technological development – so soon to be surpassed both in inventiveness and application by the United States.

But the technical world of *Moby-Dick* is a peculiar one. Whaling as expounded and explored by Melville combines the ancient skills of seamanship, boat-handling, and hunting, with a complex high-pressure industrial process carried out at sea to meet the demands of a mass market in whale oil, itself a vital element in the territorial expansion of America. Ship-board processing made it possible to secure a maximal return on capital by hunting whales where they were concentrated at particular times of year, ensuring a high-quality product, and employing the full capacity of the whaling-ships' holds. Advances in the techniques of navigation, in geographical knowledge, in the suppression of piracy, and in the understanding of whales' migratory behaviour now made it possible for ships to range throughout the Pacific.

Poising Ahab, Starbuck, Queequeg, and Ishmael between the expanding world of power, money, and material production, and the epic past where survival had depended on physical strength, on manual skills and courage, and on the psychological and spiritual resource of religion, as it still does so problematically on board the *Pequod*, subject to the warped religious impulses of Ahab, Melville is able to expose his characters and his readers to a bewildering but purposive process of disorientation. He constantly subverts any assumed sense, on the reader's part, of a discontinuity between physical and mental space. What I will attempt to demonstrate might be done with reference to many other chapters of *Moby-Dick*; but I will restrict myself chiefly to Chapter 96, 'The Try-Works' (Melville 1957: 417-21). Like any other epic writer, Melville tends to epitomise major themes in small-scale objects, and I will linger for a while in the '*left* hand try-pot' between the main mast and foremast of the whaling ship *Pequod* (i. e. one of the two cauldrons in which whale oil was produced: the one situated on the starboard side of the ship – i. e. the *right* side looking forward). I want to propose a follow-up to Captain Ahab's observation, addressed to the departing and despondent ears of the First Mate, Starbuck, but heard – or imagined – by the narrator Ishmael and recounted in Chapter 132 (Melville 1957: 531-35): 'By heaven, man, we are turned round and round in this world, like yonder windlass, and Fate is the handspike'. But if we as readers are to entertain Ahab's view, by conforming our imagination to the experience of Melville's sailors, what levers cause our rotation – and the force consequently exerted through us? And what features of the text point us towards the mindset of Melville's readers and of Melville himself as he engages with them, adapting his persuasive technique to the technology of his time and the changing orders – physical, economic, and intellectual – with which it interacts? Might our perceptions, themselves, constitute those 'levers', if they work with cumulative effect in one dominant direction? Is it possible by close examination of Melville's language to demonstrate how it works on our cognitive processes, through our sense of immediate physical space (within a ship or a whale boat, a spot in the sea), and through our more personal sense of who, or what, is *above, below, beside, beyond* or *within* us – in short, through everything that locates us, deictically, within the text? Since deictic language derives its meaning from the immediate space and time common to speaker and listener, and from the apprehended position of each individual within that space, the fact that Ahab, thinking that Starbuck is still standing next to him, compares them both to '*yonder* windlass' puts a special poignancy into the word – to get their bearings, readers must place themselves momentarily, and imaginatively, at the deictic centre that Starbuck has vacated.

2. Deixis: the try-pot's perspective

The 'standard account' of deixis typified by Stephen Levinson (Levinson 1983: 54-96) centred such language on the ego of each successive speaker, as its only meaningful point of reference. But the one-legged Ahab himself, tortured by the neural sensation of his lost limb, has already in effect refuted this in conversation with the Carpenter: 'Look, put thy live leg *here* where mine was [my italics]; so, now, here is only one distinct leg to the eye, yet two to the soul' (Melville 1957: 466). More recent thinking has at once queried the 'egocentric' view, and linked deixis to broader ideas of cognition. In his contribution to *New Essays in Deixis* (Green 1995: 27-48), Peter Jones shows that the paramount authority cited for this view, Karl Bühler, himself points beyond it. As quoted by Jones, he observes that:

> If one person wants to point out something to another, then both together, the
> guide and the person guided, must possess a sufficient measure of harmonious
> orientation within an order in which what is to be pointed out has its place.

Before considering how schema theory might help us distinguish a whole range of such 'orders' (*harmonious* or otherwise) within *Moby-Dick*, let us consider 'orientation' within 'The Try-Works' chapter. How does the reader 'see the sea' on that night of wind, waves, and fire – and *which* sea – 'monomaniac' Ahab's, Ishmael's, or a hallucination rising from the fire itself? And how can we clearly *see* anything whilst subject to such constant disorientation? We have just emerged from one of the most 'wicked' chapters of all Melville's 'wicked book', as he called it in the famous letter to Hawthorne included in Tanner's edition of the novel (Melville 1988: 601), i. e. Chapter 95, 'The Cassock'. That is the one about the skin of the sperm whale's penis, used as protective clothing by the mincer cutting up the blubber; and it ends in a staggering series of puns *mincingly* flaunting its own ambiguity, flickering between cetological, industrial, ecclesiastical, and sexual schemes of things. Moving on from there, we fall back at first into a vein of calm exposition and logic, explaining what makes 'an American whaler' outwardly different from any other ship. But even here we have a 'curious anomaly'. Something like 'a brick-kiln' – normally associated with a scene giving greater scope to human action than the open sea, 'the open field' – is 'transported to her planks'. For the greater part of the next paragraph we attend to a methodical general description of this particular piece of manufacturing equipment, addressed to us like a lecture in human geography.

The try-works, its ponderous inorganic substance 'planted' so incongruously on the deck, is contemplated as though in an isometric drawing or a fitting-out basin. Readers are made aware of its core materials, bricks and mortar, before being told how it would actually appear to them on board the completed ship, when not in use – 'cased with wood' and covered by a 'battened hatchway'. Then – as though a rabbit were being produced from a hat – the vital part not mentioned before the woodwork was (mentally) put in place, is revealed, as '*we* expose the great try-pots'. In its immediate context, it isn't clear whether the pronominal subject 'we' represents Ishmael as the lecturer with his attentive audience looking at *any* 'American whaler', or Ishmael and his shipmates setting to work on board the *Pequod*. But in any case, this exposure relates to the structure itself, not to its immediate use; and *we* as human agents are kept at a distance in the next two sentences, with their passive verbs telling us how the pots are 'kept remarkably clean . . . [and] polished', centring our minds on them as extraordinary objects, without respect to their purpose – though that is reflected in their cleanliness. It requires the comparison of this shipboard scene with one of extravagant luxury ashore, the pots 'shin[ing] within like silver punch-bowls', to remind us – through the opposed associations of work and leisure – that this is a working environment. Then, as if to subvert any simple opposition of sea, work, and hardship to land, leisure, and luxury, we see the image of 'cynical old sailors' shirking work, who '[d]uring the night watches ... will crawl into them and coil themselves away there for a nap'. They are 'coiled' reflexively 'away' as the passive objects of their own rogue activity, like ropes, dogs, or foetuses, in the try-pots – like the Cynic Diogenes in his fabled barrel, the sailors disdaining the proprieties of watch-keeping at sea as the philosopher renounced the luxuries and scorned the civic values of terrestrial Athens.

In recollecting his own active or passive role within this 'order', Ishmael recalls his experience as polisher of 'the left hand try-pot', as viewed from the standpoint of the furnace doors, facing aft – in other words (and within another, larger 'order') on the starboard side of the ship as viewed from his alternative position at the 'midnight helm':

> It was ... with the soapstone diligently circling around me, that I was first indirectly struck by the remarkable fact, that in geometry all bodies gliding along the cycloid, my soapstone for example, will descend from any point in precisely the same time.

The 'diligence' of '*my* soapstone' ('my' bespeaking the order of the task, not of personal possessions) has gone beyond the realm of *hypallage* or transferred quality, detaching itself from Ishmael the operative to such an extent that lapses in his outward attention lead to him being struck repeatedly around his bent knees, buttocks, or ankles by its rapid descent from a slackening grasp, as he 'drowses at the helm' in this small, shining world. This will be easily verified by the reader, granted such apparatus as a hemispherical salad bowl and a couple of grapes, one poised at the rim and the other half-way down, released simultaneously. Both collide precisely at the bottom in the same instant. As this fact, placed in his way by the technology on which – ostensibly – his livelihood depends, 'strikes' Ishmael, we are at once *in* the cauldron with him, choosing 'any' point on its punch-bowl surface (*any* having vivid immediacy in that imagined enclosure), and *outside* it, appreciating an abstract geometrical truth as though sitting in a lecture room. The deixis of place, 'up there' or 'down here', makes no difference to the deixis of time, the interval between the stone's release and its painful impact, though it may to the *force* of the impact. Here, too, Ishmael seems to be located within two 'orders' at once.

3. Schema theory and the plant in use

Before we consider the far more radical and disturbing disorientation which is to follow, let us extend our theoretical base a little further. The title of our chapter, '*The* Try-Works', reflects that broad order of things, that *scene* which the whole novel progressively elaborates for the reader, namely the American sperm-whale fishery, as carried on at this epoch by every ship involved in it, at every stage – though this chapter relates initially to one specific stage, the preparation and use of a ship's whale-oil processing plant. A definite article '*The*', attached to a compound noun half exotic and half familiar, '*Try-Works*', announces another stage in our familiarisation with the mystery of whaling, assuming our interest and attention to something pointed to by that definite article, as part of the *work* of the ship. Nobody could suppose that the titles of other chapters like '*The* Symphony' and '*The* Chase – First Day', or in this chapter '*The* pit' of Hell to whose fiery reek the burning blubber is compared, referred to things of a similar order – though whaling provides a context for both of them. Schema theory, as developed by Roger Schank in his *Dynamic Memory* (Schank 1982) and as summarised by Elena Semino in her *Language and World Creation* (Semino 1997: 119-59), may show us how Melville's world is both created and convulsed – as he works on the reader's existing memory, implants fresh imaginative experience to be drawn on, *as* memory, in succeeding chapters, and plays his climax against both of them. Schema theory of course, views our perception and cognition as largely shaped by pre-existing *schemata* in our minds, based on prior experience and cultural conditioning – which are in their turn modified by fresh experience and perception and which may be consciously activated – by our reason, our persuasive intent, or our imagination (or by all three as in the case of Melville).

Schank's account would represent every stage of the *Pequod*'s voyage as a 'scene', from the mustering of the crew to the sighting of Moby Dick. Most readers know that ships have to be manned, linking this to the broader capitalistic scenario of contractual agreement; and by the end of Ishmael's extended discourse on this area of human geography and oceanography, they have become acquainted with every stage of the process including watching for whales, lowering the boats, and perilously pursuing the prey – as necessity still demands prior to the invention of steam-driven whale-catchers and explosive harpoons – and they are cognitively prepared for the climactic encounter. Particular 'scripts' play on our expectations as defined by these scenes. As early as Chapter 16 we learn what makes whaling ships different, and what makes the *Pequod* extraordinary even in its mustering of a crew, presided over by one of its two Quaker owners, Captain Peleg, from a black whale-bone wigwam on the deck. And by the end we know that there are special conditions (and one bizarre participant, Ahab himself, hoisted aloft in a basket) attached to the *Pequod*'s watch for whales.

Schank would view each separate stage of the voyage as put together from progressive, and repeated, scripts and scenes – movement through the tropics, shipboard routines – made coherent to us by means of what he calls *Memory Organisation Packets* (MOPs for short). Our pre-existent ideas regarding deep-sea fishing voyages will help us to assimilate more and more information into a larger pattern of MOPs – departure, travel to the grounds, work on the grounds, difficulties encountered, ultimate success or disaster, return or non-return. This overarching or containing schema constitutes what Schank calls a meta-MOP; and Melville both plays *with* it – as storms are encountered, whales caught and processed, oil barrels stowed and re-stowed, and the prospect of a happy return to Nantucket raised as late as Chapter 132 – and *against* it. How he does this is our real concern; and four final categories of schemata, namely *goals, plans, themes,* and TOPs (*Thematic Organisation Points*) might help us find out how. *Goals* as characterised by Schank and his earlier collaborator Abelson in 1977 include *Achievement Goals* and *Instrumental Goals*, and *themes* serve to explain goals in terms of social position (or role), interpersonal relationships, and aspirations in life. *Thematic organisation points* embody our capacity to compare things, to see similarities of goal, situation (and, presumably, differences), etc.

So, how do the goals, relationships, and aspirations of Ahab's company relate to his own? Returning to the 'Try-Works' chapter and following the narrative from the position of Ishmael, sharing his five senses and his imaginative vision as he stands at the *Pequod*'s tiller, hearing Stubb's distant deictic address to the unnamed and unspecified members of the trying-out gang, "'All ready there?'", smelling the whale that has been chased, killed, brought alongside, peeled like a gigantic orange into strips of blubber which are then 'minced' into slices as thin and flammable as 'bible leaves' – as (in the discursive geographical present tense) 'he supplies his own fuel and burns by his own body', we also *look* forward down the length of the deck to the pitching of boiling oil, the flaming flues and furnace doors, the fiend-like harpooneer-stokers, and the equally fiendish watch 'lounging' on the 'sea-sofa' of the windlass, swapping stories, whose physical sensations Ishmael anticipates as 'their eyes . . . [scorch] in their heads'. Once reduced to 'fritters' and transferred to the furnace, what's left of the 'bible leaves' of blubber smells remarkably human (Melville 1957: 418):

> … his smoke is horrible to inhale, and inhale it you must, and not only that, but you must live in it for the time. It has an unspeakable, wild, Hindoo odor about it, such as may lurk in the vicinity of funereal pyres. It smells like the left wing of the day of judgment; it is an argument for the pit.

Using another affordance linking Melville with his implied reader as inheritors of a long tradition of faith, the deictic bearings of the Bible and Christian art are imposed on those of the ship; in other words mental space is mapped onto the physical frames of reference – the processing plant and the vessel under sail – so that what is seen and smelt along the centre line of the hull is simultaneously referred forwards and downwards towards 'the pit', for smell, and (for sight) forwards, upwards and outboard to a position somewhere over the port side, towards the divine reprobating judge. In paintings of the Last Judgement like that on the east wall of the Sistine Chapel, the damned are on our right as we face the scene – while for the reader familiar with Matthew 25, and the Judge's empathetic oneness with everybody helped by the good, and neglected by the bad (vv. 35-45), they are down there on 'the left wing', alternately reflecting the reader's own bad conscience, and his or her memories of rejection, as these are channelled through the ultimate spiritual insight of Christ as Judge. And the composite physical and social scene surrounding the try-works, so reminiscent of the hellish scene below the earth (as in Dante) or below the universe (as in Milton), seems at first to reflect a hardness of heart comparable to that of the damned. But whose, predominantly – the harpooneers' and the raconteurs', or Ishmael's own? His account reflects both the lounging watch's callous and shameless inhumanity, and Ishmael's willful demonising, both of them and of the trying-out team itself (Melville 1957: 419):

> As they narrated to each other their unholy adventures, their tales of terror told in words of mirth; as their uncivilized laughter forked upwards out of them, like the flames from the furnace; as to and fro, in their front, the harpooneers wildly gesticulated with their huge pronged forks and dippers; as the wind howled on, and the sea leaped, and the ship groaned and dived, and yet steadfastly shot her red hell further and further into the blackness of the sea and the night, and scornfully champed the white bone in her mouth, and viciously spat round her on all sides; then the rushing Pequod, freighted with savages, and laden with fire, and burning a corpse, and plunging into that blackness of darkness, seemed the material counterpart of her monomaniac commander's soul.

Here we see the 'full operation' of the try-works of Ishmael's imagination as, point by comparative point, it forges a flaming hell out of two working shifts – one, the blubber-boilers, hyperactive; and the other, the seamen on watch, standing (or sitting) easy. Ishmael's own life-theme, his values and his horror at the universal denial of kindness envisioned here, whether by Ahab towards his fellow-men, or by those men towards their fellow-creatures, turns the comic scripts and scenes recounted by the watch into his own 'tales of terror'. Thus, however temporarily, he is alienated from those whose hands, as recently as Chapter 94 (Melville 1957: 412-15), he recalled squeezing so affectionately, intermingled with the globules of precious spermaceti from the whale's head, as they worked together to homogenise it, and as he glimpsed a concordant vision of this-worldly happiness, to be based on human fellowship and material progress: 'the wife, the heart, the bed, the table, the saddle, the fire-side, the country' (Melville 1957: 413). As the order of factory work effaces that of the hunt, his friend and former bed-fellow the harpooneer Queequeg, is transformed into a devil flourishing a pitchfork. Meanwhile the ship herself (reflecting the sound and movement of a sea neither seen nor smelt), enacts the recurrent 'scene' of the seaway, her diving and plunging repeated, stressed, and made metaphorical as she extends Ishmael's mood, his inward 'blackness of darkness', into 'scornful' and 'vicious' belittlement of the sea itself – her *rising* to the waves only inferred from our default knowledge of this scene. As though referring back to the point when the flames first reached their full height, Ishmael steers them deictically with the ship, '*further* and *further*' into the dark.

4. Conclusion: coming or going?

Deprived as he has been, repeatedly, of any fixed mental, emotional, or spiritual bearing, it is more understandable that Ishmael, who as the helmsman is immediately responsible for the safety of the ship, should doze off like a tired motorway driver, pivot on one heel, wake up facing aft – and for a moment construe headlong retreat as heroic advance. He has the sensation of 'rushing from all havens astern' but is still, cognitively, suspended in the scene of his duty as the steersman, grasping the helm and gazing *ahead* (Melville 1957: 420):

> Nothing seemed before me but a jet gloom, now and then made ghastly by flashes of redness. Uppermost was the impression, that whatever swift, rushing thing I stood on was not so much bound to any haven ahead as rushing from all havens astern. A stark, bewildered feeling, as of death, came over me. Convulsively my hands grasped the tiller, but with the crazy conceit that the tiller was, somehow, in some enchanted way, inverted. My God! what is the matter with me? thought I. Lo! in my brief sleep I had turned myself about, and was fronting the ship's stern, with my back to her prow and the compass. In an instant I faced back, just in time to prevent the vessel from flying up into the wind, and very probably capsizing her.

The tiller seems 'inverted', pivoted forwards towards the bows rather than backwards towards the stern. Then, seemingly, Ishmael realises that he is, in reversal of normal deictic associations '*fronting* the ship's *stern*' – i. e. within mental, more than physical space, *con*fronting what grows more remote rather than what looms ahead, perceiving Ahab's abandonment of every haven, every goal of preservation. Through his disorientation he achieves a truer sense of the inexorable 'rushing' movement noted earlier by Ahab himself, in Chapter 37 ('Sunset') after gazing over the ship's wake. There the 'demoniac' compared his unswerving 'path' towards a 'fixed purpose' with the railroad's advance across continental America (Melville 1957: 166):

> Over unsounded gorges, through the rifled hearts of mountains, under torrents' beds, unerringly I rush! Naught's an obstacle, naught's an angle to the iron way!

He acknowledges in the same chapter that in enflaming others with his own purpose, 'the match itself must needs be wasting'; but then he reassumes mass and momentum, availing himself of the supreme image of wilfully abandoned choice afforded by the technical and economic power of mass-produced steel, coal, and steam.

The contrary attraction of those 'havens astern' is to be finally represented in Chapter 132, 'The Symphony' (Melville 1957: 531-35), by imagery of another order, again involving many shifts in direction and alternating strains on that 'windlass' towards which Ahab finally seeks to turn Starbuck's attention (after he has 'stolen away'). In that same last-chance chapter Ahab 'drop[s]' a tear into the sea', leaving '*that* one wee drop' in the Pacific – indicated deictically as though in a precise location, just as its atoms disperse – as an index of his humanity. He looks '"into [Starbuck's] human eye"' only to avert his gaze from his own wife and child, which it reflects. He is drawn from the '"green land"' back to the inverted orders of sea and sky where the sun as 'royal czar and king' yields up 'the pensive air … transparently pure and soft, with a woman's look' to the powers of 'sword-fish and sharks' which 'rush' below, personifying the 'murderous thinkings of the masculine sea' (and of Ahab). When in due course he looks over the side, the eyes of his evil genius, Fedallah, are reflected in the water – from which in the following chapter Moby Dick's inverted jaw will rise like an open marble tomb. All of this could well be investigated with a fuller use of deixis and schema theory; but, in the meantime, Ishmael's superimposition of forward and backward movement, figuring as it does the pain of loss fuelling Ahab's driving rage, already represents the narrative's overall direction.

References

Green, Keith (ed.). 1995. *New Essays in Deixis*. Amsterdam: Rodopi.

Jones, Peter. 1995. 'Philosophical and Theoretical Problems in the Study of Deixis: A Critique of the Standard Account' in Green (1995): 27-48.

Levinson, Stephen. 1983. *Pragmatics*. Cambridge: Cambridge University Press.

Melville, Herman. 1957. *Moby Dick: or The Whale* (ed. Newton Arvin). New York: Holt, Rinehart & Winston.

__. 1988. *Moby-Dick* (ed. Tony Tanner). Oxford: Oxford University Press.

Schank, Roger. C. 1982. *Dynamic Memory: A Theory of Reminding and Learning in Computers and People*. Cambridge: Cambridge University Press.

Semino, Elena. 1997. *Language and World Creation in Poems and Other Texts*. London: Longman.

Narratives of Transgression: Challenging the Boundaries of Competent Discourses

Anna Elizabeth Balocco

Abstract

In this paper narratives published in the Brazilian magazine *Época* are analysed: the narratives are part of a cover story entitled 'Brazilian homosexual women occupy public space and affirm their sexual orientation with dignity'. The main theoretical assumption of this paper is that social identities, across different dimensions, are discursively constructed (Hall 1997; Sarup 1996). The analysis is concerned with the *interdiscursive* (Chouliaraki & Fairclough 1999) dimension of the narratives, with a view to identifying the discourses (or discursive formations) that constitute the storytellers' voices. It is argued that although storytellers challenge the boundaries of 'competent discourses' (Chauí 2000), constituted to erase cultural, linguistic, ethnic, gender or sexual differences, their narratives are contained within a dominant code, which defines a particular type of representation for homoerotic women.

Key words: identity; interdiscourse; homoeroticism.

1. Introduction

The discussion of female homoeroticism, which was once undertaken exclusively within the limits of specialised discourses (medical, psychiatric, literary discourses, among others), has lately been emerging in different genres of the media. Well-known examples in the Brazilian media are: a soap opera produced by a powerful television channel, in which a lesbian couple played an important role; a TV programme for wide audiences, whose theme was dating among lesbians; an online feature story about teenage girls 'who kiss each other on the mouth', available at the site iGirl (Behaviour Section: *Meninas que beijam meninas*).[1] The questions that immediately emerge from this picture are the following: what are the conditions which might allow for discussion of an issue which was once circumscribed in specialised publications? What role do popular media genres perform in contemporary society, from the point of view of constructions of the real? To what extent can these genres be seen as territories for the circulation of non-hegemonic meanings?

In this paper, narratives published in issue 22 of the Brazilian magazine *Época* are analysed: the narratives are part of a cover story entitled 'Brazilian homosexual women occupy public space and affirm their sexual orientation with dignity'.[2] Narratives of this kind are often called *coming-out stories*, and represent a 'narrative of transgression' (Caldas-Coulthard 1996: 256), associated with the public affirmation of a sexual identity which is still seen by many people as 'deviant' (cf. Giddens 1992: 23).

The argument in this paper runs in two directions. First, these narratives function as a representational resource (Kress 1996: 18) through which a public identity is constructed for homoerotic women. However, as will be argued below, the narratives are contained within a dominant discourse, which defines a demarcated space for homoerotic women, and constructs a specific type of representation for them.

2. Theoretical Framework

The main principle informing this paper is the notion that social identities, along different parameters (ethnic, gender, or sexual identities, among other possibilities), are discursively constructed. They are seen, in this paper, as the result of linguistic and discursive processes: it is through dialogue with different discourses circulating around us that we constitute our identities (Hall 1997: 55).

Narratives represent a very powerful discursive practice in our culture, through which we attach meaning to our social experiences and construct our identities (Mischler 2001; Sarup 1996; Brockmeier & Harré 1997: 263). Like other practices of meaning production, narratives are culturally and historically grounded (Woodward 2000: 10): the meanings or representations expressed in narratives vary over time, and within different social groups.

With a view to investigating the cultural, historical, and ideological variables that affect the production of the *coming-out stories* published in *Época*, the decision was taken to focus on the interdiscursive dimension of the narratives (Chouliaraki & Fairclough 1999: 45). The study of interdiscourse in the coming-out stories will, it is hoped, enable us to explore the ways in which the subjectivity of homoerotic subjects is constituted, the voices that resonate in this process, and the perspective or point of view from which representations of these subjects are constructed.

In this paper, *interdiscourse* is understood as the complex articulation of discursive formations (Foucault 1987) in the narratives studied. This important, constitutive dimension of discourse enables us to analyse *coming-out stories* from the point of view of the broad cultural context in which they are situated, associating them with certain *orders of discourse* (for example, medical discourse about sexuality), as well as with particular *discursive formations* (patriarchal discourse, for example, or homophobic discourse).

The analysis also deals with the social relations established between the storytellers and the assistant editor of the feature article: attention will be paid to the factors that position the female subjects' voices in a relationship of subordination to a macro-narrative (the article within which the narratives appear) whose point of view is male (Caldas-Coulthard 1996: 256). In tackling this issue, we are concerned with how the meanings in the article are implicated in relations of power, specifically between the assistant editor who is writing about the topic and the women who are being written about.

3. Narratives of transgression: the genre of 'coming-out stories'

Magazines play an important role in the construction of social representations, thus constituting an invaluable source of reference for the study of identity, in its dimensions of gender, race, sex, and profession.

The reports published in *Época* satisfy the four criteria for narratives proposed by Bruner (1997: 46): 1) they are temporally organised; 2) they establish relationships between the exceptional and the common, or canonical (criterion of exceptionality); 3) they meet the criterion of dramatic quality; and 4) they feature two discursive dimensions: that of the story proper, whose protagonists are the female storyteller and her parents or friends; and the dimension of the context of utterance, in which the storyteller addresses the reporter who collected the narratives.

If, on the one hand, criteria 3 and 4, exceptionality and dramatic quality, make these narratives 'reportable' (cf. Labov & Waletsky 1967), on the other hand they constitute the elements which characterise them as narratives of transgression. These are narratives that are not socially sanctioned: to some, it still seems 'natural' to classify people as either 'homosexual' or 'heterosexual', to treat these two categories as stable (Lacqueur 2001: 18) and '[to view homosexuality] as a perversion (…), that is, as specifically non-natural and morally condemned' (Giddens 1992: 23).[3]

The narratives may be characterised as a sub-genre of narratives of personal experience (cf. Labov & Waletsky 1967), henceforth *narratives of identity*, given that they throw up questions of identity through discussion of issues related to the sexuality of the storytellers (cf. Caldas-Coulthard 1996: 256). These narratives report the circumstances in which the subjects 'disclosed' their sexual identity to their family or friends.

4. Coming out of the closet

In the language of magazines, titles often function as the Abstract and Orientation of a narrative (cf. Labov & Waletsky 1967), telling readers what the story is about, and who the people are who are involved in it. Brought together below are: the titles on the cover of *Época* 22; the titles that feature in the table of contents; and the heading that initiates the article:

COVER	Lesbians.[4]
	They reveal [their sexual orientation].
	Brazilian homosexuals occupy public space and affirm their sexual orientation with dignity.
TABLE OF CONTENTS	Behaviour.
	Lesbians, like psychologist Angela Prado, from São Paulo, are more and more at ease and do not hide a sexual option which is gradually ceasing to be a taboo.
	A conquered space.
FEATURE ARTICLE	Lesbians come out of the closet, want to have children, and even admit to having a relationship with men.

The Orientation in the cover provides us with the theme of the feature article (female homoeroticism), the people involved ('Brazilian homosexuals') and the situation which justifies the article insertion in the section on Behaviour ('they occupy public space'). Point of view is anonymous in the cover and in the table of contents, but represents that of the assistant editor, who signed the feature article in the magazine.

The beginning of the feature article provides us with more Orientation: 'there is something new in the streets...'; 'lesbians are more at ease...'; 'they walk around holding hands'; 'they dare to caress each other...'. The initial segment appears to have a double function: it re-establishes the Orientation, and functions as an attempt on the part of the editor to justify the article.

By describing what is 'out there in the streets', the editor presents the article as though it *reflected* changes in society ('this is a fashionable theme', he writes), thereby fulfilling his social role of *mirroring* society, bringing forward themes pertaining to Behaviour. However, as will be argued below, the feature article in *Época* does not merely *reflect* changes in society; rather, it *constructs* a specific type of representation for homoerotic women.

Kress, Leite-Garcia & van Leeuwen (1997: 270) argue that we ought to analyse the way language interacts with visual elements in a text, in ideologically marked ways. Although there is not enough room in this paper to introduce an exhaustive analysis of the 'semiotics of the visual space' of the text, the function of the photographs featured in the cover, in the table of contents, and inside the magazine proper should not be neglected. These photographs perform a double function: they indicate that the narratives published were produced by real people (and not fictionalised people, as is often the case in magazines), but they also act as the main anchorage for the characterisation of these women as representatives of 'new lesbianism': the photos show young, well dressed, and well groomed women, who wear tight clothes, high-heeled shoes and their hair long. The point of view which incorporates these women into our collective memories is male: on account of their attributes (their 'femininity', in the editor's words), they remain within the scope of the male gaze, being easily eroticised.

The narratives themselves are detached from the matrix-text, appearing as they do in boxes containing the storytellers' names, ages and professions. These narratives have been edited, with deletions and minor changes, as becomes clear from an inspection of the online version of the magazine, which features the published narratives and the full versions, as well as two narratives produced by parents of the storytellers.

4.1. Identity and interdiscourse

The narratives which were analysed articulate various orders of discourse (religious discourse; medical discourse; moral discourse), and are shaped by competing discursive formations (among others, patriarchal discourse; a more liberal discourse on sexuality; homophobic discourse). In the fragment below, for example, sexuality is constructed within moral discourse, as signalled by the terms 'values' and 'education':

> Fragment 1: Revealing my desire for other women was no easy task. Education in northeastern parts of Brazil is organised around traditional family values. (Ita Catrina)

The evaluation contained in '[it] was no easy task' signals a point of tension in the constitution of the storyteller's subjectivity. If in the fragment discussed the tension is discussed in moral terms, in the fragment below it is framed in religious discourse:

> Fragment 2: I have been dating women for three years. Before that, I had a relationship with a boy, hence my mother's disappointment when I told her the news. It was quite a shock for them. Well, I do not feel guilty from a Christian point of view. (Rafaela)

The notion of Christian guilt in this narrative represents a residual element of a discourse of the 19th century, which treats homoeroticism as a 'sin against the soul' (Freire Costa 2002: 43).

The same discursive configuration can be seen in the following fragment:

> Fragment 3: I was never afraid I would lose my job on account of my decision, but I lost friends when I disclosed my sexual identity. I knew my parents would accept me, but I was afraid of hurting them because they are from a different generation. When I told them, the weeping scene was inevitable, but the tears did not burst from my eyes, but from theirs. (Carolina)

The expressions *lose one's job, lose one's friends,* and *hurt one's parents* support the discursive construction, in the previous fragments, of homoeroticism as conduct within the domain of the prohibited, and under disciplinary constraints (Foucault 1987: 18).

From the point of view of the discursive formations articulated in the narratives, most of them introduce both a conservative conception of sexuality, and a more liberal one:

> Fragment 4: I have been dating both boys and girls since I was 16. I had a few boyfriends, as I wanted to experiment with men and make sure this is what I really wanted. I had a lot of problems in the family. I am an only child, I had a very strict education, and was brought up by my grandparents. (Ana Paula)

In this fragment, the storyteller's sexual identity is discursively constructed as a process of experimentation ('I wanted to experiment with men'), within the boundaries of a discursive formation in which the plurality of one's sexual practices may be enunciated. But the storyteller's conduct is condemned by her family ('I had a lot of problems in the family'). From an interdiscursive point of view, the fragment articulates competing discursive formations: the discourse of 'pure relationships' (see Giddens 1992: 48), which construes the notion of emotional AND sexual equality between men and women, and a conservative discourse, voiced through 'the family', which condemns such practices.

Many narratives feature the discourse of 'plastic sexuality', in which, according to Giddens (1992: 10), a distinction is drawn between *sex* and *reproduction*:

> Fragment 5: ... the fact that two women are together does not mean that they do not think of having children. I would like to have children. Insemination is very expensive and I'd prefer to have children naturally. (Ana Paula)

In this fragment, the storyteller establishes, through negation, a relationship between 'being together' (a euphemism for having a sexual attachment to someone) and 'having children'. From an interdiscursive perspective, the negation only makes sense within a discursive formation in which sex is subordinated to reproduction.

It is the discourse of plastic sexuality, which dissociates sex from reproduction, that allows for the emergence of the discourse of 'pure relationships' (Giddens 1992:10):

> Fragment 6: The idea of separating love from sex, which men have always felt comfortable with, is a recent discovery for women like me. ... [W]omen have learnt that it is possible to separate love from sex. (Raíssa)

The narrative constructs men and women as living in different temporal and cognitive universes: if for men the conception of sex as separate from love is a given ('they have always felt comfortable with it'), for women it is 'a recent discovery', one which 'women have learnt'. The temporal markers (*always, recent*) and the dynamic durative verb *learn* (Greenbaum & Quirk 1990: 55), which denotes a change of state taking place over a period of time, all play an important role in discursively constructing a temporal and conceptual divide between men and women. From an interdiscursive perspective, this construction of two separate worlds for men and women only makes sense within patriarchal discourse, that is, a discursive formation that positions men and women differently with respect to sexual rights and obligations (the so-called 'model of the two sexes').

Patriarchal discourse features in many narratives, in different guises. In the next fragment, it takes the form of a dominant discourse which encourages emotional restraint for men and sensitivity, warmth, and camaraderie for women (Nixon 1997: 296):

> Fragment 7: A relationship with a woman is more satisfying. She is more of a companion, more of a friend, more of a lover. She laughs with you, cries with you. (Raíssa)

The fragment actualises a discursive formation (from 18th-century rationalist Enlightenment discourse, but which dates back to the ancient Stoics[5]) which attaches positive value to cognition and reason, and negative value to affection, or the expression of emotions. This is but a small step to associating the former (cognition) with the public sphere, and the latter (emotion) with the domestic, or private domain, and to the coding of established notions of masculinity and femininity. From this perspective, patriarchal discourse limits not only women's social experience, restricting it to the domestic sphere, but men's as well, locating it in the public sphere and ruling out emotions and feelings from this social space.

Turning to the possible conducts and practices adopted by homoerotic subjects in dealing with social exclusion, the following discourses are articulated in the narratives:

> Fragment 8: I spent my whole life thinking that a dyke was the kind of woman that kicks out other women in bars and that a gay man is the kind of guy who sees cockroaches and runs away. (Rafaela)

Fragment 9: My parents know [about it], my friends know, my colleagues at work know, my friends at school know. I never felt any kind of prejudice against me, nor did anybody give me any queer looks and I believe I have benefited from the changes [that have taken place]. The end of the stereotype of the masculine lesbian has helped a lot, it is as if this were less aggressive [for people]. People realise that a woman can be a lesbian without losing her femininity. (Daniele)

Fragment 10: It was only when I turned 26 that I attended a GLS party. I realised that this was not much of a problem. I found out there were girls [there] just like me, and not only masculine women. (Ita Catrina)

The discourse of 'camp subculture' (see Sontag [(1961)] 2001: 275-76) is articulated in these fragments, which introduce a representation of lesbians based on parodic models of heterosexual men. In these models, lesbians are depicted as behaving in exaggerated ways and as adopting male ways of dressing and speaking. The discourse of 'clandestine ghetto culture' (Freire Costa 2002: 94) is also adopted by this storyteller, in the last fragment ('It was only when I turned 26 that I attended a GLS party'), and is present in other narratives:

Fragment 11: As for me, I do not go to gay places. I do not believe it is necessary to get together with other people to fight for this. I believe that a political attitude begins at home, with my family members. (Rafaela)

To Freire Costa, the 'ghetto subculture' is made up of a restricted number of exclusive meeting places, and carries social values that reinforce the prejudice against homoerotic subjects and their feelings of *anomie*. In the same narrative, the discourse of 'gay activism', very common after the Stonewall riots in June 1969 (Berutti 1999) is introduced only to be rejected: 'I do not believe it is necessary to get together with other people to fight for this'.

The last mode of conduct adopted by homoerotic subjects, that of 'sexual acting out' (Freire Costa 2002: 94) was also identified in these narratives:

Fragment 12: But there are still other girls, mainly here in Recife, who have a boyfriend just as a façade. (Ita Catrina)

The discourse of sexual acting-out refers to a double standard of behaviour whose aim is to 'disguise' the subject's sexuality, and thus subscribes to a conservative conception of sexuality which determines a social position for the homoerotic subject. In the following fragment, for example, the storyteller reports an incident when she did not 'respect' the subject position prescribed for homoerotic subjects (which encourages 'disguising' their sexual orientation) and ended up having to deal with homophobic discourse and attitudes:

> Fragment 13: …we were once attacked by a man. We went to the police station and reported what had happened. He attacked us both physically and morally. I believe this accounts for lesbians not [wanting] to expose themselves so much. We are physically weaker in a fight. (Ana Paula)

Apart from articulating homophobic discourse in her speech, through the voice of the man who attacked her, the storyteller establishes a relationship between this discourse and one of the strongest signs of lesbianism, that of invisibility (Berutti 2001: 90): 'I believe this accounts for lesbians not [wanting] to expose themselves so much', says the storyteller.

4.2. Discursive heterogeneity

Analysis of the narratives suggests that they are characterised by their discursive heterogeneity. This heterogeneity produces an 'identity in the making' or a 'shifting identity', which challenges the static, essentialist conception of the homoerotic subject. Evidence of this is in the storytellers' concern to make clear that their sexual orientation is not fixed, and may change at any time in the future. In general terms, this kind of remark, on the part of the subjects, occurs in the final segment of the narrative (in its Coda), which features a 'final evaluation' of the contingencies of disclosing one's sexual identity:

> Fragment 14: I can't say that I will never date a man again, especially because I never saw myself as a homosexual. The prejudice is there, there is no denying it, but the tendency is [for prejudice] to weaken. Society needs somebody to crucify (or blame). (Carolina)
>
> Fragment 15: By and large, I don't want anybody to judge me. I am a missionary of my own ideas and if along the way [= in the future] I find out that this doesn't work any more, I [would] change my route. (Raíssa)

The storytellers' concern with stating the 'malleability' of their sexual orientation signals the open nature of identity in late modern society, in which dominant sexual stereotypes are challenged (Giddens 1992: 41). This concern is also evident in the development of the narratives, in Evaluative segments, in which storytellers address the reporter:

> Fragment 16: I never presented myself as a bisexual, but I can't say that my decision is definitive, because I do not loathe men.[6] (Rafaela)
>
> Fragment 17: Since then, I never dated men any more. I don't feel like doing so, but this does not mean that I might not do so again in the future. (Rosane)

In these fragments, the storytellers construct personal narratives projected towards the future: they function as 'a reflexive self-project – a more or less continuous interrogation of the past, the present, and the future', which characterises social life in late modernity (Giddens 1992: 71).

As to the ordering relations among the discourses, they seem to be paired in dichotomous sets: every time a progressive discourse on sexuality, for example, is articulated, a conservative one is placed alongside it. This distinct patterning constructs a subject position for homoerotic women which is the discoursal position of the Other of hegemonic discourses, or 'competent discourses' (Chauí 2000: 7). For the Brazilian philosopher Marilena Chauí, 'competent discourses' are those discourses constituted by a single voice and which function towards erasing difference, whether cultural, linguistic, and racial or gender difference, or difference in terms of sexual orientation.

These mechanisms for 'fixing up subjects in positions prescribed by a structural system' reveal, to Freire Costa (2002: 35), the work of ideology. Lesbians are doubly inscribed as the Other of hegemonic discourses on *sex* and on *gender*: in opposition to hegemonic male heterosexual discourse, as well as to patriarchal discourse, embedded in the ideological struggle over *gender* and *power*. Thus, the constitution of a lesbian identity of a particular kind ('chic lesbianism', according to the assistant editor of the feature article) can be accounted for only within the context of a discussion on *gender* and *power*. Adapting Lacqueur's claim (2001: 23) about sexuality, 'everything that one wants to say about [lesbianism] already contains in itself a claim about gender'.

5. The genre of coming-out stories and the construction of a discourse of resistance

The genre of coming-out stories is a representational resource that constructs a new form of social representation for the lesbian. The homoerotic subjects of these narratives have traditionally been the object of other people's discourse, in texts that discuss homoeroticism from different perspectives: clinical, psychiatric, religious, and moral, among other perspectives. There is no denying that in their coming-out stories these women constitute themselves as subjects of their own discourse.

However, these narratives are subordinated to a text which is the locus of ideological struggle: although the feature article presents itself as though it were aligned with progressive discourses on sexuality (which reject the absolute separation between 'homosexualism' and 'heterosexualism'), the text is laden with values associated with discourses that bound women within the scope of male gaze and desire, as its emphasis on chic lesbianism suggests. In this respect, it is never enough to argue that femininity is socially constructed, not a 'natural' condition for women, and that the meaning attached to the term 'femininity' carries the discursive memory of a historical and cultural context which institutionalised male sexual domination and the submission of women (Guedes 2001: 100).

The narratives themselves are permeated by contradictory discourses. In Kress's words (1989: 7), 'discourses do not exist in isolation, but within a broader system of opposing, contradictory, competing, or simply different discourses'. Indeed, these narratives seem to be aligned with progressive discourses on sexuality, which treat sex as 'autonomous in relation to other forms of relationship', as one of the storytellers says: 'women have learnt that it is possible to separate love from sex'. However, the same narratives construct stereotypical representations of men: 'men should not be trusted'; 'they separate sex from love'; 'boys only want a one-night stand'.

If on the one hand these women disclose their sexual orientation and do so 'with dignity', as the assistant editor argues, on the other hand they are still locked into a linguistic and conceptual universe which represents them as the object of male desire: 'men make a fetish of [seeing] two women together', says one of the storytellers. These narratives are thus contained within a patriarchal visual discourse of seeing/being seen, which represents a male fantasy of mastery and control over female sexuality.

Apart from residues of conservative discursive formations in the narratives themselves, the coming-out stories are performed in a small, demarcated space, contained within a dominant code (the matrix text which introduces the narratives). However, in spite of these limitations, the coming-out stories challenge competent discourses in operation at this point in time, in our culture: it is through these stories that homoerotic women's collective memory is structured and social meaning is attached to their private experiences.

Endnotes

[1] *Revista iGirl*, available at http://igirl.ig.com.br/website/sexo/comportamento.

[2] I retain the terms 'homosexual' or 'heterosexual' when these are used in the works referred to. Otherwise, the terms 'homoerotic' and 'heteroerotic subjects' are adopted (see Freire Costa 2002 for justifications for this discoursal practice).

[3] My translation into English from a Portuguese version (cf. 'References' below).

[4] The translation into English is a relatively free version aimed at capturing aspects of content only, rather than exact form of expression.

[5] Cf. Rajagopalan (in press): 'William James (1884) famously argued that emotions have no mental content but are merely bodily states. James' position thus echoes a long tradition – dating back to ancient Stoics – of regarding emotions as generally deleterious and in need of being reined in by robust reason: the hysterical woman who must be brought under control by man's cool and sober reasoning power. Incidentally, this tradition is still kept alive in contemporary practices of cognitive therapy for emotional disorders'.

[6] Literally, 'take no aversion to men'.

References

Berutti, Eliane Borges. 1999. 'Gays e Lésbicas: Vozes da Literatura Norte-Americana Contemporânea' in *Matraga* 12: 1-7.

___. 2001. 'Gays, Lésbicas e AIDS: uma Perspectiva Queer' in Oliveira Lima & Monteiro (2001): 98-109.

Brockmeier, Jens, and Rom Harré. 1997. 'Narrative: Problems and Promises of an Alternative Paradigm' in *Research in Language and Social Interaction* 30(4): 263-83.

Bruner, Jerome. 1997. *Atos de Significação*. Porto Alegre: Artes Médicas.

Caldas-Coulthard, Carmen Rosa. 1996. 'Women Who Pay for Sex and Enjoy It: Transgression versus Morality in Women's Magazines' in Caldas-Coulthard & Coulthard (1996): 250-70.

Caldas-Coulthard, Carmen Rosa, and Malcolm Coulthard (eds). 1996. *Texts and Practices: Readings in Critical Discourse Analysis*. London: Routledge.

Chauí, Marilena. 2000. *Cultura e Democracia: o Discurso Competente e Outras Falas*. Campinas: Cortez.

Chouliaraki, Lilie, and Norman Fairclough. 1999. *Discourse in Late Modernity: Rethinking Critical Discourse Analysis*. Edinburgh: Edinburgh University Press.

Foucault, Michel. 1987. *A Arqueologia do Saber*. Rio de Janeiro: Forense-Universitária [original French ed. 1969].

Freire Costa, Jurandir. 2002. *A Inocência e o Vício. Estudos sobre o Homoerotismo* (4th ed.). Rio de Janeiro: Relume Dumará.

Giddens, Anthony. 1992. *A Transformação da Intimidade. Sexualidade, Amor e Erotismo nas Sociedades Modernas*. São Paulo: Editora da Unesp.

Greenbaum, Sidney, and Randolph Quirk. 1990. *A Student's Grammar of the English Language*. London: Longman.

Guedes, Peônia Viana. 2001. 'Desafiando Mitos de Feminilidade: o Grotesco e o Erótico em *Nights at the circus* e em *The passion'* in Oliveira Lima & Monteiro (2001): 100-15.

Hall, Stuart (ed.). 1997. *Representation: Cultural Representations and Signifying Practices*. London: Sage.

Kress, Gunther. 1989. *Linguistic Processes in Sociocultural Practices*. Oxford: Oxford University Press.

___. 1996. 'Representational Resources and the Production of Subjectivity: Questions for the Theoretical Development of Critical Discourse Analysis in a Multicultural Society' in Caldas-Coulthard & Coulthard (1996): 15-31.

Kress, Gunther, Regina Leite-Garcia, and Theo van Leeuwen. 1997. 'Discourse Semiotics' in van Dijk, Teun A. (ed.) *Discourse as Social Interaction*. London: Sage: 257-91.

Labov, William, and Joshua Waletsky. 1967. 'Narrative Analysis: Oral Versions of Personal Experience' in Helm, June (ed.) *Essays on the Verbal and Visual Arts*. Seattle, WA: University of Washington Press: 12-44.

Lacqueur, Thomas. 2001. *Inventando o Sexo. Corpo e Gênero dos Gregos a Freud*. Rio de Janeiro: Relume Dumará [original English ed. 1992].

Mischler, Elliott G. 2001. 'Narrative and Identity: The Double Arrow of Time'. Paper presented at *Discourse and Identity Conference* (Rio de Janeiro: PUC).

Nixon, Sean. 1997. 'Exhibiting Masculinity' in Hall (1997): 291-336.

Oliveira Lima, Tereza Marques, and Conceição Monteiro (eds). 2001. *Representações Culturais do Outro nas Literaturas de Língua Inglesa*. Rio de Janeiro: Vício de Leitura.

Rajagopalan, Kanavilil (in press). 'Emotion and Language Politics: The Brazilian Case'. To appear in *Journal of Multilingual and Multicultural Development*.

Sarup, Madan. 1996. *Identity, Culture and the Postmodern World*. Edinburgh: Edinburgh University Press.

Sontag, Susan. [1961] 2001. 'Notes on Camp' in *Against Interpretation and Other Essays*. New York: Picador: 275-92.

Woodward, Kathryn. 2000. 'Identidade e Diferença: Uma Introdução Teórica E Conceitual' in Silva, Tomás Tadeu (ed.) *Identidade e Diferença: a Perspectiva dos Estudos Culturais*. Petrópolis: Vozes: 7-72.

The Translator's Craft as a Cross-Cultural Discourse

Mirjana Bonačić

Abstract

Dialogue between cultures which avoids cultural assimilation into a global form of communication still depends on the translator's ability to negotiate the space between cultures. Therefore, along with the writer in the context of globalisation, it seems relevant to redefine the translator as well. The traditional view of translation is expressed from the theorist's vantage point involving two potentially opposing concepts: translation equivalence with respect to the source text vs. translation acceptability within the target culture. The paper argues that important questions are closed off by an emphasis on the translated text that acquires its identity by virtue of either being equivalent to the source or acceptable within the target literary system. Postmodern logic can redefine the translator's craft in terms of access to the potentially manifold modes of mutual refraction of the source and target. Such refraction occurs in the space between them which is opened up by the concept of translatability as the mode of a cross-cultural discourse. Different translations of a poem are analysed from a linguistic and critical perspective to try to account for the individually established, multiple routes of reference where translatability means the chance to embrace more than was possible before.

Key words: poetic translation; equivalence; translatability; cross-cultural discourse; cognitive linguistics.

1. Introduction

Rather than being culture-specific, present-day high technology has become the active constituent of the driving force behind current processes of globalisation. Thus, one of the main purposes of the Internet is to facilitate international communication and access to information. The question is: Does the Internet function effectively through the use of a dominant world language or as a means of specific cultural representation through a Babel of languages? I think that in the domain of creative writing, dialogue between cultures which avoids cultural assimilation into a reductive global form of communication will continue for a long time to depend on our ability to comprehend other cultures through learning their languages or on the translator's ability to negotiate the space between cultures without subsuming it into preconceived generalities. Thus, along with the writer in the context of globalisation, it seems relevant to redefine the translator as well, since translation still plays a significant role in cross-cultural relations.

In this paper, I will first briefly discuss some crucial theoretical questions relating to the redefinition of the translator's craft in the light of postmodern logic. Then I will use translations of a poetic text from English into two different Slavic languages to examine translation as a dialogic, two-way process which can be described in terms of translatability as the mode of a cross-cultural discourse.

2. Theoretical issues

The theoretical account of translatability as a key concept in the encounter between cultures, recently put forward by Iser (1995), although not concerned with translation proper, can be seen as highly relevant for a process-oriented approach to interlinguistic translation. I see such an approach as being diametrically opposed to traditional translation theories. The majority of translation theorists and commentators on translation define or describe the nature of the relationship between source text and target text in terms of two opposite poles of the continuum relating to the norms used in the translation process: translation equivalence as the source-text-oriented pole vs. translation acceptability as the target-text-oriented pole.

The source-text-oriented models of translation define equivalence in terms of particular dimensions in the source text: formal, functional, communicative, textual, cognitive (e. g. Catford 1965; Nida & Taber 1974; Ivir 1981; Neubert & Shreve 1992; Tabakowska 1997). They prescribe aspects of translation in advance, primarily on the basis of the source text and its environment. On the other hand, the target-text-oriented models of translation rely on the notion of acceptability which they define in terms of adherence to the norms, linguistic and textual (literary, stylistic, etc.), of the target system. Thus, their aim is to provide a framework for describing existing translations against the background of the target language and culture (Toury 1995).

However, the fact that there is little agreement over the proper application of the term *adequacy* is symptomatic of a major problem underlying the idea of a continuum with two opposite poles. Namely, the term *adequacy* is used sometimes synonymously with, sometimes instead of, and sometimes in contrast to the related term *equivalence* (Shuttleworth & Cowie 1997: 9). Translation is described as adequate if the translator seeks throughout to follow source rather than target linguistic and literary norms. In this case, *adequacy* is used synonymously with *translation equivalence*. On the other hand, *adequacy* is generally defined as the quality of being good enough to be acceptable. So in this sense, *adequacy* is used synonymously with *acceptability*. This terminological confusion is related to basic problems of the two-pole continuum which is perceived and assessed from the theorist's vantage point. It is only from the theorist's vantage point that the two potentially opposing concepts of translation equivalence vs. translation acceptability seem to be clearly distinguished. In reality, the determination of translation equivalence depends on the extent to which the theorist and the translator extract converging patterns of signification from the text's language. Likewise, when translation phenomena are explained in relation to a hypothetical construct of acceptable translation, the parameters of conformity to the target-culture norms of adequacy may be variously defined by the theorist and the translator respectively.

The problem of the traditional two-pole (source vs. target) continuum of translation adequacy is related to the aporia between freedom and faithfulness. Does translation have to be faithful to the original, or does it have to be free for the sake of the idiomatic and cultural relevance of the target language? The question haunts the problem of translation assessment. However, from the translator's internal perspective, a translation is both faithful and free. It is faithful to his or her interpretation of the original. At the same time, it is free because it displaces the original into yet another context and, like interpretation, can never be complete or definitive.

I think that important questions are closed off by an emphasis on the translated text that acquires its identity by virtue of being either equivalent to the source text or acceptable to the target end. Postmodern logic can redefine the translator's craft in terms of access to the potentially manifold modes of mutual refraction of the source and target. Such refraction occurs in the space between them which is opened up by the concept of translatability as the mode of a cross-cultural discourse.

Translatability, as defined by Iser (1995), is a counter-concept to cultural assimilation in the encounter between cultures. It aims for comprehension and therefore makes us focus on the space between cultures that allows them to mirror one another, opening up the experience of otherness. Translatability requires a discourse that allows the transposition of a foreign culture into one's own by negotiating the space between foreignness and familiarity. This is an open-ended interpretative process in which the mutual translation of cultures brings about comprehension. In this, translatability represents the ever-present chance to embrace more than was possible before.

Theories of translation that rely on the concept of the continuum with two poles relating to source-vs.-target norms tend to isolate translation from interpretative processes of sign production. They totalise the text into an all-inclusive meaning or interpretation that can be transmitted as a given message or predetermined conceptual content and rendered into a target text according to the two alternative sets of given norms.

In my view, translation is best understood as a process of semiosis in which a sign of another language is an interpretative response translating and at the same time fragmenting and displacing the meaning of the first sign. The variability of the sign-function becomes an essential precondition for translation, which, like understanding, is never complete. It is always relative to the shifting modes of reference and the purpose in view. Textual indeterminacy does not prevent translation but rather sets reading, writing, and translating in motion (Bonačić 1998: 42).[1]

3. Critical analysis

3.1. The poem and two translations

In her article 'Translating a poem, from a linguistic perspective', Elżbieta Tabakowska states that her aim is to demonstrate 'how intuitive interpretations and assessments are corroborated by a strictly linguistic analysis, which is carried out in the cognitivist vein' (Tabakowska 1997: 25). The example she uses is Robert Frost's poem *Nothing Gold Can Stay* and its Polish translation by one of the most prominent contemporary Polish poets and translators, Stanisław Barańczak. Her article is presented in chronological order which is in itself a telling clue to the type of translation assessment based on the traditional source-vs.-target continuum of translation adequacy. First, she describes the meaning of the original poem on the basis of ready-made interpretations by literary critics. Then she provides linguistic evidence that this meaning resides in the poem's formal structure. In this, she relies on some central concepts of cognitive linguistics which she explains and then applies to those linguistic aspects of the poem that structure its previously established content. Finally, she analyses the Polish translation according to the conflicting principles of the traditional source-vs.-target continuum. Namely, she focuses on determining translation equivalents vs. translation losses – some of the latter unavoidable because of systematic discrepancies between linguistic conventions, others apparently non-obligatory but nonetheless justified as a compromise imposed by the target-end literary conventions.

In her approach to translation, Tabakowska seems to follow theories of translation which claim that interpretation is the first, preparatory, stage of the translation process, while the rendering process is the second (e. g. Nida & Taber 1974: 33; Steiner 1992: 49; Neubert & Shreve 1992: 7). To my mind, translation is a continuous, two-way and two-fold dialogical process in which the rendering process involves further acts of interpretation beyond any interpretative process regarded as a separate phase. Interpretation is both a prerequisite and an effect of the rendering. In the first phase of interpretation, we may become aware of the flexibility of meanings, and ask ourselves not only which features of context are relevant in the determination of meanings but also which textual patterns have the status of meaningful expressions. We may believe we have arrived at a valid interpretation, but then the actual rendering process forces us to engage in the further process of adjusting the possibilities of interpretation. Each version of the translated text looks back and reflects on the original, often producing a new reading of it. So one continues the process, begun by one's previous reading, of diversifying the original.

Thus, the meaning of the expression 'translating a poem' (from the title of Tabakowska's article) cannot be fully understood unless you examine translation as a concrete interpretative experience by trying to retranslate the poem yourself. Then translation becomes a discourse, the analysis of which can reveal important aspects that remain concealed in a contrastive linguistic analysis of the source and the target text as cut-and-dried products derived from somebody else's or even one's own previous interpretation. That is why my translation of Frost's poem into Croatian is added to the Polish translation. As a Slavic language, Croatian is closer to Polish than to English. Yet the two translations are very different. It is through their interpretative effect on each other that their relevance to the original is to be measured.

The poem:

Nothing Gold Can Stay

1	Nature's first green is gold,
2	Her hardest hue to hold.
3	Her early leaf's a flower;
4	But only so an hour.
5	Then leaf subsides to leaf.
6	So Eden sank to grief,
7	So dawn goes down to day.
8	Nothing gold can stay.

—Robert Frost

A Polish translation:

Wszystko, co   złote, krótko trwa
[Everything which gold briefly lasts]

1   Złotem   przyrody – pierwsza zieleń
[Gold (N) of-nature   first   green (N)]

2   Po   niej – już   nic   prócz spłowień, zbieleń.
[After it   already nothing except fadings   whitenings]

3   Rozkwitu   szczyt – to   pierwszy listek,
[Of-efflorescence peak   this first   leaf (Diminutive)]

4   Lecz przez godzinę ledwie; wszystek
[But for   hour   only   all]

5   Zwykleje   w   liść   natychmiast potem.
[Commons into leaf (Acc.) immediately afterwards]

6   Tak Eden zszarzał nam   w   zgryzotę
[So Eden grayed   us (Dat.) into worry (Acc.)]

7   Tak świt nam   blaknie w śiatło   dnia.
[So dawn us (Dat.) fades   into light (Acc.) of-day]

8   Wszystko, co   złote, krótko trwa.
[Everything which gold briefly lasts]

—Translated by Stanisław Barańczak (1992)

A Croatian translation:

Ništa   zlatno ne ostane
[Nothing gold (not) stays]

1   Prva je zelen   zlato,
[First is green (N) gold (N)]
(The first greenness/verdure is gold)

2   Prirodu   krasi kratko.
[Nature (Acc.) adorns briefly]
(It adorns nature briefly)

3   Njen rani list je cvijet;
[Her early leaf is flower]

4   Al   začas   već   je blijed.
[But in-moment already is pale]

5   List struni   list u   pad.
[Leaf shakes-loose leaf into fall (Acc.)]

6   Raj   potonu u   jad,
[Paradise sank   into grief (Acc.)]

7   Zora   u dan se   utrne.
[Dawn into day itself extinguishes]

8   Ništa   zlatno   ne ostane.
[Nothing gold (Adj.) (not) stays]

—Translated by Mirjana Bonačić (2001)

Let me comment briefly on some important points in Tabakowska's analysis. According to critics quoted by Tabakowska (1997: 26-28),[2] Frost chooses the pastoral technique, which means using similes in a pattern of natural analogies. The cycle of nature becomes a symbol of human life. The first five lines are purely descriptive of the transience of natural beauty. Then follows a sequence of similes suggesting ever-widening circles of correspondences in the human sphere. The three images in succession present a change from better to worse: the transience of man's happiness in Eden and the transition from purity to decay as part of a larger scene in the cosmic image of the daily cycle. The last line is a final shift into statement – the adage, simple and explicit: all things change. Tabakowska concludes that 'the permanent recurrence of cycles leading from beauty and innocence to decay... is the subject of the poem' (Tabakowska 1997: 28). Then she supports this impressionistic interpretation with linguistic arguments (Tabakowska 1997: 29-36). She analyses three aspects of the poem's language: structural iconicity, metaphors, and grammatical categories. With regard to metaphor, she relies on Lakoff & Johnson (1980). Her analysis of structural iconicity and grammatical categories is based on Langacker's model of grammar as image (Langacker 1990). Lastly, she examines how these three linguistic aspects of the original text are realised in Barańczak's translation (Tabakowska 1997: 36-39).

My aim is to examine how the Polish and Croatian texts relate to each other with respect to these and some other aspects and how this interrelationship reflects on the interpretation of Frost's poem. At the same time, I will consider how useful or relevant it is to apply the concepts of equivalence and acceptability to translation as discourse.

3.2. Grammatical imagery

According to Langacker (1990: 12-13), grammar is 'imagic' in character, and grammatical constructions have 'the effect of imposing a particular profile on their composite semantic value'. Thus, Tabakowska points out that due to the word order in l. 1, '*Nature's first green* becomes the most prominent element of the image, or what is called the figure, with *gold* providing the background, to which the green is related' (Tabakowska 1997: 30). The effect of the grammatical image is similar to a painter's visual image. She rightly points out that in the Polish translation the reversed order of green and gold in l. 1, and leaf and flower in l. 3, changes the figure/ground composition of the two images. In l. 1, we first see the 'gold of nature' and then map it against the domain 'green'. Likewise, in l. 3, it is 'of the peak of efflorescence' that the 'first little leaf' becomes merely an exemplar. However, her conclusion about all such (as she terms them) *translation losses*, is that they are 'doubtlessly dictated by the necessity of using an equivalent poetical convention' (Tabakowska 1997: 38).

Do the norms of an 'equivalent' poetic convention really constrain the translator's choices to such an extent? It is metre and rhyme that Tabakowska primarily has in mind when she justifies the reversed word order due to the necessity of 'preserving' the convention. Is the convention really 'preserved' or 'equivalence' realised? The Polish translation is in iambic tetrameter (with extrametricality at the end of the lines) while the original is in iambic trimeter. Longer lines are sometimes considered to be necessary in translating English verse into Slavic languages because of a larger number of polysyllabic words in Slavic languages. While in some instances, as in l. 1 of the Polish translation, the tetrameter may accommodate all necessary words, in others it may encumber the translation with additional words. This happens in all other lines of the Polish text. So we get *spłowień* 'fadings' and *zbieleń* 'whitenings' (2), *listek*, a diminutive leaf (3), and especially the pronoun *nam* 'us' in dative, 'to us' (6, 7), which reduces the perspective of the images to the personal sphere, as Tabakowska herself notices.

In contrast, the Croatian translation is written in iambic trimeters with rhymes and assonant half-rhymes (frequent in Croatian modern poetry). Some lines (3, 4) have a regular rhythmic pattern (x / x / x /), some have trochaic inversion at the beginning (1, 2, 7) or a stressed monosyllabic word (5, 6), and some have extrametrical effects at the end (1, 2, 7, 8), while the last line (8) with its more irregular rhythm (/ x / x x / x x) stands out from the rest and concludes the poem (in a manner similar to the effect of the last line in the original poem). In the Croatian text, there are frequent instances of alliteration, assonance, and mirror-image sound patterning (e. g. l. 5: *List struni list u pad*). So it seems that the prosodic and phonological structure of the Croatian text, although quite different from the structure of the Polish text, can also be described as governed by an 'equivalent' poetic convention. In fact, the more economical craft of the Croatian trimeters shows that the target norms are flexible enough to permit a very different translational interpretation of the images. The Croatian translation interprets the mode of iconic meaning of the original in such a way that the first green and the early leaf are projected as figures on the background of gold and flower. Also, the Croatian text avoids circumlocutions. Thus, for instance, while the Polish translation ends with a complex affirmative statement, the last line (and the title) of the Croatian text is a succinct negative statement beginning with emphatic *ništa* 'nothing'. To conclude, it seems unwarranted to justify the translator's choices and strategies on the grounds of 'preserving' the poetic convention. The convention alone is an empty rule. It comes to life when it is adapted to ever-changing, concrete substance.

3.3. Metaphors

The same controversial question of equivalence to the source text or conformity to the target literary convention applies to the interpretation of metaphors. Tabakowska refers to Lakoff & Johnson (1980) to explain that the second aspect of the linguistically symbolic structure of Frost's poem is the consistent use, in ll. 5, 6, and 7, of what cognitive linguistics defines as an orientational-axiological metaphor, namely UP IS GOOD and DOWN IS BAD. The three verbs in ll. 5, 6, and 7, *subsides*, *sank*, and *goes down*, have the concept of movement with the orientation DOWN built into their semantics. The conceptual metaphor CHANGE IS MOVEMENT combines with the axiology of the orientational metaphor to produce the meaning MOVEMENT DOWNWARDS IS BAD. Thus, all three verbs symbolise decay (Tabakowska 1997: 31-32).

The Polish version contains numerous words from the domain of colour. Inference generation proceeds in a much less direct way: LOSS OF COLOUR IS LOSS OF BEAUTY, LOSS OF BEAUTY IS LOSS OF VALUE, and LOSS OF VALUE IS DECAY. Tabakowska concludes that in this way the translator 'compensates' for the missing orientational-axiological metaphor (Tabakowska 1997: 37).

I think that the Polish version cannot be read simply by evoking the concept of compensation. The translation is a specific interpretation of the original. My version also interprets the original, but in a very different way by making it possible to infer the orientational metaphor of downward movement from the verbs *struni* 'shakes loose' (as if making petals of a flower fall down, l. 5) and *potonu* 'sank' (6), as well as from the more explicit prepositional phrase *u pad* 'into fall' (5). These verbs and the reflexive verb *se utrne* 'extinguishes itself' (7), used to describe the vanishing of dawn into daylight, evoke the central meaning of decay and loss in a much more direct way than the repetitive allusions to fading colours in the Polish text. The Croatian version reflects on the original by drawing attention to its powerful and economical craft of figuration. Thus, the two versions differently refract inference generation which sets into motion the patterning of language and metaphorical mapping during translation.

3.4. Grammatical categories

The third aspect of the poem's language involves the interplay of two grammatical oppositions, namely between countable and mass nouns and between perfective and imperfective verb forms. Tabakowska explains at length Langacker's concept of boundedness. Boundary is a conceptual contour that delimits the extension of an entity or process. Thus, countable nouns and perfective verbs are bounded, while mass nouns and imperfective verbs are unbounded. Langacker emphasises that 'bounding is a function of how we construe the conceived entity, and is not invariably motivated by objective considerations' (Langacker 1990: 66). Language allows for more complex construals. In English, the conceptualisation of count-in-mass is expressed by using a countable noun without an article. An entity, although bounded, is not grounded in any particular pragmatic context. It loses its individuality and is conceptualised as a mass of individual entities. Slavic languages have no articles, so the difference in conceptualisation can only be inferred from the linguistic or situational context. Within the category of verbs, the linguistic and/or situational context is decisive for some 'special' interpretation, e. g. when a perfective verb occurs in present-tense form and is construed as 'habitual', hence imperfective (Langacker 1990: 90).

In Tabakowska's opinion, Frost's poem conveys 'the concept of permanence composed of impermanences' through 'a conspiracy of imperfective habitual verbs (*subsides, goes down*) and ungrounded countable nouns (*leaf, dawn, day, green, gold*)' and that this concept 'confronts the translator with a true case of untranslatability' (Tabakowska 1997: 38). As Polish does not lexicalise the notion of (in)definiteness, there can be no equivalent to the 'conspiracy' between nouns and verbs. So she praises the noteworthy compensation strategy used by the Polish translator. In the Polish version, the two gerunds in l. 2, *spłowień* 'fadings' and *zbieleń* 'whitenings', are 'derived from perfective verbs, and used in the plural, thus becoming conceptually equivalent to Langacker's "imperfective habitual"' (Tabakowska 1997: 38).

Tabakowska's analysis is an excellent example of how an overemphasis on one aspect of the poem's meaning can blur another. Her analysis shows how any analysis, even if it carried out in the vein of a sophisticated present-day model of cognitive linguistics, leaves behind something in the language of the poem which is just as important or even more important for the poem's interpretation. To my mind, it is precisely those expressions in the Polish version which Tabakowska regards as conceptually equivalent to 'imperfective habitual' that actually become an obstacle to a different cognitive process of inference generation. The Polish version contains a large number of different noun phrases, such as *spłowień* 'fadings' and *zbieleń* 'whitenings' (2), *rozkwitu szczyt* 'peak of blossoming' (3), diminutive *listek* preceded by deictic *to* 'this' in the expression *to pierwszy listek* 'this first little leaf' (3), and *liść* 'leaf' (5), as well as pronouns *nic* 'nothing' (2) and *wszystek* 'all' (4). I must emphasise that all these different words apparently refer to the entity LEAF and, according to Tabakowska, contribute to the overall image of 'permanent recurrence'. An overemphasis on the grammatical category of count-in-mass, whereby it is claimed that an entity such as a leaf loses its individuality, makes one ask the important question: What happens to the individual leaf? The use of so many different and additional words (partly due to the choice of tetrameter instead of trimeter) prevents the reader from inferring the crucial meaning of change occurring in the same individual thing. The Polish version makes one try to translate the poem again in a very different way.

3.5. Different refraction

In the Croatian version, the same word *list* 'leaf' is repeated three times: *Njen rani list je cvijet* 'Her early leaf is flower' (3), *List struni list u pad* 'Leaf shakes-loose leaf into fall' (5). The translation draws attention to the repetition of the word *leaf* in Frost's poem: 'Her early leaf's a flower' (3), 'Then leaf subsides to leaf' (5). The repetition of the same word evokes the concept of difference in the sameness, as in the well-known verse by Gertrude Stein: 'A rose is a rose is a rose is a rose'. The repetition makes one suspect that each time the same word returns, it means something slightly different, so the expression gives the impression of saying something that is semantically rich and therefore ambiguous (Eco 1976: 270). In the Polish version, the enjambment between ll. 4 and 5 and the use of the indefinite pronoun *wszystek* 'all' (4), instead of the same word for 'leaf', make such instantaneous and rich meaning construction impossible. In Frost's line (5), and in its Croatian version likewise, the implied meaning of internal change in the thing itself combined with downward movement is just as important as the concept of permanent recurrence or even more so.

Perhaps the 'conspiracy' of habitual verbs and ungrounded countable nouns of the original poem does not confront the translator with such a 'true case of untranslatability'. This is a true case of untranslatability from a narrow linguistic perspective, since it is a linguistic fact that in English the notion of count-in-mass can be expressed by using a countable noun without an article, and that Croatian has no articles and does not lexicalise (in)definiteness. However, from the perspective of translatability as discourse, the concept of count-in-mass is evoked by the anaphoric reference of *list* 'leaf' in l. 3 to *zelen* 'verdure', the topic of the opening lines, and by the repetition of the same word *list* 'leaf', used without any deixis, in l. 5. The first two lines already create a context of the general and habitual. Thus, we interpret *list* 'leaf' as referring to a mass of leaves that make up nature's greenery as well as being an individual leaf which changes into a different leaf. As for the verbs, the concept of imperfective habitual relationship is expressed by the Croatian perfective verbs *struni* 'shakes loose' (5) and *utrne* 'extinguishes' (7), which are in present-tense form. Unlike English perfectives, Croatian perfective verbs are morphologically marked. But like English perfectives (Langacker 1990: 85, 90), when they occur in the present-tense form, they receive a 'special' interpretation (e. g. habitual, historical present). In the Croatian version, the perfective verbs in the present tense refer to any conceivable time in which the designated events recur permanently.

4. Final reflections

The absence of initial connectives in ll. 6 and 7 of the Croatian version needs to be commented on. The first part of the poem concludes with l. 5, *List struni list u pad*, which is not purely descriptive but emphatically evokes a new meaning of inner change. The relationship between l. 5 and the rest of the poem is open to multiple interpretations. Lines 6 and 7 are not only similes in the mode of pastoral convention. A semantically rich discourse is created by the relationships of cause and consequence, reason and conclusion. It is the imminence of inner change that brings about the events described in the lines. The possibility of multiple interpretations brings to life a poetic world which is much more complex than the overall image of permanent recurrence.

In conclusion, this analysis seeks to demonstrate the plurality of translational discourses derived from a single original text by exploring how different frames of reference are reflected in, or created by, the use of language during translation. Rather than simply assess the translation from the perspective of the original, we must also understand the original from the perspective of the translation.

Translated texts provide evidence of how different meaning representations are constructed. The analysis shows how translation procedures become interpretative decisions and how translating open-endedness into graspability involves the individually established, multiple routes of reference where translatability is the chance to grasp more than before.

Endnotes

[1] A theory of translation that takes this factor into account is fully expounded in Bonačić 1999.

[2] Tabakowska quotes from Gerber 1982; Greenberg & Hepburn 1961; Lynen 1960; and Squires 1969.

References

Bonačić, Mirjana. 1998. 'Context, Knowledge, and Teaching Translation' in de Beaugrande, Robert, Meta Grosman and Barbara Seidlhofer (eds) *Language Policy and Language Education in Emerging Nations: Focus on Slovenia and Croatia and with Contributions from Britain, Austria, Spain, and Italy.* Stamford, CT: Ablex: 37-48.

___. 1999. *Tekst Diskurs Prijevod: o Poetici Prevođenja* (Text Discourse Translation: On the Poetics of Translating). Split: Književni krug.

Catford, John C. 1965. *A Linguistic Theory of Translation.* Oxford: Oxford University Press.

Eco, Umberto. 1976. *A Theory of Semiotics.* Bloomington: Indiana University Press.

Gerber, Philip L. 1982. *Robert Frost* (rev. ed.). Boston: Twayne.

Greenberg, Robert A., and James G. Hepburn (eds). 1961. *Robert Frost: An Introduction.* New York: Holt, Rinehart & Winston.

Iser, Wolfgang. 1995. 'On Translatability: Variables of Interpretation' in *The European English Messenger* 4(1): 30-38.

Ivir, Vladimir. 1981. 'Formal Correspondence vs. Translation Equivalence Revisited' in *Poetics Today* 2(4): 51-59.

Lakoff, George, and Mark Johnson. 1980. *Metaphors We Live By.* Chicago: University of Chicago Press.

Langacker, Ronald W. 1990. *Concept, Image, and Symbol: The Cognitive Basis of Grammar.* Berlin: Mouton de Gruyter.

Lynen, John F. 1960. *The Pastoral Art of Robert Frost.* New Haven: Yale University Press.

Neubert, Albrecht, and Gregory M. Shreve. 1992. *Translation as Text.* Kent, OH: Kent State University Press.

Nida, Eugene A., and Charles R. Taber. 1974. *The Theory and Practice of Translation*. Leiden: E. J. Brill.

Shuttleworth, Mark, and Moira Cowie. 1997. *Dictionary of Translation Studies*. Manchester: St. Jerome.

Squires, Radcliffe. 1969. *The Major Themes of Robert Frost*. Ann Arbor: University of Michigan Press.

Steiner, George. 1992. *After Babel: Aspects of Language and Translation* (2nd ed.). Oxford: Oxford University Press.

Tabakowska, Elżbieta. 1997. 'Translating a Poem, From a Linguistic Perspective' in *Target* 9(1): 25-41.

Toury, Gideon. 1995. *Descriptive Translation Studies and Beyond*. Amsterdam: John Benjamins.

Illustrated Literature:
Future Style, Fertile Spirit, or Futile Waste?

Marika Schwaiger

Abstract

This paper concerns the comparison of standard text-book format and illustrated comic-book format of a literary text, using the parable *Before the Law* as told in Franz Kafka's novel *The Trial*. This text was chosen because Kafka is known as an author who often causes anxiety and difficulties in reading and understanding among students – even among those who have had a certain amount of experience with so-called high literature. Two classes of a German grammar school, one of them aged 15, the other aged 17, on average, participated in a reception study investigating readers' different reactions to a literary text offered in two different text formats, one merely textual and the other presenting both textual and visual information. The results of the study concern the relations drawn by the students between the parable and their own reality and identities.

Key words: comic book; format; illustrated literature; image; text.

1. Yesterday's literature – tomorrow's readers

One of the most obvious consequences of recent developments in information technology is the radical change of means of communication. Soon after a world-wide electronic networking concept was born, both presentation and exchange of information and knowledge changed their format, to say nothing of their speed. It was only a question of time until those developments had effects on all kinds of text, even literary texts: new forms of literary practice arose from new opportunities to deal with verbal and non-verbal information; reading habits were adapted to changing and new literary formats and vice versa. Interesting questions worth closer investigation arise when we examine current trends in textual presentation and revisit former reading traditions, expectations, and habits as well as instructional ways of dealing with literature for educational purposes ['teaching literature?'].

Does yesterday's literature presented in its original textual format still attract today's readers', especially today's young readers', attention and interest? Does literature, read and treated in class as it was traditionally done, still satisfy students' expectations as well as motivate them to continue reading literary classics outside the classroom for their own interest? Does the textual format of literary classics still manage to imbue meanings and/or messages into modern classrooms and young people's minds or do literary classics fail to show themselves to be worth reading, because of their old-fashioned textuality? These are some of the questions I believe present-day stylistics and poetics should address and help resolve.

One might imagine situations which require special means and methods in order to help young or inexperienced readers to recognise and understand meanings evoked by literary texts. This might be especially the case for texts which seem at first sight to have nothing to do with readers' current realities, because of the temporal or spatial distance between the author's and the reader's circumstances or of linguistic differences between the author's mode of expression and the reader's interpretative abilities.

If doubt arises whether yesterday's literature is able to keep its relevance for present and future readers, what does literature have to look like in order to attract and excite today's young readers? Do teachers (or any other persons who feel responsible for promoting anyone's literary interest and abilities) have to develop special means, methods and strategies to confront students with so-called high literature? Do they perhaps have to think of transitional steps or a kind of compromise between yesterday's literature and today's students' reading habits or their perceptive faculties, which are undoubtedly highly influenced by new media?

Due to recent technological developments our eyes as well as our brains have to get (and are getting) more and more used to a kind of holistic and multisensory reading, i. e. perceiving, distinguishing and processing many different kinds of information at the same time. We have to deal with verbal and nonverbal, visual and audible information simultaneously, especially when we receive and read data from electronic network systems like the internet, which requires well developed and/or well trained skills of integrated reading and thinking. Those developments fit current constructivist claims for holistic processing of knowledge and integrated learning.

Without foreseeing the actual extent to which visual media should influence today's reading and communication habits, the publisher Albert L. Kanter decades ago sought to meet young readers' needs by suggesting the comic-book format as a new way to introduce children to the great classics of literature and to motivate them to read classic literature for their own pleasure. Started in 1941 under the title *Classic Comics*, the series changed to *Classics Illustrated*, which soon became one of the most popular series of comics ever produced anywhere in the world. The main aim of the series was to encourage readers to read the original book after having overcome their reservations about literary classics and after having given up the idea that one might not have the necessary intellectual and emotional resources to deal with them. The comics were amazingly popular all over the world, with many foreign language editions being produced. They were continually reprinted in hundreds of different editions until 1967 when the title was sold to Twin Circle, who published for a further four years until they ceased due to poor distribution. The American editions ran to 169 titles with many specials. The British editions ran to 162 titles with 13 titles that never appeared in America, plus other variations in cover design. There were also numerous special hardcover deluxe editions, which are very hard to find nowadays and are true collectors' items.

More recently, Acclaim Books have published new editions, re-coloured and including essays by accomplished scholars and specialist teachers about each book, as a study aid. The series *Classics Illustrated* forms a nostalgic part of many a childhood, and there are readers who may not be interested in other comics but still collect individual copies of *Classics Illustrated*. Although there is no equivalent series of illustrated German literary classics, at least not to that extent, a small number of single issues can be found. I once came upon *Kafka – kurz und knapp*, an illustrated synopsis about Franz Kafka's life and works written by David Zane Mairowitz and illustrated by Robert Crumb, who ranks as one of the pioneers of American underground comics (e. g. *Fritz the Cat, Mr. Natural,* and other popular cartoons), and upon *Give it up!*, a collection of Kafka stories illustrated by Peter Kuper, a famous American political cartoonist, who has been publishing his illustrations in well-known American newspapers and magazines (e. g. *The New Yorker, Time, The Washington Post,* and *The New York Times*). As I found myself developing a special liking for these appealing and critical high-quality illustrations, I wondered whether students would like them more than the ordinary textbook Kafka, whether students would experience fewer difficulties in understanding and interpreting them, and whether the additional visual elements would exert an influence on connections drawn by students and their own realities and identities.

The study described below aimed to concentrate on textual and visual information only, excluding any other (e. g. audible) multimedia components. Looking for previous research concerning the role of text and illustrations for learning purposes, one can fall back upon a number of widely acknowledged studies that show the significance and the indisputable effects of pictures on memory and learning. The question whether, where, and how multimedia environments can be used as promising learning environments has played an important part in current debates on instructional methods and educational designs. Those approaches, which predominantly concentrate on learning situations and processes requiring tasks of recognition and recall (e. g. in first- and second-language acquisition), are based on neuro-physiological findings that promise best learning outcomes when the left and right brain hemispheres are simultaneously involved. Neurophysiological tests show that left and right hemispheres of the brain process information in two different ways (often complementing each other) and suggest a bipolar division into a logical vs. an intuitive, or a rational vs. a non-rational processing mode, both possessing specific attributes and functions. In accordance with the assumption that the left-brain hemisphere has a verbal component (using words to name, describe, define etc.), and the right-brain hemisphere has a non-verbal one (awareness of things, but minimal connection with words), it seems reasonable to conclude that pictures and words are processed differently by the human brain: most individuals read text with the left-brain hemisphere, whereas the right-brain hemisphere is responsible for processing visual stimuli, i. e. recognizing pictures (Benson 1981: 82).

Based on these and further deliberations, the following study was designed. It reflects on the place of the writer's craft in a world of technological change, where everyday culture is characterised by multimedia exposure and processing.

2. Processing Kafka through text and image

The present study investigates readers' responses to a text, both in a standard text-book format and an illustrated comic-book format. These two formats reflect the traditional way in which literature has been mediated over the past centuries (i. e. as 'text') on the one hand, and the present-day mode, in which cultural artifacts and symbols are encountered through several channels simultaneously (i. e. as 'text AND image'). As a text, the parable *Before the Law* as told in Franz Kafka's novel *The Trial* was used. This text was intentionally chosen, as Kafka is known as an author who often causes difficulties, or even anxiety or aversion among students, even among those who have had a certain amount of experience with so-called high literature. Because a parable contains many symbolic components, which, in the case of Kafka's text, date from ages ago, it is not as easy to handle and understand as other literary text types which show more transparency in both language and content. Since I have often met students as well as teachers who showed quite a prejudiced attitude towards Kafka and his texts, I developed this study in order to find out whether the media format of a text influences readers' reactions and attitudes to such author and/or text.

A further aim of the study was to find out whether illustrating a literary text had any positive effect on young people's reading motivations. It is a widely held opinion among teachers that students are more motivated when they provide them with visual and/or multimedia material. Cartoons are used to boost understanding, collages for brainstorming activities, comic strips for keeping students in a good mood. According to constructivist learning theories these multi-sensory strategies are highly functional. But there might be cases where presenting visual stimuli in addition to textual ones does not necessarily lead to the hoped-for success.

With respect to the illustrated Kafka text, it is important to observe the following: illustrated literature differs from ordinary comic books in so far as it shows temporal discontinuities between the time of the text's original edition and the illustrated version, whereas ordinary comic books can, as a rule, be dated in the same period of time, in so far as author and illustrator are often one and the same person. The time difference involved in illustrated literature results from the artist's attempt to give an adequate interpretation of the original literary text. Thus, the reader of *Before the Law* in comic-book format must be aware of the fact that Crumb presents an individual interpretation of Kafka's words by using his drawing pencil. Whereas pure text offers the chance to build up more than just one single image in one's mind, illustrated text can have a restraining effect on the reader's interpretative freedom.

Furthermore, studies like the present one have to deal with individual differences and preferences: age, for instance, is an important factor concerning the processing of texts and pictures. Whereas children tend to prefer pictures in order to imagine, understand, and recall certain situations, facts and coherences, adults often prefer dealing with pure texts as they gain experience with reading words, as their reading becomes faster, and as the processing of words (unlike the processing of pictures) becomes automatic through practice (Noldy, Stelmack & Campbell 1990: 418).

3. Design of the study

The sample of the present study consisted of 40 students, two classes of a Bavarian grammar school, one of them aged 15, the other aged 17, on average. I chose these two different age groups to make sure to work with a mixed group of students, the one almost without any knowledge of Franz Kafka and the other with basic knowledge and first experiences with some Kafka texts. With the help of the students' German teachers, I split the classes into two groups of the same size, taking into consideration that each group should consist of a mix of students usually having good results and those usually coming off worse in working on literature tasks, in order to make sure that the two groups were homogeneous concerning their literary and interpretative skills, at least to a large degree. One group was the 'text-group', the other one the 'comic-group'. Text-group members read the German text, which means Kafka's parable *Before the Law*, in the common textbook format. Comic-group members read the same text in illustrated comic-book format. Both texts contain almost the same textual information. After reading the text, both groups had to fill in the same questionnaire. I used closed questions to be answered on interval scales as well as open questions to be answered in their own words. Each student had to work completely on his or her own.

3.1. Hypotheses

The hypotheses can be divided into five different categories: (1) reading motivation and aesthetic judgement; (2) estimation of degree of textual difficulty; (3) understanding and interpretation of the text; (4) connections drawn by readers between the central meaning of the parable and their own reality; and (5) the readers' emotional reactions to protagonists.

Before I carried out the research I discussed my research project with some teachers, not least to get an idea of their spontaneous assumptions concerning the results of the survey. They expressed considerable enthusiasm for the comics I had shown them: they all suggested that they would integrate them into their lessons as soon as they had to read Kafka in class. Most of them affirmed that their students would prefer reading Kafka comics to reading Kafka texts and they assumed that the comic-readers would achieve better results in understanding the text than the text-readers.

When I was to put forward my own hypotheses for the research, I remembered my own experiences, first as a student who had to read what the teacher proposed and later as a teacher who proposes readings to students and who unceasingly tries to motivate students to read. Both experiences led me to hypothesise the following causal chain: the more illustrated, the more interesting; the more interest, the more motivation; the more motivated, the more concentrated; the more concentration, the better the understanding; the better understood, the easier applied... and so on.

Shortly I too was as good as convinced that an illustrated comic-book format would achieve successes in at least the first three of the five categories above. And I hoped that, concerning the fourth category, with the help of illustrations, not only the protagonists but also the central idea of the text would get more concrete and that the students would therefore manage to transmit abstract elements of the text into their own reality. Let us now look at the results of the study.

3.2. Observational and empirical results

When the students were working on their questionnaires I made several interesting observations. While I was distributing the materials in class, some students were complaining about the grouping, which had been made in advance. Some students who had been assigned to read the text, when they noted that other students were given comics, were moaning and protesting that they would like to swap groups. With members of the comic-group it was the other way around: they were happy and content with their lot as comic-readers. After the lesson the students were free to keep the texts or comics for their own use or to return them. 95% of the texts came back but only 29% of the comics. When the students handed in their questionnaires, some of the text-group members even asked for a copy of the comic for their own use. Thus, the illustrated text was more likely to be reread at home than the plain text or, at least, students found it worth keeping.

Furthermore, I noticed a difference between the two age groups: the younger students were much more excited about and keen on the comic than the older ones. These different reactions may underline the theory that children are more familiar with processing images whereas adults – in the present case young adults – get more and more used to processing text.

There was also a noticeable difference between text- and comic-groups concerning their working methods: Many of the text-group members showed concentrated and disciplined working, as if they were working on an exam. Some of them even seemed to be quite nervous and anxious about not making any mistakes. Most of the comic-group members, however, seemed to be more relaxed and less anxious about the exam-like situation. I had the impression that they did not take the situation as seriously as their text-reading classmates did, that they tackled the tasks with less discipline and concentration, but with more self-confidence. Another remarkable difference was that comic-group members simply had more fun: they seemed to enjoy their activity more than the text-group readers did. These were only my observations and impressions. Students were not asked to confirm them explicitly.

The evaluation of the questionnaires was conducted using the statistics computer program SPSS for Windows. On the one hand I carried out tests of the difference in means between the two groups, on the other hand I calculated correlations between students' emotional reactions and the behaviour they would show if they took on the role of one of the protagonists, the man from the country. Much to my surprise, especially with the previously mentioned observations in mind, there were no significant differences between the text- and the comic-group concerning students' motivational and aesthetic attitudes towards the story. Both groups tended to choose the middle value of the scales, indicating that they partly liked the parable. I also wanted to know how much they liked filling in the questionnaire and doing the tasks on the story, and whether they could imagine reading something similar again. No noticeable differences between the interest of text-group and comic-group members were observed.

The question of how difficult they found the parable did not show significant differences between text- and comic-groups either. The average student chose a value between 2 and 3, which means that the average statement concerning the students' estimation of the degree of difficulty of the parable is somewhere between 'medium' and 'difficult'.

Another series of questions aimed to investigate students' general understanding of the text. Among other things they were asked to characterise the protagonists of the parable, the doorkeeper and the man from the country, as I wanted to see whether the students were in a position to sift out character traits from textual or textual-plus-visual information. Again, the evaluation of these questions did not reveal any noticeable differences between text-group and comic-group members.

Questions concerning the interpretation of the text did not show significant differences between text- and comic-groups either, though the comic-group members' formulations of the central message of the parable showed a slight tendency to be more convincing than those of the text-group members. Concerning one particular task, for instance, where students had to write their own story including the central idea of the parable, I noted that comic-group members wrote stories containing more concrete, imaginable, and realistic elements, elements from their own lives and experiences, whereas text-group members wrote stories which showed quite symbolic and abstract traits, similar to the parable itself.

Further questions investigated students' attitude towards the behaviour of the protagonists as well as their own behaviour in case they were in a situation like that described in the parable. Again I could observe a highly similar distribution of students' answers, no matter which group they belonged to.

Investigating the students' emotional reactions to the protagonists, I discovered some significant differences between text-group and comic-group concerning their reactions to the doorkeeper. There were differences in both the students' anger toward, and their pity for, the doorkeeper. Comic-group members show perceptibly more anger and less pity for the doorkeeper. This observation means that the visualisation of the doorkeeper, which is the artist's personal interpretation of the character, resulted in the intensification and lessening respectively of the emotions 'anger' and 'pity' among comic-readers, whereas text-readers tended to experience less strong emotions.

3.3. Analysis and interpretation

All present results (except my personal observations in class) indicate that the choice of the text format does not really influence students' motivation, interest, understanding, and interpretation. This was much to my own (and most teachers') surprise.

As it will never do any harm to disprove some widespread assumptions from time to time, I tried to find reasons for these results: I spoke again with teachers and pedagogues and tried to put myself in the position of the students. The more I did the latter, the closer I came to some plausible explanations. One of the conclusions I came to was that today's students, who are confronted (and often even flooded) with visual (and multimedia) stimuli day by day and nearly right round the clock, may sometimes be glad and grateful to deal with textual material in its pure and original form. Taking into consideration that pure text is likely to be the opposite of students' everyday reading experiences, I can understand that they quite welcome and appreciate this kind of plainness from time to time.

Finally, I wanted to have a closer look at the students' emotional reactions, as that was the complex of questions with the most interesting and most noticeable results. I wonder whether the visualisation of the parable had an influence on connections and correlations between the students' different emotional reactions and their own behaviour. In fact, the comic-group members showed more significant correlations than the text-group members. Let me highlight one example.

In the comic-group, there was a clear connection between students' estimation of the fictional situation, which means the fictional universe of the protagonists, their comments on the behaviour of the protagonists, their emotional reactions to the protagonists, and their own behaviour if they were in a similar situation. Text-group members showed hardly any such connection. One possible interpretation of this result could be that those who read only the text answered each question separately, whereas those who had text and pictures showed more homogeneity between their answers and even more connections between their estimation of the protagonists' fictitious and their own reality. That could mean that they were, with the help of visual elements, in a better position to translate the content and meaning of the parable into their own life. The theory of the two different brain hemispheres mentioned above could give a suitable explanation for that result: working with words and pictures means stimulating and integrating both the left (words) and the right (pictures) hemispheres of the brain. As the right-brain hemisphere is also responsible for seeing relationships between things, for understanding metaphoric relationships and for relating to things as they are at the present moment, the clearer and more homogeneous transmission into the students' own reality could derive from the more intensive stimulation of the right-brain hemisphere during the reading process.

4. Conclusion

Although the question of how to deal with yesterday's literature in today's classrooms cannot easily be answered, the results of the present study reveal that there are certain factors which should be taken into account and perhaps also further scrutinised. The study showed that the more difficulties the readers have in tackling the text, the more they are interested in and grateful for additional visual aids, and, conversely, the more familiar the readers are with the degree of difficulty of a text, the less they need visual elements in order to cope with the text. Thus, age plays an important role when the question arises whether to add visual material. Furthermore, one can say that even experienced readers who do not need visual aids to grasp the meaning of a text may profit from illustrations when they are asked to relate traits of fictitious characters and parts of fictional worlds to their own identity and reality. This might be connected to the study's finding that students experienced stronger emotions concerning both the fictitious scenery as well as their own situation when they had additional visual stimuli.

The results of my study lead me to question the widespread classroom theory of 'the more illustrated the better'. Rather, these results argue for a well-directed use of illustrations in specific classroom situations. For example, illustrations might be helpful for young and inexperienced readers; they might also help students to draw parallels between literary fiction and their own reality. I consider these results an encouragement to further explore the relationship between the writer's craft and new cultural technologies, especially to have a closer look at the differences between processing text and processing multimedia information.

References

Benson, D. F. 1981. 'Alexia and the Neuroanatomical Basis of Reading' in Pirozzolo, Francis J., and Merlin C. Wittrock (eds) *Neuropsychological and Cognitive Processes in Reading*. New York: Academic Press: 69-92.

Kafka, Franz. 1925 [posthum.]. *Der Prozess*. Berlin: Verlag Die Schmiede.

Kuper, Peter. 1997. *Gibs auf! und andere Erzählungen von Franz Kafka*. Hamburg: Carlsen Verlag.

Mairowitz, David Zane, and Robert Crumb. 1995. *Kafka – kurz und knapp*. Frankfurt: Zweitausendeins.

Noldy, N. E., R. M. Stelmack and K. B. Campbell. 1990. 'Event-Related Potentials and Recognition Memory for Pictures and Words: The Effects of Intentional and Incidental Learning' in *Psychophysiology* 27(4): 417-28.

PART III

CHANGING CULTURES OF REPORT

Who said that? Who wrote that? Reporting, Representation, and the Linguistics of Writing

Geoff Hall

Abstract

Quotations appearing in newspaper stories tend to be at best rather inaccurate, at times completely imaginary or probabilistic, though important parameters impacting on the faithfulness of the representation are suggested by Short (1989), Short, Semino & Wynne (2002) and van Dijk (1988). Tannen (1989), Mayes (1990), Sternberg (1982) and others have proposed altogether abandoning the notion of 'reported speech' in favour of more 'presentational' pragmatic views of what is seen as primarily a rhetorical device. The investigation reported here is informed by this debate, including the comparative rarity of accurate reproduction as opposed to loose representation even in cases when technology would seem to have made more precise reporting easily possible. Testing the proposed 'faithfulness parameters' reveals that while Short et al. have undoubtedly given us a better nuanced picture than was once the case, their schema may still be premised upon too limited a model of communication. I conclude with wider reflections on the need for stylistics to develop and apply a better elaborated linguistics of writing.

Key words: news reporting; verbatim quotation; faithfulness; linguistics of writing; authorship.

1. Discourse representation vs. 'reported speech'

A critical linguistic interest in media representations led me, like many others, initially to notice the improbability, if not downright inaccuracy of many quotations attributed to speakers in newspaper reports of events purportedly of public significance, where conventions of a 'universal pragmatics' (Habermas 1979) would lead a reader to expect greater faithfulness to factuality. The insight is hardly startlingly original in itself, as a brief review of the literature reveals in what follows. My larger claim, however, is that the issue and its handling in stylistics to date, throws into relief a characteristic aporia of mainstream stylistics, given the extent to which writing is central to the field, in regard to the central issue of a linguistics of writing, particularly of writing under conditions of new technologies and 'new work orders'. The notion will be elaborated in my conclusion by reference to the previous discussion and analysis, but in essence a linguistics of writing argues that writing is a distinct linguistic representational form, not secondary to speech as in some Bloomfieldian scheme of things, whether in fiction or newspaper reporting or in any other written medium. I contend that too much work in stylistics, whatever intellectual arguments might be accepted, operationally speaking, does not sufficiently recognise this alternative rather than secondary nature of written communication (cf. Linell 1982). Finally, I accept that the linguistics of presentational writing I sketch here inevitably problematises the fundamental fact-fiction distinction in a way which many will find uncomfortable, but which may more accurately reflect the ways in which language in the postmodern world works.

An early, pre-theoretical, even pre-analytical pedagogical label for the kind of phenomenon to be investigated here was 'reported speech'. Indeed Toolan's undergraduate stylistics textbook (Toolan 1998) has a chapter entitled 'Recorded Speech', as if a novel were some kind of spectrograph, though a few pages later this label modulates without explicit commentary to 'represented speech' (Toolan 1998: Ch. 5), a more critical orientation, and also the preferred verb in the more monograph-level study of *Narrative* (Toolan 2001: Ch. 5: 'representing character discourse'). The 'ownership' of the subordinate clause in 'reported' structures exercises Toolan (1998), presumably including the ownership of the last two sets of single inverted commas ('scare quotes'?), as it will exercise us all in what follows. The most refined linguistic taxonomy of speech representation was initially offered by Leech & Short (1981), distinguishing DS and IS (Direct Speech and Indirect Speech), FDS (Free Direct Speech), NRSA (Narrative Report of a Speech Act), and FIS (Free Indirect Speech). The seemingly infinitely open, quasi-Borgesian attempt to map this complex territory continues to the present with ongoing additions and refinements to the scheme and its categories (adding Thought, Writing, Embeddedness etc.), nowadays importantly assisted by corpus research (see Semino, Short & Culpeper 1997), and insistence on the importance of context. At the same time a literary tradition, nurtured on Vološinov ([1929] 1986: *double voicing*), Pascal (1977), Banfield (1982), Fludernik (1993) and McHale (1978), among others, emphasised the slippery indeterminacy, and the social rather than individual nature of represented voices (Bakhtin 1981) in fiction, just as Toolan (1998) emphasises the slippages that seem to occur in his own attempted textbook examples. So, too, new literacies research and media studies emphasise the problematics of traditional notions of writing, including questions of authorship and attribution (Gee 1990). Vološinov ([1929] 1986), indeed, seems to suggest that in so far as literary writing has any *differentia specifica* from other kinds of discourse, its essence might be apprehended in the consideration of FID (Free Indirect Discourse). Later literary successors, however, seem to suggest that the literary/non-literary divide could be more problematic than this, with indeterminacy reaching far into the more ordinary and everyday uses of language.

However, Short, Semino & Wynne (2002 [hereafter SSW]), in the best-argued paper on the subject to appear to date, acknowledging the validity of many criticisms that have been made, nevertheless wish to resist what is seen as the fashionable impingement of such literary and discoursal perspectives onto 'non-literary' areas like newspaper reporting. The very uneasiness with the perceived vagueness of the term 'discourse' can be taken as symptomatic of the effort to fix boundaries (SSW: 333). The efforts of those such as Banfield (1982), Fludernik (1993), Tannen (1989, 1995) or Sternberg (1982), who wanted to go further than Short and his colleagues in querying the value of understanding speech or thought representation by reference to any supposed anterior or 'real world' utterance at all, are resisted, often fruitfully critiqued. Verbatim, precise 'word-for-word' reproduction, it is accepted, can only rarely occur. A more 'functional', almost Gricean notion of 'faithfulness' of representation is proposed. At the least it is felt, quite understandably, that the newspaper report is of a different order, or stands in a different relation to the world, or should do, than the fictional representation. There are times and instances, it is argued, when what was said does matter, and in life, as opposed to fiction, people do actually speak, and what they say can make a difference. The article sets out parameters for such times and instances. It is this debate which forms the setting for my own examples and the conclusions I draw, which ultimately suggest that the hard boundaries the Lancaster Speech and Thought Representation group (SSW; Semino, Short & Culpeper 1997) wish to draw are not fully tenable, however instructive the attempt has undoubtedly been. I conclude that the idea of faithfulness certainly haunts many of our communicative practices, but is however necessarily finally imprecise and negotiable.

SSW concede that Sternberg (1982) or Fludernik (1993), to begin, are held to make some valid points regarding the impossibility of tracing origins for speech reported as 'his face spoke volumes' or 'my students say they can't find the books in the library', or 'the Pope said' (where English translation is used) and the like. In this vein Mayes (1990) or Tannen (1989, 1995) question on empirical grounds the coherence of the notion of 'reported speech' if it is taken to imply the invariable existence of an actual previous speaker whose precise words are being faithfully reported. There is 'no such thing, literally, as reported speech' (Tannen 1995: 148). Mayes (1990) calls DS a 'misnomer' (after Tannen 1989: 133), and notes rather the functions of 'direct speech' utterances in building affect, dramatising, and bidding for credibility in the conversations she studies. Nevertheless, the defence (SSW) is that these examples come from literature, conversation, or are 'hypotheticals', all of which are specific kinds which need to be treated specifically, and in any case, the Lancaster corpus indicates, are not particularly characteristic types of reported speech. SSW acknowledge the importance of drawing attention to 'presentational' rather than '*re*presentational' issues in speech representation, but insist that such work draws on investigations of reported speech in conversations, and as such is not easily generalised to the very different genre of newspaper reporting. The injunction to beware of carrying over generalisations from one field to another, related but not identical, is well taken.

Perhaps a more serious challenge comes from investigators such as Slembrouck (1992) or Caldas-Coulthard (1994), who note the habitual inaccuracy, or at best challengeability, of apparent reproductions of speech in, respectively, *Hansard* (the transcriptions of proceedings in the British parliament) or in journalism. These are documents where faithfulness should matter surely. Similarly, Waugh (1995), on the basis of her investigations of the French newspaper *Le Monde*, proposed a dichotomy between fiction and conversation, on the one hand, and concern with issues of referentiality, truth, reliability, and accountability in serious newspaper reporting. Where, it is proposed, a prototypically literary form of 'reported speech' is the finally undecidable voice-mingling of Free Indirect Discourse (compare Vološinov, Banfield, McHale), *Le Monde* writings carefully maintain DS and IS, where DS will not necessarily be precise *verbatim* reproduction, but is expected to be 'functionally equivalent' (cf. 'faithful'), and IS allows for more journalistic – rather than original text – determination. Sanders & Redeker (1993: 74), indeed, in one of the few studies I have found in the area to actually study real readers, report that perspectival embedding of IS, far from being a problem, is something that readers *expect* from journalism. Waugh's idea of 'functional equivalence', and the suggestion of parameters determining when readers should be given the actual words at issue to judge for themselves, echoed by investigators like van Dijk (1988), is a more fruitful avenue for Short et al. and certainly introduces more precision into the debates.

Certainly, what quickly became evident from the more precise investigations of Leech & Short (1981) and then Short and other collaborators in what became the Speech and Thought Representation project at Lancaster University, was that a label like 'reported speech' or even 'reported speech and thought' attempted to include too many disparate forms under one umbrella. Increasingly subtle taxonomies, likely to be familiar to readers of this paper, were – and continue to be – proposed in an effort to tame the beast(s), and important efforts have been made to distinguish contextual parameters which will impact on the accuracy of speech reports in newspapers. The weakness or incompletion of Slembrouck or Caldas-Coulthard's work from this perspective would be its neglect of these parameters.

The most elaborated and very valuable listing of factors determining the degree to which faithfulness is a salient issue for readers occurs in SSW, which readers interested by this paper clearly need to consider carefully for themselves if they are not already aware of the work. Nevertheless, I list them again for convenience now, though it is important to note that these proposals, however intuitively and retrospectively valid they may seem, have yet to be empirically tested, so far as I am aware, in (say) protocol studies of readers reading newspaper reports. My own 'report' of these parameters, many instances of which are found in the examples I offer, would include:

- Anterior discourse accessibility (without access there could logically be no report). Accuracy of written report is more easily checked. Analyses of examples below suggest this may be a more critical factor than SSW recognise.
- The importance of what is being reported – obviously relative, but for most, war with Iraq will be more of an issue than the state of the weather.
- Status, social role, and personality of the original speaker/writer (President Bush vs. Church of England vicar or 'a Bedouin').
- Attitude, social role, and personality of the reporter – sympathy or antipathy to the source could promote either greater or less accuracy, but are likely to be relevant factors.
- Text type and speech context: popular magazine vs. respected broadsheet; court of law vs. conversation in bar.
- Part of the text in which the reporting occurs: e. g. Short (1989) on headlines as less accurate than main story quotations.
- The memorability of the original – form, context, etc. – though what we know about memory and language suggests that even 'peace in our time', or 'the lights going out across Europe', etc. will have been crafted in transmission over time (after SSW: 351-52).

A particularly suggestive earlier publication was Short (1989), who writes of 'Speech presentation, the novel and the press'. The first key point to emerge from the research described there is the importance of 'speech summary', including apparent (IS) Indirect Speech, to newspaper reporting, as contrasted, for example, with fictional novel writing. Giving the 'gist' is clearly felt to be more important than precise reproduction of words uttered for the first genre. Second, and related, anticipating SSW, various parameters are proposed to impact on what Short denominates the 'faithfulness principle' (Short 1989: 74). Overall, however, the perceptive proposal of this earlier publication is that newspaper reporting be viewed as primarily a storytelling activity, using attention-gaining devices such as (purported) direct speech (enclosed in quotation marks or italicised), however cautious Short might be about such a formulation today. A headline, as already observed, is likely to be a 'macro-proposition' (in Kintsch & van Dijk's 1978 terms) representing what might well have been said (but in fact never was in those words), rather than – as perhaps only the academic trained in citation practices and the like expects – making strict claims to reproduce faithfully what was said, regardless of circumstances, simply because it is punctuated by quotation marks of some kind. My own analyses have tended to validate the general bearing of these proposals, though I feel they fall short of a completely satisfactory account of the data. For the moment, I note with Bray (2002), Short (1989), and Fairclough (in Short 1989) that: 'the reporting of speech is never mere reproduction, but a representation, even in the case of DS or FDS [Free Direct Speech], because the writer can choose "what parts of the speech reported to include, in what order, and within what discoursal matrix"' (Short 1989 in Bray 2002: 66; now in Hall 2001). This is Bakhtin's point that every individual utterance is always totally 'novel' (we need to return to this characterisation) and unique (because of its new context, regardless of its form, which will necessarily also vary anyway). But at the same time, (Bakhtin points out), all language is pervasively intertextual, all utterances are constructed from a tissue of quotations, so that choosing to punctuate a given utterance as a quotation is seen as a pragmatic or rhetorical rather than a factual decision in this perspective (compare Fairclough 1992: Ch. 4). We may also be reminded of the Derridean notion of 'iterability' of language: language always exceeds and pre-exists the speaker's intention (Derrida 1977). In any case, we can all agree, surely, that words can never speak for themselves, nor be evaluated or responded to (dialogically) in a context-free Chomskyan vacuum.

Here too some historical perspectives are in order, since it could be argued that modern journalistic practices have come full circle – or perhaps they never turned at all – to return to earlier written communicative norms. Parkes (1992) describes with fascinating examples the early appearance of what would become our various differentiated 'quotation marks' used by scribes from the sixth century, when 'diples' (< >) began to appear in manuscripts to highlight the importance of Biblical quotations relative to any surrounding text. Here a reader should 'pause' for contemplation. ('Pause and Effect' is Parkes's title). Printers from the 16th century experimented with an increasing range of fonts and technological possibilities becoming available to (for example) highlight the words of international or prestigious authors, increasingly in vernaculars other than the classical languages (Latin especially), with italics or 'textura'. Diples occur increasingly in the margin to indicate Biblical or Church Fathers' quotations, later moving from margins into the body of the text from the end of the 16th century (Parkes 1992: 58ff.). We should also note that '*sententiae*', wisdom whose provenance was often unknown or irrelevant, their aura sometimes preserved in Latin or another foreign language, lost in history, were normally equally punctuated as direct speech. By the 18th century, with authors like Fielding, Swift, and Sterne, something like modern conventions of quotation punctuation were in operation, though Parkes emphasises that, as 'the novel' emerged and differentiated itself into fiction and newspaper (cf. Davis 1983), punctuation was used increasingly for presentation, and with much creativity, exploiting what Parkes terms 'the pragmatics of the written medium' (72), writing increasingly coming into its own as a separate, alternative linguistic system, with its own unique affordances, as intended by my own phrase, 'the linguistics of writing'. While, as Bray (2002) usefully outlines, literary history now takes a more nuanced view of Davis' proposal for the blurring of fact and fiction at the moment of the emergence of the novel and the newspaper and modern historiographical writings in the early 18th century, Davis' point that the three modes of writing have not always been as distinct as we would like to imagine, and as rapidly evolving printing practices came to suggest (the punctuation of speech representation), is to the point in this discussion too.

2. Three new examples

In my own efforts to explore some of these ideas even as they were being developed and published I began with a text like that of the 'shoplifting vicar' (*Express on Saturday*, 15 March 1997), whose headline 'A Moral Duty to Shoplift' (with single inverted commas) under the banner 'Astonishing outburst by Church of England priest' seems to suggest that the priest concerned spoke those words. In fact, as Short (1989) suggests, a closer reading of the article (if the reader is inclined to read more closely rather than have his prejudices confirmed) suggests that these words were never uttered by the priest, nor was there actually any 'outburst', but rather some over-reported comments made in the context of a larger sermon, now all but obliterated (a committed reader would have to follow the story on to a slight column on an inner page even to know this). Under the main headline are three further quotations, it seems from their bullet-point presentation, though now there are no inverted commas. Further reading confirms that two are more or less faithful quotations, while the first has lost its hedging and specificity from the original sermon. (Newspaper: Big stores are evil because they destroy local community life; sermon, as reported later, with double inverted commas: "These big stores are thoroughly evil because they are really destroying local community life."). The report goes on to suggest in its leading paragraph that the priest said it was "quite right" to steal from giant supermarket chains, when further reading suggests (if only by its absence) that the Rev. Mr. Papworth used no such expression, and that in fact he was even careful to speak against the idea of stealing, even though he regarded supermarkets as being themselves immoral. (This newspaper, ironically or not, was given to me free by a local supermarket!) In the period of a run-up to a general election, we should also note, the *Express* emphasises that the priest had been a Labour parliamentary candidate earlier in his life. Here, in sum, is a popular newspaper, (mis)reporting a minor personality on a tangential issue to confirm reader prejudices. The accuracy of reporting seems to increase as the story progresses over the page on to a minor column which will not usually be read in case any legal proceedings should arise, though there seems a low risk of this. A good example of Short (1989) and Fairclough on 'slants' and embedding in reporting, 'reporting' as evaluation, but perhaps also raising questions about the form of the presentation, where the single, double, and zero inverted commas seem to relate almost inversely to whether or not the words thus marked were actually spoken as attributed or not. A lot of inferential work needs to be done to see past the presentation by a sceptical reader. At the least we can say that this is not how we were taught to punctuate at school!

A second and more problematic text to consider could be the report of a serious event in a serious newspaper, 'Gaza Strip explosion kills four Palestinians' (*Guardian Unlimited*, 4 Feb. 2002, credited to 'Staff and agencies'). Here an Internet news text highlights usefully the way modern journalistic practices of writing and (co-)authorship throw some doubt on ideas of a world in which single writers can be held to account for faithful reporting of individual voices, an instance where I find the Short et al. parameters and model suggestive but not fully adequate to capture what seems to be going on. This is reporting as bricolage with collective voices and multiple embeddings much in evidence as a complex actual and fast developing real-world situation is reported. I identify at least ten individual or collective voices here, with confusions of DS and DW (Direct Writing) and interesting modalisation through double quotation marks: thus, "terrorist groups", for example. Does this indicate the controversial nature of such designations? a distancing of the newspaper from an official Israeli pronouncement? presentational rather than reporting? Since sources mentioned include press releases as well as spokespeople (anonymous as well as named) it cannot be clear at what stage those double inverted commas were introduced or by whom. (We remember SSW's point about the accessibility of the original utterance.) One anonymous participant is a 'Bedouin' who is ventriloquised here in English. Collective speakers include the Israeli military, the UN, and the Red Cross; embeddings include the report of a report of an interview with Arafat (where Sharon is available in a less mediated voice, suggesting the 'importance' of the speaker [SSW] as ideological bias). Who said that? Who wrote that? The questions admittedly arise, but the answers are not clear. Short et al. might want to argue that this is because of the online, up-to-the-minute nature of this reporting (though it must be said that events became no clearer in subsequent days before the event was removed forever from our horizons). But surely also, however, the report is a highly confused and confusing one (when read with these questions of attribution in mind) because of the conditions of communication and composition, specifically of journalism here, in the modern world. I would also suggest, though certainly intuitively and without benefit of quantitative or corpus-based evidence, that such a style of reporting is increasingly the norm.

In support of such a contention, however, it is fitting to turn for a moment to Allan Bell's (1991: 41) strictures on 'authorship' in journalism, as part of his book-length argument that applied linguists have tended to misinterpret journalistic writings because of profound ignorance about the conditions of production of news reports:

> Much of what a reporter writes is [therefore] paraphrased or quoted from what someone else said to him.... [J]ournalists can draw on written as well as spoken sources. Very few stories consist entirely of wording newly generated by the journalist from his own observation or verbal interview. Much news comprises updates and rewrites of previous stories....

> [M]any stories contain material selected and reworked from documents generated by newsmakers or other media – reports, agendas, proceedings, transcripts, speech notes, news agency copy, newspaper clippings, press releases. Some stories are entirely cut-and-paste jobs from such sources ....

> [A] basic feature of media communication: embedding....

> The journalist is therefore as much a compiler as a creator of language, and a lot of the news consists of previously composed text reworked into new texts.

This kind of process of composition, then, is increasingly the typical case in contemporary journalism of all kinds, just as poststructuralist and postmodernist accounts of authorship and intertextuality have problematised traditional approaches to written communication in literary studies.

The final text to be offered here was deliberately selected to test the 'faithfulness parameters' validity most directly when SSW came to my attention. SSW's own offering (SSW: 344) is the most senior BBC political reporter's recorded and broadcast question to Prime Minister Thatcher just before her resignation as reported in a senior colleague's diary. Only a few minor variations are reported by SSW, thus apparently validating their proposals, though it is stressed that the parameters could probably be supplemented and better understood. My own example is the 'axis of evil' speech (as it very rapidly came to be known) of President George W. Bush, a very public and very significant event, released by the President's own press secretary onto the Internet (as written sources) almost immediately, and then immediately reported in prestigious newspapers world-wide (Bush 2002). The Website also offered the opportunity to view a video of the State of the Union address and the option of listening as well as reading. Here if anywhere, the condition of retrievability of the original instance of utterance applies. We could thus confidently expect *The Washington Post* (WP) to report from the horse's mouth, and indeed, with other quality newspapers, as SSW found, that is mostly what occurred (Goldstein & Allen 2002), and DS seemed, as predicted, to be mainly used for variety and 'colour': 'tens of thousands'; 'I will not stand by' (credibility); and of course 'axis of evil'. And yet I find the example again prompts questions about modern technologies of story composition, and the inescapability of media frames.

The important variable here is of course the length of the speech (10 pages, half an hour to deliver including applause and razzamatazz). The WP report will clearly highlight what are felt to be key phrases, and these our model would predict to be very accurate. In fact, of 18 purported DS quotations, 10 were completely accurate, just over 50 percent, not an unusual figure in my own research, but far from 'highly accurate' in anyone's statistics. The differences in most cases are small and clearly due to inattention ('typos' like 'our economic is in recession'); or house style (systematic replacement of semicolons by commas, removal of hyphens); or naturalisations (expansions such as 'we have' from 'we've', 'we will' from 'we'll'); minor lexical substitutions. 'Faithful', then, broadly. Nevertheless, different is not the same, and even small changes make a difference to our understanding, perhaps cumulatively. Consider 'So long as Congress acts in a fiscally responsible manner' (speech text) which becomes 'in a financially responsible way' (newspaper text is arguably vaguer), or 'our war on terror', reproduced as 'our war on terrorism' (more specific?). At the least, however, these changes are evidence that the text of the speech has not simply been downloaded into the article at appropriate points, as it could have been if faithfulness and accuracy was the object (as the journalism training manuals suggest it should be). Rather the story has been thoroughly *written*, word by word, using the official release as a source, otherwise all these minor changes are difficult to explain. Frames recur to guide our interpretation throughout ('Sounding mindful of the divides in politics that often typify election years...', etc.). Moreover, arguably, not all the changes are minor. I was particularly struck, even from looking at this single example, by the report in this newspaper and in all other media reports I heard, watched, and read of the charge that Iraq, Iran, North Korea, and others were 'developing weapons of mass destruction'. Where did this verb come from? The President actually said: 'seeking weapons of mass destruction'. (e. g. *Washington Post*: '[H]e [Bush] said that ... North Korea, Iraq and Iran, represent "an axis of evil" that is attempting to develop nuclear, biological and chemical weapons').

So what's all the fuss about? The gap between my own investigations and those of the Lancaster group is clearly not unbridgeable. I do want to suggest, however, that Short et al. taxonomies do not go far enough to recognise the realities of the linguistics of writing, particularly under modern technological conditions. In the light of evidence such as the texts discussed here, it is difficult not to conclude that there is still a certain clutching on to straws of presence (Derrida), modes of representation and communication which do not fully recognise the realities of modern media communication production and reception, where the relevance of the referent, recoverable or not, is attenuated, of less import than the representation in its own right as a representation. The Bush speech could simply have been reproduced, but the journalists had a story to write. And we should note, too, that the two named journalists, who would have been edited and sub-edited in any case, were demonstrably subject to house style, and drew on the Internet release, also were assisted in unspecified ways ('contributions') by three named 'staff writers', as a credit at the end of the article reveals. Of course the story comes from somewhere (someones), but the processes of transmission and reproduction, in my view, raise very real questions about models predicated on (at least some) recoverable and faithfully reproduced words.

3. Concluding Remarks

In my abstract I suggested that the wider field of stylistics may be more generally at fault here, and it is encouraging to note one or two examples of 'linguistics of writing' appearing in the field (see Hall 2001). The kind of discussion found in Austin's (1994) careful reading of apparent quotations in Shelley's 'Ozymandias' is exemplary in this respect and should be consulted by those who would like to understand better the wider point I wish to raise, but which lies beyond the limits of this single conference paper. ('I met a traveller... who said... written...', etc.: multiple levels of indirection). It is not at all the case that 'faithfulness' is an irrelevant idea. It is a condition we aspire to much of the time. My point is rather that this undoubtedly central principle of communicative practice is at the same time often highly problematic or instable on closer investigation as I have tried to show from my own admittedly very limited set of examples.

References

Austin, Timothy R. 1994. *Poetic Voices: Discourse Linguistics and the Poetic Tradition*. Tuscaloosa: University of Alabama Press.

Bakhtin, Mikhail M. 1981. *The Dialogic Imagination: Four Essays*. Austin: University of Texas Press.

Banfield, Ann. 1982. *Unspeakable Sentences: Narration and Representation in the Language of Narrative*. Boston: Routledge & Kegan Paul.

Bell, Allan. 1991. *The Language of News Media*. Oxford: Blackwell.

Bray, Joe. 2002. 'Embedded Quotations in Eighteenth-Century Fiction: Journalism and the Early Novel' in *Journal of Literary Semantics* 31: 61-75.

Bush, George W. 2002. 'State of the Union Address'. 29 Jan. 2002. Online at: http://www.whitehouse.gov/news/releases/2002/01/20020129-11.html (consulted 02.04. 2002).

Caldas-Coulthard, Carmen Rosa. 1994. 'On Reporting Reporting: The Representation of Speech in Factual and Factional Narratives' in Coulthard, Malcolm (ed.) *Advances in Written Text Analysis*. London: Routledge: 295-308.

Davis, Lennard. 1983. *Factual Fictions: The Origins of the English Novel*. New York: Columbia University Press.

Derrida, Jacques. 1977. 'Signature Event Context' in *Glyph* 1: 172-97.

Fairclough, Norman. 1992. *Discourse and Social Change*. Oxford: Blackwell.

Fludernik, Monika. 1993. *The Fictions of Language and the Languages of Fiction*. London: Routledge.

Gee, James Paul. 1990. *Social Linguistics and Literacies: Ideology in Discourses*. London: Falmer Press.

Goldstein, Amy, and Mike Allen. 2002. 'Bush Vows to Defeat Terror, Recession' in *Washington Post* (30 January 2002). http://www.washingtonpost.com/ac2/wp-dyn?pagename=articel&node=&contentId=A58475-20 (consulted 03.04.2002).

Habermas, Jürgen. 1979. *Communication and the Evolution of Society*. London: Heinemann Educational.

Hall, Geoff. 2001. 'The Year's Work in Stylistics: 2000' in *Language and Literature* 10(4): 357-68.

Kintsch, Walter, and Teun A. van Dijk. 1978. 'Toward a Model of Discourse Comprehension and Production' in *Psychological Review* 85: 363-394.

Leech, Geoffrey, and M. H. Short. 1981. *Style in Fiction: A Linguistic Introduction to English Fictional Prose*. Harlow: Longman.

Linell, Per. 1982. *The Written Language Bias in Linguistics*. Linköping: University of Linköping Press.

Mayes, Patricia. 1990. 'Quotation in Spoken English' in *Studies in Language* 14(2): 325-63.

McHale, Brian. 1978. 'Free Indirect Discourse: A Survey of Recent Accounts' in *PTL: A Journal for Poetics and Theory of Literature* 3: 249-87.

Parkes, Malcolm B. 1992. *Pause and Effect: An Introduction to the History of Punctuation in the West*. Aldershot: Scolar.

Pascal, Roy. 1977. *The Dual Voice: Free Indirect Speech and its Functioning in the Nineteenth Century Novel.* Manchester: Manchester University Press.

Sanders, José, and Gisela Redeker. 1993. 'Linguistic Perspective in Short News Stories' in *Poetics* 22: 69-87.

Semino, Elena, Mick Short and Jonathan Culpeper. 1997. 'Using a Corpus to Test a Model of Speech and Thought Presentation' in *Poetics* 25: 17-43. Online at: http://www.comp.lancs.ac.uk/computing/users/eiamjw/stop/papers/poetics.html (consulted 02.04.2002).

Short, Mick. 1989. 'Speech Presentation, the Novel and the Press' in van Peer, Willie (ed.) *The Taming of the Text: Explorations in Language, Literature and Culture.* London: Routledge: 61-81.

Short, Mick, Elena Semino and Martin Wynne. 2002. 'Revisiting the Notion of Faithfulness in Discourse Presentation Using a Corpus Approach' in *Language and Literature* 11(4): 325-55.

Slembrouck, Stef. 1992. 'The Parliamentary Hansard "Verbatim" Report: The Written Construction of Spoken Discourse' in *Language and Literature* 1(2): 101-19.

Sternberg, Meir. 1982. 'Point of View and the Indirections of Direct Speech' in *Language and Style* 15(2): 67-117.

Tannen, Deborah. 1989. *Talking Voices: Repetition, Dialogue, and Imagery in Conversational Discourse.* Cambridge: Cambridge University Press.

__. 1995. 'Waiting for the Mouse: Constructed Dialogue in Conversation' in Tedlock, Dennis, and Bruce Mannheim (eds) *The Dialogic Emergence of Culture.* Urbana: University of Illinois Press: 198-217.

Toolan, Michael. 1998. *Language in Literature.* London: Hodder.

__. 2001. *Narrative: A Critical Linguistic Introduction* (2nd edition). London: Routledge.

van Dijk, Teun A. 1988. *News as Discourse.* Hillsdale, NJ: Lawrence Erlbaum Associates.

van Dijk, Teun A., and Walter Kintsch. 1983. *Strategies of Discourse Comprehension.* New York: Academic Press.

Vološinov, Valentin N. [1929] 1986. *Marxism and the Philosophy of Language.* (tr. Ladislav Matejka and I. R. Titunik). Cambridge, MA: Harvard University Press.

Waugh, Linda R. 1995. 'Reported Speech in Journalistic Discourse: The Relation of Function and Text' in *Text* 15(1): 129-73.

'Print Culture' and the Language of the 18th-Century Novel

Joe Bray

Abstract

Recent technological developments, including the Internet, have led some textual scholars to identify a 'destabilizing crisis in the world of production and meaning'. This essay shows that such a crisis also occurred in the early 18th century. A rapidly expanding 'print culture' created many of the conditions that have preoccupied the late 20th and early 21st centuries, including 'mobility, instability, the permeability of text to text, and of authorial property to readerly reinterpretation and alteration'. These features are particularly well demonstrated by the first novel of the successful London printer Samuel Richardson. Not only did *Pamela; or, Virtue Rewarded* (1740) generate an explosion of print in the form of satires, continuations, and imitations, it also embodies the slipperiness of text and meaning in the period. The fluidity and instability of Pamela's own written text is a key theme in the novel, as too is the way that her journal is open to the 'readerly reinterpretations' of Mr B.

Key words: textuality; print culture; the *Pamela* media event; embodied discourse; misreading.

It has long been fashionable in modern textual criticism to observe that recent technological developments pose a challenge to traditional understandings of textuality. As Kathryn Sutherland notes (1997: 1), both enthusiasts and critics of electronic technology

> take it for granted that the shift is monumental, involving a reconsideration of such large and difficult issues as the nature and extent of authorial property, the stability/fluidity of text and its relation to material forms, the globalisation or dis-/relocation of knowledge and the threat to or likely changes in reading practices.

For Sutherland, the 'dominant procedures of the electronic medium' are 'mobility, instability, the permeability of text to text, and of authorial property to readerly reinterpretation and alteration' (14). Her claim that 'we are in the late twentieth century living through [a] destabilizing crisis in the world of production and meaning' (3) has been echoed in the first few years of the 21st. Describing the 'move into a more insistently, intensely multimodal world', made possible by technological developments such as the internet, Gunther Kress and Theo van Leeuwen announce a 'deep change in the representational world' (2001: 127). As Jerome J. McGann somewhat wearily observes in Sutherland's 1997 volume, 'lofty reflections on the cultural significance of information technology are commonplace now' (1997: 19).

In this essay I will argue that this 'destabilizing crisis' is also nothing new. Similarly anxious debates about the nature of text have been occasioned at other moments of rapid technological change. Here I will focus on one such moment in particular: the early 18th century.[1] This period witnessed an unprecedented proliferation of printing technologies and printed material, which helped to promulgate, amongst other genres, the early novel. The result was a sometimes confusing 'print culture' in which texts circulated in an often bewildering variety of forms. The 'mobility' and 'instability' of text were everywhere evident, as too was 'the permeability of text to text, and of authorial property to readerly reinterpretation and alteration'. These factors created crises of meaning and interpretation of the kind which have preoccupied critics of postmodern culture. However, this essay does more than argue that technology has caused textual instability at an earlier historical period. It also grounds some of the lofty reflections about the interaction between technology and literary culture. I show that many of the concerns about textuality and meaning which have recently come to prominence are actually *embodied* in one particular early 18th-century text. This was produced by a man who, as the most successful printer in London at the time, was at the centre of the expanding 'print culture'.

Following its publication in November 1740, Samuel Richardson's *Pamela; or, Virtue Rewarded* generated what Thomas Keymer and Peter Sabor call an 'explosion of print' (2001: xvi). The first pirated edition appeared in Dublin in January 1741, less than three months later. Henry Fielding's witty satire *Shamela* arrived in April, the same month as *Pamela Censured*, an anonymous criticism of the novel's morality. An unauthorised continuation by John Kelly, *Pamela's Conduct in High Life*, was published in May, and Eliza Haywood's response, *Anti-Pamela: or, Feign'd Innocence Detected*, was brought out in June. Further pirated editions, sycophantic imitations, critical attacks, and spurious continuations followed later in the year, as well as a French translation (in October), a stage play by Henry Giffard (in November) and even an opera (in May of the following year). As Keymer and Sabor put it, '*Pamela*'s success inspired a swarm of unauthorized appropriations, a Grub Street grabfest in which a hungry army of entrepreneurial opportunists and freeloading hacks [...] moved in for the action' (2001: xiii).

Almost as numerous as these grubby appropriations by others were Richardson's own rewritings of the novel. He became increasingly desperate to control and limit readings of the novel of which he did not approve, particularly those which were hostile to its heroine. His response to criticism of *Pamela*, as with all of his novels, was to keep obsessively rewriting and revising the text in order to try and prevent the possibility of it being misread. As Eaves and Kimpel bluntly put it, 'Richardson, who read little else, read his own works constantly and seldom read them without changing something' (1971: 91). The second edition of *Pamela* appeared just three months after the first, in February 1741, with a new, self-promoting introduction based on six commendatory letters from Aaron Hill. A third edition followed in March, a fourth in May, and a fifth in September, before, irked by those that were already circulating, Richardson published his own continuation of Pamela's married life in December. A sixth edition came out in May 1742 in luxury octavo format, together with what was called the 'third' edition of the continuation. Three further revised editions of the original novel appeared in Richardson's lifetime, in 1746, 1754, and 1761.[2]

Yet despite Richardson's best attempts, the 'permeability' of *Pamela* into other texts meant readings that were far from his original intentions continued to circulate, and he could not control the ensuing debates about the novel. This 'readerly reinterpretation and alteration', to use Sutherland's terms, is highlighted by William B. Warner in his discussion of 'the *Pamela* media event'. For Warner, 'the elevation of novels' was 'a creative early modern response by media workers and entertainers to the onset of market-driven media culture' (1998: xiii). Praising Richardson's understanding of the workings of this media culture, Warner argues that 'the extraordinary popularity of *Pamela* involves more than a transient shift in taste, a mere "vogue"; it is a media event that helps to inaugurate a shift in reading practices' (178).[3] Thus 'the *Pamela* media event evidences a mutation in the print-media culture in Britain' (224), reinscribing the novel 'within a contentious public sphere, where what a text means will be the negotiated outcome of sustained critical scrutiny by sophisticated adult readers' (208).

These sophisticated critical scrutineers were generally divided into two camps: on the one hand those who defended Pamela's morals and recommended them as models to be followed, and on the other those who found her unbelievable and were inclined to suggest that she had been a schemer all along. The argument between the 'Pamelists' and the 'Antipamelists', as these two groups were known, reveals wider cultural debates within the period, as Keymer & Sabor (2001: xix) point out:

> below the surface of arguments about character and motive, also in play were the larger conflicts and questions of an age in which the traditional ideologies were increasingly open to question or challenge: the relationships between virtue and class, or between virtue and gender; the rival claims on the Christian soul of faith and good works; the vague and troubled borderline between moral and immoral discourse. *Pamela* was not only a novel but also a site of ideological contestation, and in the focus given by writers of the controversy to these and other areas of dispute we can read a whole culture and its discontents.

For Warner, it is an important point that this 'ideological contestation' soon spins out of the original author's control. He characterises the print market in which *Pamela* appeared as 'a system of production and consumption in which no one can control or guarantee the meanings that sweep through its texts' (1998: 181), and claims that 'there is something in the very structure of both the system of early modern entertainment wherein the letter-novel *Pamela* is composed and circulates and the space that opens around Pamela's performance of her virtue that produces meanings that disrupt claims to an interior univocal meaning' (197-98). In his view 'it is precisely because it is set in motion by someone who strives so hard to get his message to its proper destination that the *Pamela* media event is an especially rich matrix for reading the perversely plural effects of communication' (199).

The rapidly proliferating network of texts that followed the publication of *Pamela* was thus characterised by the 'permeability of text to text, and of authorial property to readerly reinterpretation and alteration'. Richardson's original novel soon became transformed into other versions, and, try as he could, he was unable to control the vast spectrum of 'readerly reinterpretations' which the text generated. As a result unresolvable debates over *Pamela*'s destabilised 'meaning' arose. In the rest of this essay I will argue further that uncertainties of interpretation and possibilities of misreading were actually inherent in the text from the beginning, in its first edition.[4] The 'perversely plural effects of communication' are not just evident in the controversy that surrounded the publication of *Pamela*, but are also embodied within the text itself. In fact the metaphor of embodiment is central to accounts of the 'print culture' in which *Pamela* appeared.

Referring to the 'proliferation of print commodities' in the early 18th century, which saw 'printing-processes in overdrive', Deidre S. Lynch (1998: 24) identifies a 'typographical culture', in which 'communication was a matter of marking, imprinting, and *embodying*' (28). Her study of the period's understanding of 'character' points to the earliest meanings of the word associated with marking and engraving,[5] and notes 'an interest in the material grounds of meaning and a fascination with the puns that could link the person "in" a text to the printed letters (alphabetic symbols, or "characters" in another sense) that elaborated that text's surface' (6). 'Understanding how character mattered in eighteenth-century Britain entails, first of all', she claims, 'understanding the curiously *embodied* terms in which literate people conceptualised their reading matter' (30). The '*Pamela* media event' offers several examples: aside from the play and opera mentioned earlier, other material forms into which Richardson's text was transmuted include paintings and engravings, a fan, and even a waxwork.[6] Referring to 'a semantic complex in which the ethical, the physiognomic, the typographic, and even the numismatic merge' (30), Lynch (1998: 30) claims that:

> The eighteenth century inherited from the seventeenth the conviction that it was best to *image* the linguistic grounds of human knowledge and an eagerness to apprehend the constituents of knowledge through analogies with the human body. According to the understanding of linguistic behaviour that prevailed at the opening of the century, discourse was *embodied* – at ease with its immersion in a print culture in which language necessarily assumes visible, corporeal form. At the same time, the body was discursive, a telltale transcript

> of the identity it housed. Ideas of the Book of Nature invited people to think
> of human bodies and the cultural texts humans produced in tandem *and*
> invited them to think of both humans and their texts as linked to the animal,
> vegetable, and mineral works of Creation – to natural forms, which
> themselves were said to possess 'signatures' indexing their affinities.

The idea that human bodies, like humanly produced texts, can be read, was of course not new. Alberto Manguel traces the long history of the notion that 'human beings, made in the image of God, are also books to be read' back to St. Augustine, showing that it was important for Shakespeare and Whitman, amongst others (1997: 163-73). According to E. R. Curtius, 'the idea that the world and nature are books derives from the rhetoric of the Catholic Church, taken over by the mystical philosophers of the early Middle Ages' (Manguel 1997: 168). The metaphor was strengthened at the end of the 17th century by John Locke's *Essay on Human Understanding*, which explicitly forges a connection between the materiality of text, particularly its typography, and the body. In his *Essay* Locke rejects the 'received Doctrine, That Men have native *Ideas*, and original Characters stamped upon their Minds, in their very first Being' (1975: 104), arguing that 'if there were certain Characters, imprinted by Nature on the Understanding, as the Principles of Knowledge, we could not but perceive them constantly operate in us' (67). Instead, Locke asserts, 'let us suppose the Mind to be, as we say, white Paper, void of all Characters, without any *Ideas*' (104). This 'Experience' is composed of 'Sensation' and 'Reflection'. No one has '*any* Idea *in his Mind*', Locke insists, '*but what one of these two have imprinted*' (106). The human mind is thus, for Locke, a text on which ideas have been imprinted, or, as Lynch puts it, 'at the centre, then, of the *Essay*'s account of the operations of human understanding is an analogy that links the getting of ideas, the techniques of typography, and the process of individuation' (1998: 34). She refers to the early 18th century's 'Lockean conception of the person', according to which, 'people figure as bodies of writing' (42).

This textual 'conception of the person' is certainly apparent in *Pamela*. As will shortly be demonstrated, the heroine is often represented by and equated with a body of writing. Similarly, many observers equated the text with its heroine, including its author himself. In a letter of 1753 to Lady Bradshaigh, Richardson predicted that 'I will give Pamela my last Correction, if my Life be spared; that, as a Piece of Writing only, she may not appear for her Situation, unworthy of her Younger Sisters' (Forster Collection, XI, 30).[7] Others viewed Richardson's texts as sisters. An example is the German scientist Albrecht von Haller, whose review of *Clarissa* appeared, translated, in the *Gentleman's Magazine* of June 1749. For von Haller, '*Clarissa* may be said to be the younger sister and imitater [*sic*] of *Pamela*', though he claims that the author, a Mr S. Robinson, 'appears to have drawn great advantages from the criticisms which have been made on the prior work', and praises the younger sister for 'a variety that is wanting in *Pamela*' (*The Gentleman's Magazine* 1749: 245).

This conflation of text and heroine is also apparent in the two letters with which Richardson prefaced his text in the first edition of 1740. The first was from a French translator then earning his living in London, Jean Baptiste de Freval, the other was unsigned, but probably the work of the Reverend William Webster, who had recently become vicar of Thundridge and Ware. Webster's commendation had already appeared, a month earlier in the religious periodical which he edited, the *Weekly Miscellany*. Richardson had printed the journal for four years following its inception in 1732, and had recently forgiven Webster a debt of £90 owing from this period. He had also just printed de Freval's English translation of the Abbé Pluche's *The History of the Heavens* on favourable terms.[8] De Freval's letter opens by announcing that 'I have had inexpressible Pleasure in the Perusal of your PAMELA' (2001: 5). The merging of text and heroine is apparent again in its final paragraph: 'Little Book, charming PAMELA! face the World, and never doubt of finding Friends and Admirers, not only in thine own Country, but far from Home' (6). Similarly, arguing that the text should be seen 'in its own native Simplicity, which will affect and please the Reader beyond all the Strokes of Oratory in the World', Webster condemns 'superfluous and needless Decorations':

> No, let us have *Pamela* as *Pamela* wrote it; in her own Words, without Amputation or Addition. Produce her to us in her neat Country Apparel, such as she appear'd in, on her intended Departure to her Parents; for such best becomes her Innocence and beautiful Simplicity. Such a Dress will best edify and entertain. The flowing Robes of Oratory may indeed amuse and amaze, but will never strike the Mind with solid Attention. (9)

Throughout the novel the heroine is closely associated with the text which she writes, as her body and her writing are intimately connected. This is indeed physically the case, since, as she reveals to her parents, she stitches her 'Writings [...] in my Under-coat, next my Linen' (131), in order to hide them from Mr B and Mrs Jewkes. Later she reports that her journal is 'sew'd in my Under-coat, about my Hips' (227). Desperate to see her 'sawcy Journal', Mr B realises he will have to strip her:

> Now, said he, it is my Opinion they are about you; and I never undrest a Girl in my Life; but I will now begin to strip my pretty *Pamela*; and hope I shall not go far, before I find them.
>
> I fell a crying, and said, I will not be used in this manner. Pray, Sir, said I (for he began to unpin my Handkerchief) consider! Pray, Sir, do! - And pray, said he, do *you* consider. For I will see those Papers. But may-be, said he, they are ty'd about your Knees with your Garters, and stooped. Was ever any thing so vile and so wicked! (235)

To get to Pamela's journal then, Mr B must interfere with her physically. Reading her text becomes an act of sexual assault, akin to taking her virginity. When Pamela is finally forced to hand over her papers, she says she 'will take it for a great Favour, and a good Omen' if he will 'please to return them, without breaking the Seal' (239). Yet for Mr B such restraint is impossible: 'He broke the Seal instantly, and open'd them' (239).

Indeed Mr B is driven to distraction and infatuation by Pamela's text, as much as by her physical charms. He is particularly struck by her writing style, praising her 'easy and happy Manner of Narration' (300), and admitting that he is 'quite overcome with your charming manner of Writing, so free, so easy, and so much above your Sex; and put this all together, makes me, as I tell you, love you to Extravagance' (84). He defends his increasingly violent attempts to get possession of her writing by asking 'And if I had not loved you, do you think I would have troubled myself about your Letters?' (229), and acknowledges that they have been instrumental in strengthening his feelings for her: 'Your Papers shall be faithfully return'd you, and I have paid so dear for my Curiosity in the Affection they have rivetted upon me for you, that you would look upon yourself amply reveng'd, if you knew what they have cost me' (247).

Several times in the novel, Mr B in fact conflates Pamela's text and her body, or her self. She is afraid of his reaction when he has read the bulk of her journal:

About nine o'Clock he sent for me down in the Parlour. I went a little
fearfully; and he held the Papers in his Hand, and said, Now, *Pamela*, you
come upon your Trial. (230)

It is not clear whether this '*Pamela*' refers to the heroine herself or to
her text, or to a conflation of the two. Later he merges the two again
when urging her 'to continue your Relation, as you have Opportunity;
and tho' your Father be here, write to your Mother, that this wondrous
Story be perfect, and we, your Friends, may read and admire you more
and more' (301). In her letters to her parents, Pamela exhibits a
similar confusion between herself and her text. Sending them 'a most
tedious Parcel of Stuff, of my *Oppressions*, my *Distresses*, my *Fears*'
via Mr Williams, Pamela rejoices that 'I am glad I can conclude, after
all my Sufferings, with my *Hopes*, to be soon with you' (149). Seeing
her writing will, she often insists, be the same as seeing her, and she
often finds herself apologising for both: 'But blame not your poor
Daughter too much: Nay, if ever you see this miserable Scribble, all
bathed and blotted with my Tears, let your Pity get the better of your
Blame! But I know it will' (175). The connection between Pamela's
text and her self is reinforced when Pamela has finally fallen in love
with Mr B and agreed to marry him. Her transfer from her father's
protection to that of her future husband is marked symbolically by the
transfer of her writing, as she asks for her letters and journal back
from her father and solemnly hands them over to Mr B: 'He pulled
them from his Pocket; and I stood up, and with my best Duty, gave
them into my Master's Hands' (296).

However, although Pamela's text has a very physical, embodied
presence in the novel, at times seeming to represent the heroine
herself, this materiality is no defence against 'readerly
reinterpretation'. In a letter to Pamela's father Mr B reveals that he
has contrived, by his servant John, to read 'the strange
Correspondence carry'd on between you and your Daughter, so
injurious to my Honour and Reputation' (92):

Something, possibly, there might be in what she has wrote from time to time;
but, believe me, with all her pretended Simplicity and Innocence, I never
knew so much romantick Invention as she is Mistress of. In short, the Girl's
Head's turn'd by Romances, and such idle Stuff, which she has given herself
up to, ever since her kind Lady's Death. (93)

This claim that Pamela's head has been turned by the unchecked
reading of romances is not simply invented by Mr B in order to justify

his behaviour to her father. Elsewhere he seems genuinely to believe
that her writing style is that of a romantic heroine, and indeed belongs
in a romance. He explains his curiosity to read all she has written:
'there is such a pretty Air of Romance, as you relate them, in your
Plots, and my Plots' (232). Pamela responds indignantly that 'this is a
very provoking way of jeering at the Misfortunes you have brought
upon me' (232). He also reads her correspondence with Mr Williams
as an episode from a romance:

> In the first Place, Here are several Love-letters between you and *Williams*.
> Love-letters! Sir, said I. – Well, call them what you will, said he, I don't
> intirely like them, I'll assure you, with all the Allowances you desired me to
> make for you. Do you find, Sir, said I, that I encouraged his Proposal, or do
> you not? Why, said he, you discourage his Address in Appearance; but no
> otherwise than all your cunning Sex do to ours, to make us more eager in
> pursuing you.
>
> Well, Sir, said I, that is your Comment; but it does not appear so in the Text.
> (230)

The physicality of Pamela's writing in the novel does not then prevent
Mr B from reading it in his own way, and discovering meanings far
from those she intended. In response to his reinterpretations she
resorts here to the authority of 'the Text', yet it is clear that this is a
less transparent and stable entity than she had foreseen when
reluctantly agreeing to let him read 'all my private Thoughts of him,
and all my Secrets, as I may say' (226). Though strongly connected
with the body in this novel, her text remains slippery and unstable,
and its meanings are hard to pin down. Indeed, none of the elements
of the 'semantic complex' which Lynch sees as central to the early
18th century's 'typographical culture' are perhaps as easy to read as
she suggests. It is possible to challenge particularly strongly her claim
that in this period 'the body was discursive, a telltale transcript of the
identity it housed'.

The 18th-century novel is in fact littered with physiognomical
misreaders. In Henry Mackenzie's *The Man of Feeling*, 'physiognomy
was one of Harley's foibles, for which he had often rebuked by his
aunt in the country' (1967: 44), and 'his skill in physiognomy is
doubted', not least in Chapter 27, in which he is advised that '"as for
faces - you may look into them to know, whether a man's nose be a
long or a short one"' (53). As Graeme Tytler has shown,
physiognomical readings are also often problematic in Fielding's
novels, which abound with misreadings of faces and bodies (examples

are those by Parson Adams in *Joseph Andrews* and The Man of the Hill in *Tom Jones*; see Tytler 1982: 144-151). In his 'Essay on the Knowledge of the Characters of Men' Fielding notes that 'the truth is, we almost universally mistake the symptoms which Nature kindly holds forth to us' (1882: 332). The fault is thus with the physiognomist, rather than the science itself: 'I conceive the passions of men do commonly imprint sufficient marks on the countenance; and it is owing chiefly to want of skill in the observer that physiognomy is of so little use and credit in the world' (332).

The common practice of misreading, or rather not reading, the Book of Human Nature is also a theme of an article in *The Lady's Magazine* in July 1789. The writer asks: 'Is it not strange, gentle courteous reader, is it not strange, that nobody should read what is in every body's hands? That there should be a book, full of information, entertainment, and instruction, as easily come at, as is to lay one's hand on one's heart, and yet so few give themselves the trouble to look into it?' (339). Though this book was 'printed, published and dispersed through the universe long before [...] the invention of printing was heard of' (339), the article makes an analogy with the products of 18th-century 'print culture':

> it does happen in the case of curious and old books – such as the one I am speaking of – that we rarely can complete a copy, and render it perfectly agreeable to the ORIGINAL – without collating and comparing many editions, one with the other, expunging what appears to have been interpolated – and adding what may have been omitted [....] (340)

This reference to interpolated and incomplete texts, and the need to collate and compare many editions in order to 'complete a copy, and render it perfectly agreeable to the ORIGINAL' gives a sense of the chaotic circulations of 'print culture' in the 18th century, and the unstable and fragmented nature of text. As the 'riot of print' (Keymer & Sabor 2001: xiv) which followed the publication of *Pamela* demonstrates, original meanings could soon be overtaken by the 'permeability of text to text', and the often startling transformations and alterations which texts underwent. The desperate anxiety to keep the text fixed and stable is a sign of how fleeting such fixedness and stability was in practice. Pamela promises that she will give Mr B her 'Papers [...] without the least Alteration, or adding or diminishing' (235). Yet he remains nervous:

If you have either added or diminish'd, and have not strictly kept your
Promise, woe be to you! Indeed, Sir, said I, I have neither added nor
diminish'd. (238-39)

'The *Pamela* media event' thus offers rich evidence for the way that
technology can cause a 'destabilizing crisis in the world of production
and meaning'. Richardson's first novel rode the tide of the rapidly
expanding 'print culture' and soon became drowned in the deluge of
publications which ensued. The controversy and ideological debate
which it generated illustrate that the early 21st century is not alone in
witnessing 'the permeability of text to text, and of authorial property
to readerly reinterpretation and alteration'. Furthermore, the
'instability' and 'fluidity' of text is an internal theme of the novel, as,
in Warner's words, 'misreadings are programmed into *Pamela* from
its inception' (1998: 203). The physical, embodied nature of Pamela's
discourse does not protect it from reinterpretation. Rather, given the
repeatedly stressed hazards of reading bodies and faces in the period,
it emphasises the slipperiness of her text, and the impossibility of
reducing it to a fixed meaning. The novel is indeed driven by Mr B's
misreading of her journal as a romance, and the heroine's attempt to
correct him and reassert her original meanings. Pamela's struggles
anticipated Richardson's own efforts to control the readings of his
text. Both could tell the 21st-century theorist much, from bitter
experience, about the 'perversely plural effects of communication'.

Endnotes

[1]There are, of course, other such moments of 'destabilizing crisis' brought about by
technological development. Sutherland cites 'that moment around 1800 which saw the
invention of the iron-frame hand-press with its *mechanical* power to increase the rate
of print production' (1997: 3).

[2]In the last years of his life, before his death in 1761, Richardson was working on
another revision of his first novel; this was eventually published, possibly with some
alterations by his daughters, in 1801 as the 14th edition.

[3]Terry Eagleton makes a similar point, arguing that *Pamela* is not so much a novel as
'a whole cultural event [...] the occasion or organizing principle of a multimedia
affair, stretching all the way from domestic commodities to public speeches, instantly
recodable from one cultural mode to the next' (1982: 5).

[4]I am greatly indebted to Thomas Keymer and Alice Wakely's recent (Richardson
2001) edition of the novel, which takes the first edition as its copy-text. All quotations
from *Pamela* in this essay are from this text.

[5]The first three 'literal senses' of 'character' in the *OED* are 'A distinctive mark impressed, engraved, or otherwise formed; a brand stamp'; 'A distinctive significant mark of any kind; a graphic sign or symbol'; and 'A graphic symbol standing for a sound, syllable, or notion, used in writing or in printing; one of the simple elements of a written language; e. g. a letter of the alphabet'.

[6]The most famous paintings of episodes from *Pamela* are those of Joseph Highmore, which were exhibited at his house in Lincoln's Inn Fields in February 1744. In the following year Antoine Benoist and Louis Truchy produced engravings of Highmore's paintings. In April 1741 *The Daily Advertiser* reported that 'PAMELA, a new Fan, representing the principal Adventures of her Life, in Servitude, Love and Marriage' is now on sale 'at all the Fan-Shops and China-Shops in and about London', while the same paper announced the exhibition of 'PAMELA; or, VIRTUE REWARDED. Being a curious Piece of Wax-Work' near Richardson's Salisbury Court premises in April 1745. It seems the waxwork was on display for several months and may even have been expanded to include scenes from the continuation.

[7]In the absence of a complete edition of Richardson's letters, I have consulted the Forster Collection in the Victoria and Albert Museum, London, which contains many of the original manuscripts of the letters.

[8]As Keymer puts it, 'though no doubt sincere in their admiration, both de Freval and Webster were clearly in receipt or expectation of SR's patronage, which must have helped to lubricate their praise' (2001: xlv).

References

Eagleton, Terry. 1982. *The Rape of Clarissa*. Minneapolis: University of Minnesota Press.

Eaves, T. C. Duncan, and Ben D. Kimpel. 1971. *Samuel Richardson: A Biography*. Oxford: Clarendon Press.

Fielding, Henry. 1882. 'An Essay on the Knowledge and Characters of Men' in *The Works of Henry Fielding*, Vol. VI (ed. Leslie Stephen). London: Smith, Elder & Co.: 327-353.

The Gentleman's Magazine. 1749. London.

Keymer, Thomas, and Peter Sabor (eds). 2001. *The* Pamela *Controversy: Criticisms and Adaptations of Samuel Richardson's* Pamela, *1740-1750*. Vol. I: *Richardson's Apparatus and Fielding's* Shamela. London: Pickering & Chatto.

Kress, Gunther, and Theo van Leeuwen. 2001. *Multimodal Discourse: The Modes and Media of Contemporary Communication*. London: Arnold.

The Lady's Magazine. 1789. London.

Locke, John. 1975. *An Essay Concerning Human Understanding* (ed. P. H. Nidditch). Oxford: Clarendon Press [based on 4th ed., 1700].

Lynch, Deirdre S. 1998. *The Economy of Character: Novels, Market Culture, and the Business of Inner Meaning*. Chicago: University of Chicago Press.

Mackenzie, Henry. 1967. *The Man of Feeling* (ed. Brian Vickers). Oxford: Oxford University Press.

Manguel, Alberto. 1997. *A History of Reading*. London: Flamingo.

McGann, Jerome J. 1997. 'The Rationale of Hypertext' in Sutherland (1997): 19-46.

Richardson, Samuel. 2001. *Pamela; or, Virtue Rewarded* (ed. Thomas Keymer and Alice Wakely). Oxford: Oxford University Press [based on 1st ed., 1740].

Sutherland, Kathryn (ed.). 1997. *Electronic Text: Investigations in Method and Theory*. Oxford: Clarendon Press.

Tytler, Graeme. 1982. *Physiognomy in the European Novel: Faces and Fortunes*. Princeton, NJ: Princeton University Press.

Warner, William B. 1998. *Licensing Entertainment: The Elevation of Novel Reading in Britain, 1684-1750*. Berkeley: University of California Press.

Truth and Lies: The Construction of Factuality in a Television Documentary[1]

Susan Hunston

Abstract

This paper describes a television documentary in which two contradictory versions of a story are presented. The paper explores how these two versions are given without the narratorial voice in the film appearing inconsistent. It is argued that this is achieved mainly because in the first half of the film the epistemic status of much of the material is kept indeterminate and that it is therefore open to reinterpretation in the second half of the film. The indeterminacy is maintained by features of language and of image.

Key words: film; factuality; status; averral; attribution.

1. The story

In the mid 1990s a newly published book, *Fragments*, had an impact on the reading public. It was the autobiography of a man called Binjamin Wilkomirski who, as a Latvian Jewish child during World War II, had been interned in the concentration camps at Majdanek and at Auschwitz. It was a harrowing book, describing in detail the suffering of young children in those camps. Its publication was welcomed by other child survivors, who felt that their unique suffering had at last been given a voice. A BBC film team from the 'Inside Story' series filmed Wilkomirski telling his story, with the aim of making a documentary about his life and his book.

Before the film was finished, however, an Israeli-born journalist named Daniel Ganzfried cast doubt on the book's authenticity as autobiography. He suggested that although events like those described in *Fragments* may indeed have happened, they had not happened to, or been observed by, the writer of the book. The BBC team interviewed Ganzfried and undertook further investigations. Wilkomirski had lived for most of his life in Switzerland, under the name Bruno Grosjean. Following Ganzfried's leads, the film researchers found a number of people who asserted that Grosjean had been born in Switzerland, rather than arriving there as a child after the war, that he had never been in a concentration camp until he visited Majdanek as an adult tourist, and that his parents were Swiss, not Latvian, and not Jewish.

The film *Truth and Lies* that was eventually shown on BBC television, in 2000, is divided into two parts. The first part is entitled 'Binjamin's Story', and consists mainly of interviews with Wilkomirski, along with readings from his book. Here the audience is given Wilkomirski's version of the events of his childhood. The second part of the film is entitled 'Bruno's Story', and it presents the alternative life of Bruno Grosjean – his birth to a single mother, his adoption, schooldays, and young adulthood, all taking place in Switzerland. This is the evidence against Wilkomirski's version of events. By the end of the film it is clear that viewers are positioned to believe Ganzfried and to disbelieve Wilkomirski. The book *Fragments* is not a record of the writer's life, but a work of fiction.

2. The film

Like most documentaries, the film *Truth and Lies* is a multitextual entity and incorporates a number of different voices. Its raw material is a number of individual texts, including filmed interviews, news footage from the 1940s, and reconstructions of the events in *Fragments*. Parts of these texts are extracted and recombined to make the film. The constituent texts may be described in terms of their epistemic status, using the categories 'record' and 'reconstruction', and the concurrent categories 'averred' and 'attributed'.[2] For example, a sequence of news footage is 'record' (because it is a film of actual, not acted, events) and 'attributed' (because the film-makers have not filmed it themselves). A reconstruction of the events described in *Fragments* is 'reconstruction' and is 'averred' (because the film-makers have filmed it). An interview with Wilkomirski is 'record' (because the interview is an actual event) and 'averred'. In addition, the statements spoken by the various participants in the film can also be ascribed status, based on whether they are averred by the narrator, or attributed to Wilkomirski, to other speakers, or to the book *Fragments* (extracts from which are read by an actor). Table 1 gives three examples of the combination of statuses of film and of statements.

Table 1

Content of extract	Status of film	Status of statements
News footage of Nazi troops in Riga. Voice-over (narrator): In 1940 the Red Army came in. Then in 1941 the Nazis. Jews in Riga were rounded up, herded into synagogues, and burned alive.	attributed record	narrator averral
Wilkomirski in close-up. Narrator: And how old would you have been then? Wilkomirski: I guess, I guess, three.	averred record	attribution to Wilkomirski
Black-and-white shots of steam train, close-ups of wheels, chimney. Unidentifiable person climbing onto train. Narrator: A woman in a grey uniform put him on another train. Book: 'Where to?' I asked the grey uniform, clutching on the edge of her skirt. 'Majdanek' she said.	averred reconstruction	narrator averral; attribution to *Fragments*

The question raised by the film is: how are these different texts combined so that two incompatible versions of events are presented without apparent internal inconsistency? Clearly it is not the case that the two possible stories are shown impartially, leaving the audience free to choose between them. If this were the case the narrator would aver two mutually inconsistent narratives. More plausible is the possibility that the story in the first half of the film is attributed to others while the second half is averred by the narrator. As shall be seen below, some instances of attribution-averral do occur. Mostly, however, the relationship between the two halves of the film is more subtle. I shall argue below that the second half of the film in fact reinterprets the status of the first half. This is made possible because the status of the first half is indeterminate and is therefore open to resolution in the second half.

3. The process of reinterpretation

The process by which the second part of this film reinterprets the information in the first part, and in particular reinterprets its status, can be illustrated by comparing two extracts from one of the constituent texts of the film: an interview with Anne Karpf, who is described as the daughter of a holocaust survivor. In 'Binjamin's Story' Karpf is shown giving her reaction upon first reading the book:

> I found it devastating. I've read an enormous amount of holocaust literature, a surfeit I'd say, but this I did think belonged up with Primo Levi and the other greats. It was very very powerful, very evocative, very moving. I read it in one sitting and I sobbed.

In the second part of the film she is shown giving her reaction upon hearing that the book might not be a true account:

> I had a complete sense of disbelief in the beginning and that was followed quite quickly by a sense of rage, betrayal, feeling traduced, and it almost felt blasphemous, you know, as if to take on– as if– as if being a holocaust survivor was some kind of costume that you could just don and impersonate someone. I felt absolutely appalled.

The relation of these statements to each other is important. They do not form a sequence of 'statement plus contradiction' (which would be discoursally inconsistent), but the common English discourse sequence of either 'apparently true plus actually true', or 'concession plus counter-assertion'.[3] The presence of the second extract from the interview re-evaluates the status of the first extract in such a way that it is discoursally consistent. These possible interpretations are shown in Table 2.

Table 2

Discourse pattern	First statement	Second statement
Statement + contradiction *Discoursally inconsistent*	Anne was moved by the book.	Anne was angered by the book.
Apparent + real *Discoursally consistent*	Anne thought she was moved by the book.	Actually she was angered by it.
Concession + counter-assertion *Discoursally consistent*	It is true that Anne was moved by the book.	But later she was angered by it.

The Anne Karpf sequence is a micro-sequence that mirrors the structure of the film itself. Binjamin's story comes first, and Bruno's story, coming second, reinterprets it. More specifically, the first half of the film contains many statements which appear to have the status of 'fact', averred by the narrator, but which are later reinterpreted as fictions, lies, or inventions, attributed to Wilkomirski and then contradicted. For example, in 'Binjamin's Story' the narrator says:

> Long ago in Poland his brother had played with toy planes in a sunny field.

In 'Bruno's Story' the boy playing is described as an *image*, not as an actual event:

> One of the images in the book is that of Wilkomirski's elder brother flying model planes in the fields.

Similarly, in 'Binjamin's Story' the narrator describes an event from Wilkomirski's childhood in Switzerland:

> Once he went on a school trip to a fair in Zürich. Suddenly he ran away from the other boys, squatted on the ground and begged for money from strangers. It was as if he was back in his orphanage in Poland.

In 'Bruno's Story' this becomes a *claim*:

> Wilkomirski claims that on a school trip to a fair he broke away and begged for money from strangers. Somehow he thought he was back in his Polish orphanage.

This claim is then discredited in an interview with Bruno's class teacher:

> Teacher: Could never have happened because I never went to a fair with the whole class.
>
> Interviewer: You would have heard if something like that had happened.
>
> Teacher: Yes of course. The other children would surely have told me.

As a final example, in 'Binjamin's Story', the assertion that Wilkomirski was born in Latvia is presented as a *belief*, that is, something which the speaker holds to be true:

> He began life, he believed, in a more humble home, in Riga, in Latvia, on the edge of the Baltic Sea.

In 'Bruno's Story' a former girlfriend disparages this view, and the narrator classifies it as a *lie*, that is, something which the speaker (Wilkomirski) holds to be untrue:

> Girlfriend: When he was seventeen or eighteen he told me that he came from the Baltic states. And I didn't believe it because I knew it couldn't be true.
>
> Narrator: They were small, harmless lies.

This strategy of reinterpretation may be contrasted with a less-used device, mentioned above, in which statements in the first part of the film are attributed and hedged, and then contradicted by averral in the second part of the film. For example, 'Binjamin's Story' describes the relationship between Wilkomirski and a woman named Laura Grobowski. The assertion that Laura was a fellow internee at

Auschwitz is not averred by the narrator, but is attributed to Wilkomirski:

> The victims of the experiments, he believes, include Laura Grobowski... like him a child of Auschwitz.... In their first phone conversation Wilkomirski told her he thought he remembered her...

Where the narrator does aver, it is with a hedged statement:

> [Laura] seemed to have a rare blood disease caused by the experiments...

In 'Bruno's Story', the narrator's averrals contradict these claims:

> Laura is not who she seems.... She isn't Jewish and never was in a concentration camp.... It certainly was a strange day when she and Binjamin Wilkomirski came together. Neither had ever seen each other before in their lives.

This example, however, is an exception. In most cases the status of the first part of the film is reinterpreted in the second, as in the previous examples. The reinterpretation is possible because the status of the utterances in the first part of the film is in fact indeterminate, the indeterminacy being a product of both word and image and resolved by the words and images in the second half of the film. The next section will illustrate this process.

4. The narrator's words and the resolution of indeterminacy

Indeterminacy of status can be illustrated by two extracts from the text that is the narrator's commentary. The first is from the first part of the film:

> In Poland he was separated from his mother and brothers. A woman in a grey uniform put him on another train. He was told that at Majdanek he would find his brothers waiting. Majdanek was amongst the worst of Nazi death camps. Men, women and children rounded up all over Europe were brought to a siding near the camp. Then they were marched along the black road made of broken tombstones from Jewish cemeteries.

This extract includes both 'historical fact' (*Men, women and children rounded up all over Europe were brought to a siding...*) and statements about Wilkomirski's life (*In Poland he was separated from his mother and brothers...*). These are undifferentiated in terms of their status, in that neither is explicitly attributed, or assessed for its truth value. The second extract is from later in the film, at the point where Wilkomirski's story begins to be challenged. In this extract, signals of attribution and hedging, and status identifiers, are shown in bold.[4]

The truth is long ago and far away. In Riga, which **he says** he left when he was two or three, could he really have remembered his house? ... Bernstein and Verena returned with him to Riga, which he **seemed** to know like the back of his hand. ... But **a Jewish historian says** his account of escaping with his mother and brothers across the river is **highly unlikely. The fact is that** almost everything about the Nazi occupation of Riga, and the murder of the Latvian Jews, is well known.... **Wilkomirski admits** he studied the holocaust from college onward. Before this trip to Majdanek in 1993 his passports disclose several previous trips to Poland. On any one he **could** have visited Majdanek. He **could** have stitched his story together from what he'd read. **The official historian at Majdanek says** Wilkomirski could only have survived if the SS hadn't known he was a Jew. Since **he says** he's circumcised, that **seems unlikely**.... **He claims** he was ... transferred to Auschwitz. 38 women and children were transported from Majdanek to Auschwitz in April 1944 but **as far as is known** they were killed.... **The answers in the end are** in the archives of a small town in Switzerland. **Wilkomirski claims** that when he arrived from Poland, Swiss officials gave him a false identity.... But **Ganzfried discovered** that a real Bruno Grosjean did exist.

In this extract, a dialogic argument is enacted, with points being made for and against Wilkomirski. For example, Wilkomirski's memories of living in Riga, with the evidence that he *seemed to know* the city, are set against the words of *a Jewish historian*. His claim to have been transferred from Majdanek to Auschwitz is countered by the assertion, attributed in a hedged way to unnamed persons (*as far as is known*), that there were no survivors of such a transfer. The notion of Wilkomirski obtaining his knowledge through research rather than through experience is raised as a possibility (*could have*). Three statements are asserted categorically: that facts about the Nazi occupation of Riga are common knowledge (*The fact is that*); that the debate can be resolved by consulting Swiss archives (*The answers in the end are*); and that someone with the name Bruno Grosjean existed as a Swiss citizen from birth (*Ganzfried discovered*).[5]

There is much more that could be said about the various statements in this extract, but what is important here is that the statuses of the various statements are precisely differentiated; there is averral and attribution, fact and supposition. This contrasts sharply with the undifferentiated stance of the first extract. Because of the differentiation in the second extract, the narrator's voice as an averrer is stronger. This in turn encourages reinterpretation of the first extract, where the narrator's apparent averral is weaker precisely because it is not in contrast with anything else.

A crucial additional element, however, is that neither of these two extracts stands as they have been presented here. In each case the narrator's account is interspersed with quotes, from interviews and from Wilkomirski's book. Below is an expansion of part of the first extract, showing the different voices used:

> Narrator: In Poland he was separated from his mother and brothers. A woman in a grey uniform put him on another train.
>
> Book: 'Where to?' I asked the grey uniform, clutching on the edge of her skirt. 'Majdanek', she said.
>
> Narrator: He was told that at Majdanek he would find his brothers waiting.
>
> Book: 'I pictured how it was going to be in Majdanek. We'd play in a big sunny field. But when we arrived there I didn't find my brothers'.

I suggest there is uncertainty here as to whether the narrator's statements are averral or attribution, and what their relationship is with Wilkomirski's utterances as recorded in his book. The utterance *He was told that at Majdanek he would find his brothers waiting* could be an averral: a statement which the film-makers believe, and for which evidence is provided by the quotation from Wilkomirski's book. Alternatively, it could be an implicit attribution: a report of what Wilkomirski claims, followed by more attribution in the form of quotation. Because the attribution is implicit the audience may interpret the utterance as narrator averral. However, because the attribution is possible the audience may subsequently reinterpret the utterance. In other words, indeterminacy allows for subsequent resolution.

5. The interaction of word and image

It has been argued that in the first part of this film the epistemic status of many of the utterances is ambiguous. Supporting this ambiguity is the juxtaposition of words and images of different statuses. The film is remarkable for very rapid cutting between the constituent texts of the film, each of which, as has been discussed, has a different status. For example, in one sequence, the narrator gives the following account of events in the 1940s:

> Narrator: In 1940 the Red Army came in. Then in 1941 the Nazis. Jews in Riga were rounded up, herded into synagogues and burned alive. Latvian fascists, on the orders of the Nazis, murdered thousands more. Foreign Jews were brought into concentration camps. Several thousand of the old and the weak were shot at a station and buried in pits under the track.

This is accompanied by the following series of film extracts:

> Colour shot: house and road.
>
> News footage: army vehicles, cannon firing, Jews escorted along street, Nazi troops, burning building.
>
> Colour, image blurring: Riga across river, red sunset.
>
> News footage: men being hurried along road.
>
> Colour: train moving quickly, still shot of station.
>
> Colour, image blurring: railway tracks.
>
> News footage: man in pit being shot.

No fewer than seven separate texts make up this sequence, interspersing contemporary news footage with illustrative reconstruction filmed in the present day.

Even more remarkable is a sequence which recounts the child Wilkomirski's experiences. The voice-over intersperses narrator averral with attribution to Wilkomirski as author of the book *Fragments*:

> Book: In a shadowy corner the outline of a man, his sweet face smiling at me. Maybe my father.
>
> Narrator: Wilkomirski says his home in the Jewish ghetto was raided by Latvian fascists.
>
> Book: A cry of terror echoing down the staircase – 'Watch it! Latvian militia!'
>
> Narrator: A man is dragged to the ground next to the front gate. In Wilkomirski's memory, a Nazi transport heads straight for him.
>
> Book: A big stream of something black shoots from his neck as the transport squashes him. From now on I have to manage without you. I am alone.

The following series of images accompanies this:

> Muted colour: shadow of man moving along roadway.
>
> Black-and-white: camera moves along cobbled street, along corridor towards sunlight.
>
> Colour: pen points to street map.
>
> News footage: man dragged along street by soldiers.
>
> Black-and-white: still shot of door handle, moving shot of staircase.
>
> Colour: Wilkomirski looking upwards.
>
> News footage: soldiers and large vehicles.
>
> Black-and-white: camera moves along passageway to gates.
>
> Muted colour: small boy moves out of shadow, arms shielding body, looks at camera.
>
> News footage: dead body in street, woman covers face with arm, bodies in street, woman among ruins.

Here news footage is interspersed with apparent reconstruction of the
events recorded in *Fragments* and with present-day film of
Wilkomirski pointing to a map and 'remembering' the events. Image
and voice are combined in a variety of ways. For example, a quotation
from the book, 'A cry of terror echoing down the staircase' is
accompanied by a shot of a staircase, and the words 'I am alone' are
accompanied by a shot of a small boy in a doorway staring at the
camera. The narrator's words 'Wilkomirski says his home in the
Jewish ghetto was raided by Latvian fascists' overlay the image of a
pen pointing at a map, clearly filmed in the present, followed by news
footage of a man being dragged along a street and a black-and-white
still shot of a door handle. The words 'In Wilkomirski's memory a
Nazi transport heads straight for him' are accompanied by a present-
day shot of Wilkomirski followed by news footage of Nazi soldiers
and vehicles.

It is possible to interpret this sequence simply as a dramatic
reconstruction of the events in Wilkomirski's book, but this
interpretation is uncertain. Firstly, a distinction is made in the images
between 'real' and 'unreal'.[6] Reality is present in the solid-colour
shots of Wilkomirski and his map, and also in the grainy, black-and-
white news footage. Unreality is represented by the muted colour or
the black-and-white of the reconstructions, and by the over-sharp
distinctions between light and shadow. It is not clear, however,
whether this unreality is a simple indication that we are watching
reconstruction as opposed to news footage, or whether it implies that
we are watching the product of imagination. The confusion is
compounded by the rapid movement between footage and
reconstruction and back, which is matched by the alternation between
narrator averral and quotations from the book. Such rapid changes of
status in word and image keep the audience off balance in terms of
whether they are watching fact or fiction. Finally, the sequence has a
background of emotional music which also allows for two
interpretations: horrific reality or dramatic fiction. All these things
taken together create a sequence whose status is in the end uncertain,
in which the distinction between fact and fiction is blurred. This
ambiguity allows for the reinterpretation essential to the film.

6. Reinterpretation: the 'Wilkomirski in tears' text

As a final point about reinterpretation, attention may be drawn to a number of images which recur throughout the film, each time in a different context and with a different interpretation indicated by the voice-over. One example is a home-made video text which shows Wilkomirski visiting the site of the concentration camp of Majdanek as an adult. As he walks around the site, now so peaceful, then the scene of so much human suffering, he breaks down in tears. Similar footage of Wilkomirski with a handkerchief to his face is shown several times throughout the film, and each time it is interpreted differently by the voice-over, as shown below.

First telling:
> Narrator: At the age of three or four he entered a concentration camp.

Second telling:
> Wilkomirski's partner: And I think one of the deepest impression was for me when he said you know it was so crowded and now it's so empty and the grass it was very high and and it was very very moving the– the– whole situation.
>
> Narrator: Next to the gate children were held.

Third telling:
> Narrator: Wilkomirski admits he studied the holocaust from college onwards. Before this trip to Majdanek in 1993 his passports disclose several previous trips to Poland. On any one he could have visited Majdanek.
>
> … At Majdanek his emotion seemed real enough.

Fourth telling (interspersed with news footage of elderly Jews being mistreated):
> Ganzfried: ... so this guy desperately tried to make a character out of himself. So you know what better character can you have but the victim?
>
> Karpf: If you are victimised, miserable, turbulent person because you've been adopted, because you've been badly treated, you aren't necessarily going to get the kind of sympathy that you're going to get if you are a holocaust survivor.

Fifth telling:
> Karpf: If he set out to delude people obviously that feels like a terribly calculated and very sick unpleasant thing to do. If he somehow had such a profound sense of identification that his own identity somehow merged into that of a holocaust survivor I suppose one would be more charitable. But I think it is a key question.

At the first two showings of this footage, the audience is likely to accept the reality of the emotion conveyed. The third showing casts doubt on this, and the fourth and fifth showings assume that Wilkomirski is lying and ask what his motives might be. Each time the sequence is shown, then, the emotion presented is re-evaluated: as genuine grief and then as hypocritical pretence. Because the same image is repeated it is apparent that both interpretations cannot be true, and our acceptance of the hypocrisy forces us to reject the grief.

7. Conclusion

Truth and Lies is a remarkable film that has at its heart a debate about the epistemic status of a literary work: is *Fragments* fact or fiction? I have suggested in this paper that this debate is mirrored by the interspersal of words and images of varying statuses in the film itself. Specifically, the second half of the film reinterprets the first, something that is possible without inconsistency because in the first half of the film there is considerable ambiguity or indeterminacy in the narrator's voice.

This film is, however, interesting not only for its treatment of the story concerned, but also for the attention it draws to the very nature of documentary. The first half of the film – 'Binjamin's Story' – is credible in its own terms as an account of Wilkomirski's early life.[7] It uses many of the resources common in historical documentaries, such as interviews, contemporary film, and dramatic reconstruction. I suggest that audiences tend to accept such films as accurate accounts of the historical events. In particular, they tend to accept that reconstructions of past events are true in essence if not in detail. In *Truth and Lies*, however, this acceptance is subsequently undercut by the evidence presented in the second half of the film. But that part of the film, also, is documentary and so is also open to debate. What is drawn into question by the film is not just one person's credibility, but the process of documentary itself.

Endnotes

[1] I would like to thank Malcolm Daniel, film editor of *Truth and Lies*, for assistance in preparing this paper. Responsibility for omissions and inaccuracies is of course mine. Malcolm Daniel was awarded the 2000 BAFTA award for non-fiction film editing for his work on this film.

[2] The notion of 'status' is taken from Hunston (1994, 2000) and adapted for use here. An integral part of the theory of status is the distinction between averral and

attribution, made by Sinclair (1986) and developed in Tadros (1993) and Hunston (2000).

[3]Although these are two distinct sequences, it is not possible to say which one the audience will perceive here. As Hoey (1983: 18-19), following Winter (1982), notes, relations between clauses are determined by readers, not writers (or hearers, not speakers), and there is always scope for different readers to perceive different relations (see also Hoey 1991: 12). The relation 'apparent + real' is identified by Winter (1982: 196-98) as 'hypothetical + real'.

[4]Signals of attribution include 'say' and 'admit'; signals of hedging include 'seem' and 'could'. Status identifiers include 'the fact is' and 'highly unlikely'.

[5]The first two of these are narrator averral. The phrase 'Ganzfried discovered' indicates, of course, that the following statement is attributed to Ganzfried, but responsibility for the statement remains with the narrator, as it does when a statement is averred, because of the verb 'discover' (Hunston 2000).

[6]For a discussion of colour and its relationship to perceived reality in images, see Kress & van Leeuwen (1996: 165-68).

[7]This is not strictly true, as the film begins with a summary of the whole argument, so that at the beginning of the section entitled 'Binjamin's Story' the audience is already aware that this story will be contradicted. In spite of this, 'Binjamin's Story' is a convincing and internally coherent account.

References

Hoey, Michael. 1983. *On the Surface of Discourse*. London: Allen & Unwin.

___. 1991. *Patterns of Lexis in Text*. Oxford: Oxford University Press.

Hunston, Susan. 1994. 'Evaluation and Organisation in a Sample of Written Academic Discourse' in Coulthard, Malcolm (ed.). *Advances in Written Text Analysis*. London: Routledge: 191-218.

___. 2000. 'Evaluation and the Planes of Discourse: Status and Value in Persuasive Texts' in Hunston & Thompson (2000): 177-206.

Hunston, Susan, and Geoff Thompson (eds). 2000. *Evaluation in Text: Authorial Stance and the Construction of Discourse*. Oxford: Oxford University Press.

Kress, Gunther, and Theo van Leeuwen. 1996. *Reading Images: The Grammar of Visual Design*. London: Routledge.

Sinclair, John. 1986. 'Fictional Worlds' in Coulthard, Malcolm (ed.) *Talking about Text*. Birmingham: ELR Monographs 13: 43-60.

Tadros, Angela. 1993. 'The Pragmatics of Text Averral and Attribution in Academic Texts' in Hoey, Michael (ed.) *Data, Description, Discourse*. London: HarperCollins: 98-114.

Winter, Eugene. 1982. *Towards a Contextual Grammar of English*. London: Allen & Unwin.

PART IV

CORPUS-ENABLED STYLISTICS

Technology and Stylistics: The Web Connection

Donald E. Hardy

Abstract

There are at least four potential problems in high-tech stylistics pedagogy and research: 1) high costs of purchasing individual programs or site licences; 2) front-end overloading of the technological learning curve; 3) inflexibility in the analytic tool; 4) a focus on technology for the sake of technology. The motivation, structure, and use of the author's text-analysis program – TEXTANT – will serve as illustrations of solutions to these potential problems. The 'front-end' of TEXTANT is designed with the beginning student in mind, and the 'back-end' may be relatively easily modified by the designer in response to particular needs of users. TEXTANT is written in Perl and runs on a password-protected website.[1]

Key words: computational stylistics; Perl; software; text-analysis; corpora.

1. Introduction

One obvious strategy for promoting stylistics in the curriculum and research agenda of literary and linguistic studies is the motivation of stylistic methods and analyses within computer-based pedagogy and research. There are several sets of dangers in the use of computers for text analysis: for the instructor, for the student, and for the researcher. However, most of these dangers are at least relatively manageable with the use of Web-based text processing and analysis. This chapter specifies some of the more prominent of these dangers and demonstrates how it is that a text analysis and statistical program, entitled TEXTANT (**TEXT AN**alysis **T**ools), serves as a solution in advanced development to several problems involved in teaching selected computational methods of linguistic analysis, in making available to a consortium of text researchers both corpora and text-processing software, and in using the program specifically for stylistic analysis. TEXTANT, which I wrote using Perl (**P**ractical **E**xtraction and **R**eport **L**anguage), demonstrates many of the advantages of creating and managing software and corpora on the Web for both pedagogical and research purposes. In an age of increasing technological need, drastically reduced educational funding, and the consequent shortage of technological expertise, Web programming is an attractive alternative for stylistics students and researchers needing customisable text-processing software and access to corpora.

2. Pedagogy and technological need

In an introduction to stylistics at the graduate level in the English department at Northern Illinois University (NIU), a mid-sized university quite typical in America in having no linguistics department but having a diffuse collection of linguists and linguistics students across campus (in English, psychology, foreign languages, anthropology, speech pathology), the following are the skills and materials that are taught in a typical 16-week semester: 1) the use of at least one text-search software program; 2) basic statistics and the use of at least one statistical software package; 3) basic research design; 4) the literary work of an author or authors, typically one or more authors whose texts have been scanned into ASCII form (e. g., Jane Austen, Flannery O'Connor, Henry James); 5) syntactic and morphological analysis concentrating on structures of interest to stylisticians; and 6) the answer to the most frequently asked question, 'Why would you want to go to all this trouble?' That last question is perhaps the most difficult one of the semester and is answerable only by extended demonstration, that is, the demonstration of the use of computer-aided stylistic methodology and interpretation, ideally, to contribute potentially to both linguistics and literary analysis in a way that is not feasible without the technology. About the only similarities between the stylistics course and any other literary course in our department are the literary texts themselves. The students do buy and read print editions of the literary texts, but an author is chosen at least in part on the basis of whether a significant number of the author's works are already available on the Web, as in the cases of Austen and James, or whether the professor has enough interest in the author to scan the works himself, as in the case of my interest in O'Connor. There are other computational methodologies, such as text markup and even basic programming skills, with which students ideally would be provided some practice. However, given the current pedagogical load of the course as outlined above, markup and programming are probably best left for another as yet uncreated and unapproved course. In a description of a B.A. honours module in stylistics at the University of Luton, Jon Mills and Balasubramanyam Chandramohan (1996) describe the acquisition of an almost duplicate set of skills as the goal of their course. Their module for honours undergraduates analysed one relatively short text – *Heart of Darkness* – and restricted statistical analysis to the level of percentages and ranked z-scores for collocations. One of the required courses in the stylistics master's degree at NIU is one on linguistic research methods; however, students in the introduction to stylistics may not have taken the research methods course yet, and most students in the stylistics course are not in the stylistics programme but are instead literature students looking either to complete their single Ph.D. linguistics requirement or to explore 'something different'. There is no element of the stylistics course that does not at least implicitly rely on computer technology although most of the students in the course have no background at all in statistics, research design, linguistics, or computer programming. Thus, the typical student begins our stylistics course with no background at all in the specific skills to be learned. About the only way to guarantee failure in the course would be the use of intrusive, distracting, and non-functional technology.

3. Research and technological need

There are at NIU several professors who perform or are interested in beginning to perform computer-based text research. On the strength of our combined research and pedagogical interests, the English department has invested in a membership in the Linguistic Data Consortium as well as purchased the ICAME (International Computer Archive of Modern English) corpus collection. Thus, among the corpora that we have are the Brown, LOB, London-Lund, Helsinki, Santa Barbara Corpus of American English, Switchboard, and Wall Street Journal corpora, plus several individually constructed datasets, including all of Flannery O'Connor's fiction and all of Wallace Stevens' poetry. As a group, we thus have several million words of text for analysing; as a group we also have need of an easy-to-use text analysis program and a central easily accessible repository for all of the corpora.

4. The burden of technology

For both groups – students and researchers – there are at least four internally complex problems in the use of technology in stylistic and linguistic analysis: 1) costs of purchasing individual text-analysis programs or site licences for those programs; 2) front-end overloading of the technological learning curve; 3) inflexibility in the analytic tool; 4) focus on technology for the sake of technology. Each of these problems involves hidden complexities. Thus, the frequently very time-consuming tasks of installing programs and maintaining the computers on which the programs run must be figured into the technological learning curve and cost. Any hypothetical solution to the second and third problems might seem mutually exclusive in that the easier programs are to use the more inflexible and pre-determined their structures. And focus on technology for the sake of technology is a result not only of the joy of mastering the electronic tools but also of a failure to realise how or why to use those tools in the production of significant research.

The work that Mills and Chandramohan's students performed was possible at least in part because they used the text/statistical package TACT (Text Analysis Computing Tools). Another easily obtained and widely used program is Wordsmith Tools. Harald Klein has created a useful list containing these and many other similar programs and a basic description of each (http://www.textanalysis.info/). Eric Rochester (2001) has written an insightful comparison of TACT and Wordsmith; as he points out, TACT is still in many ways the standard for prepackaged text-analysis programs. However, in reality even with a prepackaged program there are problems with individual installation and use. For example, there are serious shortcomings in the TACT program, including the limited size of text that can be processed, and the fact that the program does not run in the Windows NT or 2000 environments, the latter issue ruling out its use in our English department computer laboratory with 20 computers running Windows 2000. This laboratory is where our stylistics and research-methods courses are taught. In the version of TACT that Mills and Chandramohan used, the program must be installed on individual computers. There is a Web version of TACT under development:

http://tactweb.humanities.mcmaster.ca/tactweb/doc/tact.htm. However, it is very much still in its experimental stage.

One potential way to avoid the more obvious monetary costs and operating-system limitations of prepackaged text-analysis programs is individual programming, which provides maximum flexibility in the ability to respond not only to operating-system advances but also to individual student and researcher needs. Maximum flexibility may indeed be gained only by programming by the individual student or researcher, but custom programming can lead to unrealistic demands on those with the programming expertise to create text-processing programs of enormous complexity and specificity. The dangers for the programmer and for the field of humanities computing are 1) that the programmer is called on to produce relatively isolated pieces of programs for exceedingly specific tasks; and 2) that individual programmers reinvent the wheel multiple times. The first danger is illustrated in Eric Johnson's (1996) description of the 15-odd programs that he wrote individually either for his own students or for colleagues who became interested in text processing but who could not write their own programs. It is quite common, however, for authors such as Johnson to make their programs widely available to others, as have John Sinclair et al. (1998) with their collocation tests.

The costly reinvention of the programming wheel is perhaps unavoidable in these early stages of the mass adoption of computer-based research and pedagogy. One relatively obvious and easily avoidable error in duplication of effort is the multiple installation of a program that needs only one installation on one server. So, for example, even though the next section of this paper presents TEXTANT as an exemplar of how to avoid some of the more obvious dangers of technology, in the interests of experimentation I recently arranged for the installation of TEXTANT on a server at another location where researchers are interested in Web text processing and are experimenting with various text-analysis programs. In retrospect I realise that I should simply have loaded the research group's files to my own server for analysis and evaluation. Primarily due to internal networking complications, it took two full working days, four different computer technicians, two hours of my time in a telephone conference, and the installation of two different server software packages – IIS4 and Personal Web Server – to get Perl working with the server software at the remote location. Once Perl and Personal Web Server were installed and communicating with one another, the installation of TEXTANT was simply a matter of copying files from a floppy disk. In spite of the touted portability of Perl programs, no one except a relatively highly computer-literate user is going to have the patience or knowledge to install Perl and a Web server and then configure that Web server for the use of TEXTANT. In summarising the experience of the publishing house Chadwyck-Healey in creating, first, a CD-ROM of British and American literature, Steven Hall (1998: 290) writes that in a survey of universities that had purchased their *English Poetry* collection it was discovered that many of those universities had not made the resource available except by use on a single CD-ROM drive. Hall points out that among the many reasons why Chadwyck-Healey decided to put their collection on the Web was the aim of increasing its availability for research and teaching as well as the ease of updating their 'databases, making good omissions and correcting errors' (1998: 286). Thus, the availability of programs and data on the Web both increases availability and decreases the need for duplication of effort, or reinvention of the wheel.

Two final technological dangers to consider are that student and researcher end up 1) simply surfing through the programs with no real understanding of how or why to use the programs; and/or 2) focussing on technology for the sake of technology. Rosanne Potter (1996: 183) registers a warning about the first danger in relation to the use of hypertext in the literary classroom. She writes that 'the literature student who is clicking merrily down the lane is not re-creating that work, but sliding irresponsibly over its surface'. Potter points out that 'a research tool requires a research plan and the hard work of trial-and-error data manipulation before one is anywhere near doing research or, for that matter, even learning with it'.

All students in the NIU stylistics programme have had some experience in literary analysis. Some have had quite a bit. However, students typically have initial difficulty connecting their literary expertise with the technology available to them. A program that produces impressive frequency counts, collocational figures, and key-words-in-context displays would be worse than useless if the student had to concentrate too much on how to install and operate the program that produces the impressive computer displays. The goal for the instructor of computational stylistics is to turn the student's attention to a discovery that an empirical study of, say, O'Connor's use of body-part terms will get at some of the literary issues of interest in the term *grotesque*. Potter (1996: 182) has aptly written that 'technology does not speed up the process of doing valuable work'. In fact, as she points out, the time that it takes to learn the technology can mean the coverage of fewer literary works. Technology will not allow us to perform more quickly, subtly, or thoroughly the literary analysis that students are probably familiar with, especially if the technology itself becomes the focus of instruction; instead, computer technology should almost recede to the background as it allows students to perform a different kind of analysis, a type of analysis that begins with hypotheses about how a particular form patterns stylistically, progresses to a gathering of empirical data on that form, and then ends with a refinement of the hypotheses that the students started with. Of course, the successful execution of this type of analysis depends on successful education in the goals and methods of computer-based linguistics and stylistics.

In his summary paper on Chadwyck-Healey's experience in creating its corpus of literary texts, Hall (1998: 289) makes a trenchant point:

> We have told our customers how to use the database, through our manuals, help files and on-site training; we have perhaps failed, however, to tell them why to use it, to spell out the ways in which it might contribute to their teaching or research. (We intend, incidentally, to address this issue for *Literature Online*).

Although I do not think that it is necessarily the long-term job of Chadwyck-Healey to explain to instructors or students why such a tool is valuable, if their tool is to be used, rather than simply purchased by a library, such information is necessary until the time, if it ever arrives, when large numbers of students and researchers already know what large searchable literary texts are for.

5. Web-based technological solutions

In the stylistics and linguistics community at NIU, the dangers outlined in the section above have been at least tempered through the use of TEXTANT.[2] The free program runs on one server and is available through the Web to registered users so that the labour costs of programming and maintenance are absorbed by only one member of the research consortium. The program interface is constructed with simple drop-down menus, radio-buttons, and text boxes. The program itself may be modified in order to accommodate any particular need, within reason, of individual users. And given that TEXTANT runs almost trouble-free on the Web, users are better able to concentrate on using the program to produce their own research. This section details text markup and preparation; the architecture of the latest version of TEXTANT; planned additions; and use of the program by both students and researchers.

TEXTANT runs on a password-protected website (http://textant. colostate.edu). One of the most important features of administering TEXTANT on a password-protected site is that one may use copyright-protected materials with the protection of the 'fair-use' copyright agreement. That is, one may use copyrighted material for one's teaching and research but need not give ASCII copies of the texts to one's students. There is no feature in the program that allows students or researchers to print out or download entire texts from the corpora that are contained within it. TEXTANT currently has loaded within it many copyrighted-protected texts such as the complete stories and novels of Flannery O'Connor and the complete poems of Wallace Stevens as well as the Brown corpus and the Switchboard corpus. Thus, without having to go to a central computer laboratory, students and researchers are able to access (potentially from their own homes) copyright-protected material as well as the computer program used to search those texts and produce basic statistics. And no extra software is required on the users' computers other than a Web browser.

TEXTANT produces the standard frequency counts, word lists, and statistics that one finds in most text-analysis programs. It provides total word counts for each corpus. It can produce both alphabetically sorted and frequency-sorted type/token counts; these windows also provide ratios. In either of the type/token count windows, users may create, save, retrieve, and modify lexical groups for the purposes of efficient group searching in the search window. A separate collocations window provides both fixed-phrase and variable-phrase collocations along with frequency counts, t-scores, and mutual-information scores. The fixed-phrase collocations may vary in length between two and eight words. The distance for the variable-phrase collocations may vary from one to four words on either side of the optional target word. If a target word is specified, only those collocations with the target word are listed by the program. TEXTANT also provides the opportunity to choose alpha probability thresholds for t-scores. There are separate stoplist files for auxiliary verbs, modal verbs, determiners, coordinating conjunctions, subordinating conjunctions, and prepositions, which may be selected in any combination or alone. The stoplists may be applied to both collocation windows as well as the total word token count. The optionality of using the stoplists allows users to choose, for example, whether to include prepositions and determiners in the lists of collocations since collocations of the sort 'of the' are common but of no interest to most researchers.

Besides the statistics that are generated in the type/token pages and the collocation pages, TEXTANT also produces tables in which users may enter data for statistical processing. The descriptive statistics that may be produced are minimum, maximum, sum, count, mean, median, mode, variance, and standard deviation. Slated for addition are basic statistical tests for which probability tests may be run: chi-square, anova, and correlation.

The most commonly used features of TEXTANT in stylistic work are the search mechanisms. Some relatively simple search choices are presented in user-friendly interfaces in TEXTANT either because the choices are so simple that restraining user input on those searches does not limit at all the user's creativity or because the input of the user would need to be so complex that any minor loss of creativity is more than compensated for by relative ease of use and may easily be overcome by repeated searches. First, a user may choose zero or any number of words to include before or after the target word or phrase in the output of the program. Thus, the immediate context in the sense of number of words on each side of the target word is left to the user's choice. If one were searching for words whose relevant context might be the simple phrase, one might choose to display few words on either side of the target. However, if one were interested in cohesive ties in a text and were searching for pronouns, one might want to include a great number of words before the target. Depending on whether and how the corpus that the user is searching is tagged, the user may choose to search for words or phrases within dialogue or narrative or both; search for words or phrases within a selected chapter/story or all; and search for words or phrases in the dialogue of a particular character. Of course, the tags are at the level of detail to please those who inserted them and plan to use them. So, for example, most but not all literary texts in TEXTANT are tagged for dialogue vs. narration, usually but not always operationally defined as dialogue when the text occurs within quotation marks and is attributed as thought or speech to a character or characters. I have written a Perl subprogram that inserts the dialogue and narration tags although the tagging must be hand checked if, for example, scare-quoted words and phrases are not to be tagged as dialogue. Text divisions such as chapters or short stories are implicitly defined by formatting of the texts rather than with tags.

Unlike with the predetermined contextual search parameters, users must know something of regular expressions in order to find what they want in entering anything but the simplest words or phrases for search material in the 'Word or Phrase to Search for' box. If users don't use regular expressions carefully, they are likely to find something both unexpected and unwanted or not find the very thing they are looking for. Thus, the program has an extended help page for the use of regular expressions. That help page is reachable from the search page for each text. For example, advanced users of the program can use regular expressions to search for two or more words within a specified window of words. And, of course, all of the regular expression 'wildcards', such as \S for non-whitespace character or \d for digit, may be used.

At NIU, TEXTANT is currently used by two psychology professors, two English professors, and their graduate student research assistants in both psychology and English, as well as one Ph.D. candidate who is using the program for his dissertation research on pseudo-clefts in English. TEXTANT is also used by the American research institution North Central Regional Education Laboratory (NCREL) for the purpose of analysing text files composed of the search strings that are gathered from the search engine of their website. NCREL's specific use of the program provides a good example of the flexibility of the programming that is possible in Perl. It also illustrates the convenience of Web-based text processing, in which both program and texts may be used from any location with Web access. Thus, NCREL e-mails me the data, I load it for them into the proper directory, and they analyse the data from their own offices over the

Web. The ultimate purpose of NCREL's research using TEXTANT is to structure their website so that information that users tend to look for frequently is easily found. Researchers at NCREL indicated that they had grown weary of the labour-intensive text preprocessing that was necessary to analyse their texts in other affordable commercial or freeware programs. In TEXTANT, the text data is automatically preprocessed and loaded into the program. The program itself formats the data and deletes irrelevant information. For example, the raw data in (1) are transformed to (2):

1)   [Sun Jan 14 6:09:24 'The Thinking Curriculum'
     [Sun Jan 14 8:12:32 '(no search)'
     [Sun Jan 14 8:20:51 'education technology'
2)   The Thinking Curriculum
     education technology

Empty searches, dates, times, and quotation marks are deleted.

Student interest in TEXTANT currently takes two forms: 1) students using the program to write papers for me on texts that I have preloaded for them; and 2) students preparing their own texts for analysis in other classes. The second category of students is interesting for the reason that they must do some text preparation themselves and thus learn some issues regarding corpus preparation, such as the use of a sophisticated text processor like Textpad and the use of regular expressions in such a program. Thus, some of the more advanced areas of text processing and analysis are picked up by the students as they perform their own research on their own data.

I wrote TEXTANT in the first place to allow me to analyse Flannery O'Connor's fiction for a series of articles and a book on her style. Over a period of three or four years, I had become extraordinarily frustrated with the performance and reliability of existing text-analysis programs. The primary use of TEXTANT in my O'Connor studies has been to search for and count tokens of morphological and syntactic patterns such as *not* negation, *see* + clausal or phrasal complements, and body-part terms. Using TEXTANT, I am able to process all of O'Connor's fiction in one text file, whose size makes economical processing impossible in programs such as TACT, for example. As Biber, Conrad & Reppen (1998: 255-56) point out, there are many advantages to writing one's own program for text analysis. For example, by processing O'Connor's fiction in one file, I am able to perform many tasks at once that otherwise would necessitate several repetitive, and potentially error-inducing, processing runs. In particular, in the initial preparation of the O'Connor texts, I was able to create one 'suspect-words' list in the final check of the accuracy of the electronic scanning of the texts into ASCII files. Greater accuracy in text searches is made possible by the ease with which the results of searches can be double-checked against multiple versions of the corpus, ensuring the identification and correction of any errors introduced by coding the corpora for contextual variables such as dialogue and narration.

By means of a reliable text-analysis program, students can be led back to the text and away from an overemphasis on abstract notions of theme, characterisation, and even narrative structure. One specific way to do this is to ask them questions that can only be easily answered by means of a text-analysis program like TEXTANT. The following is an excerpt from O'Connor's 'A Good Man Is Hard to Find', in which narration, dialogue, and speaker identity are tagged.

> "If you would pray,"<G=D> <G#N>the old lady said,<G=N> "Jesus would help you."<G=D> <SP@Grand>"That's right,"<G=D> <G#N>The Misfit said.<G=N> <SP@Misfit>"Well then, why don't you pray?"<G=D> <G#N>she asked trembling with delight suddenly.<G=N> <SP@Grand>"I don't want no hep,"<G=D> <G#N>he said.<G=N> "I'm doing all right by myself."<G=D>

The information that is encoded here and throughout the tagged version of the story is normally constructed or accessed by any reader with no conscious effort. What the computer technology makes possible is simply the rearrangement and acquisition of this information very quickly and efficiently. For example, it is possible in TEXTANT to find and quantify almost instantaneously all dialogue, all narration, or all dialogue by any one character. My favourite introductory exercise with students is to ask them which of the characters in 'A Good Man Is Hard to Find' talks the most. The invariable answer is the grandmother; she is perceived as being garrulous to a fault, full of rambling detail in her stories and nosy. A raw count in TEXTANT of the number of words spoken by her and The Misfit shows that she produces 602 words while he produces 978 words. The difference between what readers expect and what results from an objective count is even more striking when it is realised that The Misfit does not even enter the story until it is half-way finished.

Thus, the disjunction between perception and reality can be discussed as perception is influenced by expectations of gendered differences in ways and quantity of talk and by narrative focus. One can also search the texts without specifying the context of dialogue, narration, or character, so one can in fact abstract out the tags in searches showing students the informational gain from having these tags. The limits of the existing tags may also be demonstrated by showing for example how it is that one might study clausal complements to cognitive verbs by first creating a group of cognition verbs, then searching for those verbs, and finally sorting through by hand the complements that are clausal rather than phrasal.

6. Conclusions

I am not naïve about the permanence of websites and the programs and information available within them. Byron Anderson (1998) laments the lack of scholarly emphasis on 'value, relevance, quality, and nature of the content' of the World Wide Web. Indeed, three of the trustworthy review sites that Anderson points us to in 1998, or 1997 since the publication date of his article is in 1998, are now in October 2002 (my writing time) no longer available as review sites: Point (http://www.pointcom.com), Magellan Internet Guide (http://www.mckinley.com/), and Infofilter (http://www.usc.edu/users /help/flick/Infofilter). However, unlike a great deal of raw information on the Web that can be found more reliably and predictably in a good library, a Web-resident program such as TEXTANT is a promising model for stylisticians and text-analysts in search of economical and reliable text-processing software.

Endnotes

[1]Although this paper was written when I was at Northern Illinois University, most of the generalisations and particulars about computer usage and need apply to my current teaching and research environment at Colorado State University as well.

[2]Readers who wish to have accounts in TEXTANT in order to evaluate the program may email the author at Don.Hardy@colostate.edu to request those accounts.

References

Anderson, Byron. 1998. 'The World Wide Web and the Humanities: Superhighway to What? Research, Quality, and "Literature"' in *Humanities Collections* 1(1): 25-40.

Biber, Douglas, Susan Conrad and Randi Reppen. 1998. *Corpus Linguistics: Investigating Language Structure and Use*. Cambridge: Cambridge University Press.

Hall, Steven. 1998. 'Literature Online – Building a Home for English and American Literature on the World Wide Web' in *Computers and the Humanities* 32(4): 285-301.

Johnson, Eric. 1996. 'Professor-Created Computer Programs for Student Research' in *Computers and the Humanities* 30(2): 171-79.

Klein, Harald. 'Text Analysis Info Page'. Online at http://www.textanalysis.info/ (consulted 15.10.2002).

Lancashire, Ian, et al. 1996. *Using TACT with Electronic Texts*. New York: Modern Language Association.

'Literature Online'. Online at http://lion.chadwyck.com (consulted 15.10.2002).

Mills, Jon, and Balasubramanyam Chandramohan. 1996. 'Literary Studies: A Computer Assisted Teaching Methodology' in *Computers and the Humanities* 30(2): 165-70.

Potter, Rosanne G. 1996. 'What Computers Are Good for in the Literature Classroom' in *Computers and the Humanities* 30(2): 181-90.

Rochester, Eric. 2001. 'New Tools for Analysing Texts' in *Language and Literature* 10(2): 187-91.

Sinclair, John, et al. 1998. 'Language Independent Statistical Software for Corpus Exploration' in *Computers and the Humanities* 31(3): 229-55.

'TACTWeb 1.0 Home Page'. Online at http://tactweb.humanities.mcmaster.ca /tactweb/doc/tact.htm (consulted 15.10.2002).

'TEXTANT'. Online at http://textant.colostate.edu (consulted 29.03.2004).

How Playwrights Construct Their Dramatic Worlds:
A Corpus-based Study of Vocatives
in Early Modern English Comedies*

Michi Shiina

Abstract

Vocatives are generally neglected in linguistic research. Carefully investigated, however, vocatives reveal themselves to be a rich source of socio-historical information about the characters found in period dramas. This paper focuses on the use of vocatives in a selection of Early Modern English comedies, and illustrates how a variety of vocatives are exploited by playwrights in staging the relationships and interactions of characters within their dramatic worlds. This is made possible through a combination of historical pragmatics, stylistics, sociolinguistics, and corpus linguistics. Theoretically, this study draws on Brown & Levinson's (1987) politeness theory and Brown & Gilman's (1960) study of address terms. A quantitative analysis teases out general patterns of vocative use, and a qualitative analysis examines deviant cases in terms of pragmatics and stylistics. The paper illustrates how computer-assisted linguistic research can help us explore the literary craftsmanship and creativity of playwrights of the past.

Keywords: vocatives; address terms; historical pragmatics; corpus-based approach; discourse markers.

1. Introduction

How do playwrights construct the characters in their dramatic worlds? Syntactically marginal as it is, a vocative is an effective linguistic device to describe the relationship between characters in a dramatic world which consists mainly of language. In this paper, I take a corpus-based approach with a historical pragmatic perspective to analyse the use of vocatives. Consequently, my research depends on several linguistic fields.

*This research was supported by MEXT. KAKENHI 15520320.

2. Vocatives as discourse markers
2.1. Politeness scale of vocatives

The theoretical framework I apply to analyse pragmatic functions of vocatives is Brown & Levinson's (1987) politeness theory. The most significant notion in their theory is face, which is people's emotionally invested self-image. Face consists of positive face and negative face. Positive face refers to appreciation by others, whilst negative face refers to personal freedom of action. The weightiness of a face-threatening act involves three factors: the relative power of and social distance between the interlocutors, and the ranking of impositions. Relative power and social distance are closely related to the vocative form, whereas the ranking of impositions is related to the pragmatic force of the utterance. Vocatives, as discourse markers, mitigate or strengthen the illocutionary force of the utterance.

I use a continuum on a sliding scale of values devised by Raumolin-Brunberg (1996) to align vocative forms and analyse them in terms of politeness. Vocative forms are classified into two types: the deferential and the familiar.

Figure 1 Politeness scale of vocatives

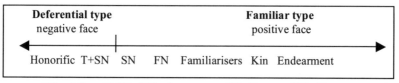

Abbreviations: T+SN = Title-plus-surname; SN = Surname; FN = First name.

As Figure 1 shows, the deferential type oriented to negative face includes honorifics (e. g. *Sir*) and title-surname combinations (e. g. *Mr. Strictland*; title-surname combinations include title and first name combinations such as *Sir Paul*), whilst the familiar type oriented to positive face includes surnames (e. g. *Wat*), first names in full form (e.g. *Thomas*), shortened first names (e. g. *Tom*), familiarisers (e. g. *Friend*), kinship terms (e. g. *Mother*), and endearments (e. g. *Dear*). Although it is not on this scale, I have also included abusives (e. g. *Villain*) in my classification.

2.2. Three-dimensional model of vocatives

Address terms have been discussed comprehensively since Brown & Gilman (1960). To summarise these past discussions, I refer to Wales

(1983), who presents a list of dichotomies of the use of *thou* and *you* during the medieval period (116). Her model provides insight into the basic concepts underlying choices of vocative form, if I assume that *thou* forms correspond to familiar vocatives, and *you* forms to deferential vocatives.

Figure 2 Dichotomies in use of vocatives (adapted from Wales 1983)

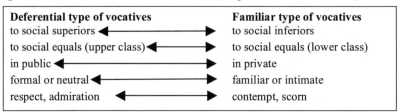

Combining the politeness scale of vocatives presented in Figure 1 with the dichotomies in Figure 2, I have constructed a three-dimensional model for vocative forms. I have transposed vocatives on the politeness scale onto three axes: power, solidarity, and contextual condition. The vertical axis of power deals with vocatives used between equals and non-equals in status and social roles. The horizontal axis of solidarity situates vocatives used between those in close or distant relationships. The contextual axis is twofold in that it refers, on the one hand, to the situational condition, such as formal/private context, and on the other hand, to the emotional state of the interlocutors, such as admiration/contempt. This is represented in Figure 3.

Figure 3 Three-dimensional model of politeness scale of vocatives

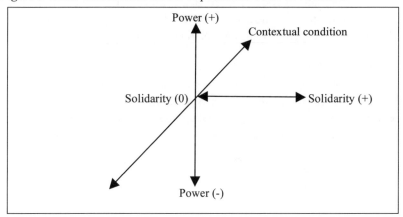

This model helps explain the factors influencing a dramatist's choice of vocative form between characters. The interlocutors are to be located on this politeness scale. If the addressee is more powerful than the speaker, s/he goes up the hierarchical power axis, and the politeness scale moves towards negative politeness. But if the addressee is lower down the social ladder, the politeness scale turns to positive. Thus if the addressee is higher in social status than the speaker, deferential types of vocatives are expected. Conversely, if the addressee is lower in status, familiar vocatives are generally used. Likewise, along the horizontal solidarity axis, when the relationship becomes closer, the degree of positive politeness increases, whilst it turns negative when the relationship becomes distant. In this case, the deferential type is used when the social relationship is distant, whilst the familiar type is used when it is closer. The third axis depends on the context. In a formal situation, the politeness scale moves towards negative politeness, whereas in an informal situation it moves towards positive politeness. Thus in formal situations the deferential type is expected (Watts 1992), whereas the familiar type is expected in informal situations. The emotional situation, on the other hand, is more complicated and it depends on context. This will be discussed further in §5.2 below.

3. Data and methodology

3.1. Data

My data come from my own 'Vocative-Focussed Socio-Pragmatic Corpus' (120,000 words), which consists of twelve play extracts between 1640 and 1760. This corpus comes from the million-word 'Corpus of English Dialogues 1560-1760' compiled by Merja Kytö and Jonathan Culpeper (Culpeper & Kytö 1997).

3.2. Methodology

There are two tagging systems in my annotation. One is the socio-pragmatic tagging system (Archer & Culpeper 2003), which describes the interlocutors by sex, role, status, age, etc., as follows:

Socio-pragmatic tagging system
1. Number of interlocutors
2. ID numbers of the interlocutors
3. Sex of the interlocutors
4. Roles of the interlocutors

5. Status of the interlocutors
6. Age of the interlocutors

The second is the vocative tagging system (Shiina 2002), which distinguishes 10 kinds of linguistic property for each vocative:

Vocative tagging system

1. Presence/absence of a vocative in the utterance
2. Pronoun used in the vocative
3. Premodifier used in the vocative
4. Vocative form
5. Vocative position in the clause
6. Number of words preceding the vocative in the clause
7. Number of words following the vocative in the clause
8. Pronominal address term used in the utterance
9. Number of words in the vocative
10. Lexical item number of the vocative

4. Quantitative analysis: General patterns in the use of vocatives

4.1. Vocatives used between spouses

Are there any general patterns to be discerned in the use of vocatives? Here let us see how the vocative form is used according to the three axes. First, let us give solidarity a positive value, and change the values on the power axis. The vocative use between spouses is an example of this kind. Table 1 shows how husband and wife use vocatives in the nobility, the gentry and the middling groups:

Table 1 Vocative use between husbands and wives

Interlocutors	Status	Familiar type					Deferential type	
		endear	kin	familiar	short FN	full FN	T+SN	Honor
husband→wife	nobility							1
wife→husband		1						21
husband→wife	gentry	8	2			1		4
wife→husband		17	2				10	15
husband→wife	middling groups	2	5	10	3			4
wife→husband			5	8		5	1	

Note: The numbers in the cells are raw numbers of tokens.

In the nobility, the wife uses the deferential type, mainly honorifics, to address her husband. In the gentry, the spouses use both the deferential and familiar types, but their preference is for the deferential type. Unlike the nobility, the gentry use the title-plus-surname as well as honorifics. In the middling groups, their vocative use leans towards the familiar type. To summarise, between husband and wife, there is a status difference in the use of vocatives in that characters of higher status prefer the deferential type and those of lower status the familiar type. This supports the observation made by Brown & Gilman (1960), i. e. the power semantic.

As Figure 4 shows, the wife is in a contradictory space in that the power semantic suggests she use the deferential type whereas the solidarity semantic indicates the opposite. How does she solve this conflict? One solution is to add a premodifier of endearment, such as *dear* as in 'Dear Mr. Strictland', to make vocatives more intimate. The husband also uses vocatives of endearment such as *Love* and *Dear,* premodifiers of endearment such as *dear* and *poor*, as well as an in-group marker *my*, to mitigate their hierarchical relationship, as in 'my Dear', 'poor Madam', and 'my Love'. These additional items of endearment on both sides seem to emphasise their solidarity relationship, though their hierarchical power relationship is simultaneously indicated.

Figure 4 Husband and wife on the two axes

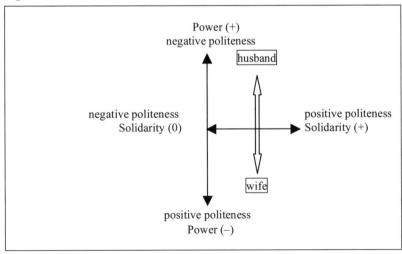

4.2. Vocatives used between customer and tradesperson

Secondly, let us give solidarity a negative rather than positive value, and change the values on the power axis. Table 2 shows vocative use between customers and tradespersons. They mainly use deferential type of vocatives, because shopping is ostensibly an activity done in a public situation in which there are other shoppers and apprentices present. Between them, there is a division in social roles in that the tradesperson must serve the customer. Concerning status, the customer could be higher, the same as, or lower than the tradesperson. In my data, when the customer is lower in status than the tradesperson, the social roles seem to override status difference. Thus the hierarchical axis seems to influence the choice of vocative form.

Table 2 Vocative use between customers and tradespersons

Relationship	Familiar type	Deferential type	
	familiariser	T+SN	honorific
customer → tradesperson	3	20	2
tradesperson → customer	1	0	41

Note: The numbers in the cells are raw numbers of tokens.

Not unlike the wife described in 4.1, the customer is also in a contradictory position, as Figure 5 shows.

Figure 5 Customer and tradesperson on the two axes

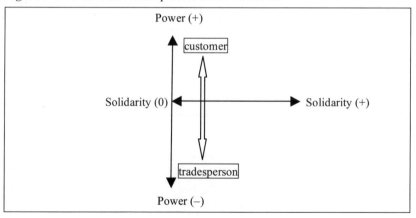

In the hierarchical relationship, the customer is in a higher position in terms of social roles, and thus entitled to use the familiar type. But the solidarity axis indicates the opposite: the deferential type oriented to negative face when they are not close friends. To resolve this conflict, both interlocutors use the deferential type to avoid embarrassment, but the degree of negative politeness differs. The tradesperson uses a more deferential vocative than the customer to show their social roles. Title-plus-surname vocatives are used from customer to tradesperson, whereas honorifics are used from tradesperson to customer. The familiar type is also used from customer to tradesperson, which may be an indication of the hierarchical order based upon social roles, but the number is too low for generalisation. This pattern changes when they have a close personal relationship. In such a case, the tradesperson is in a conflicting position similar to the wife discussed above.

4.3. Vocatives used between strangers, acquaintances, and friends

The third case is when the value along the power axis is fixed and those on the solidarity axis change, as in Figure 6:

Figure 6 Strangers, acquaintances, and friends on two axes

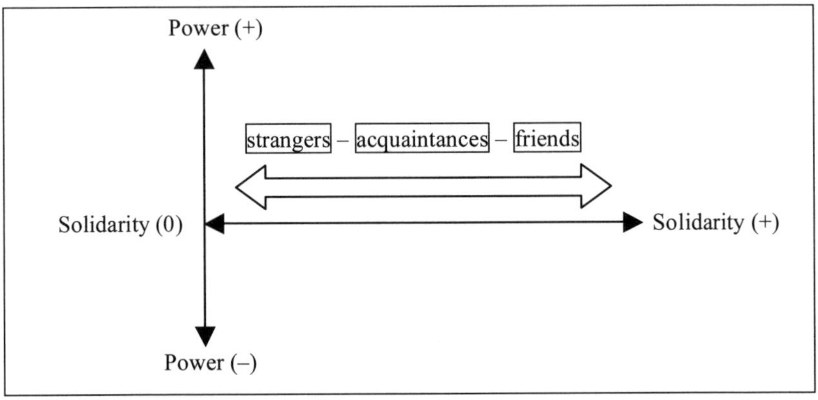

Table 3 shows how characters change their choice of vocatives when they come to know each other. Regardless of status, strangers mainly use honorifics such as *madam, lady,* and *sir.* This may be because they do not know the addressee's name, but it is also because strangers prefer to keep distance so as to avoid embarrassment. As long as the interlocutors use honorific vocatives, they cannot be regarded as impolite, and thus it is safer to use honorifics.

As characters come to know each other better, they start using familiar vocatives. When characters of lower status use vocatives to address friends of higher status they use honorifics, whereas familiar vocatives are used downwards. The two most frequently used vocative forms are first name and surname. Surname vocatives are mainly used by male friends amongst the gentry to show comradeship. These distribution patterns are also predicted by Brown & Gilman's (1960) configuration, i. e. the solidarity semantic.

Table 3 Vocatives used between strangers, acquaintances, and friends

Relationship	Direction	Status	Familiar type	Deferential type
strangers	upwards	2 → 1		3
		3 → 2		2
		5 → 1		1
	level	1 → 1		2
	downwards	1 → 2		1
		2 → 3		1
		1 → 5		1
acquaintances	upwards	2 → 1		1
		3 → 2		2
		3 → 1		20
	level	1 → 1	19	108
	downwards	1 → 2		1
		2 → 3		3
		1 → 3		16
friends	upwards	1 → 0		11
		2 → 1		6
	level	1 → 1	213	130
		5 → 5	4	
	downwards	0 → 1	11	13
		1 → 2	6	1

Status: 0 = nobility; 1 = gentry; 2 = professions; 3 = middling groups;
4 = ordinary commoners; 5 = lowest groups.

5. Qualitative analysis: A case study

5.1. Social network and vocative

This qualitative analysis takes an example from Brome's *A Mad Couple Well Match'd* (1653). Figure 7 illustrates the social networks (Milroy 1987) of some characters in Brome's text. I focus on the network surrounding Alicia Saleware, the wife of Thomas Saleware who owns a drapery shop. Table 4 summarises the vocatives used by Lady Thrivewell and Alicia Saleware.

The default forms are static sociolinguistic phenomena, and the shifts dynamic pragmatic phenomena. The shift of vocatives from the default form to other forms is pragmatically interesting, because these are the moments when the relationship between the characters can be reconfigured either to the positive or negative side of the politeness scale. These are also the moments when the third axis comes into play – that of formality or emotion.

Figure 7 Social network of Brome's characters

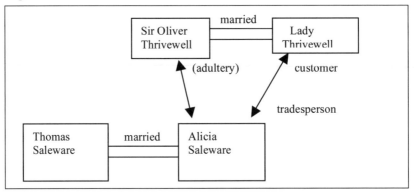

Table 4 Norms and deviations in the use of vocatives in Brome's text

speaker → addressee	Vocatives	
	default form	shift to
Alicia → Lady T.	Honorific: *Madam*	+ modifier of positive value: *most courteous*
Lady T. → Alicia	T + SN: *Mistris Saleware*	+ modifier of endearment: *sweet*

5.2. Vocatives in context: A dialogue between a tradesperson and her customer

In this section, I will discuss vocatives in a dialogue between a tradesperson and her customer. The following example is a dialogue between Alicia Saleware and her customer, Lady Thrivewell. Lady Thrivewell discovers that her husband has had an affair with Alicia (see Figure 7), and has paid her £100. Lady Thrivewell goes to Alicia's shop, buys an enormous amount of expensive lace, and pays

£100 less than the full price, saying Alicia has already received the difference from her husband. Lady Thrivewell has just exacted her revenge.

Example

1   [Alicia] **Madam** your Beere.

2   [Lady] I'le pledge you **Mistris Saleware**.

3   [Alicia] I shall presume then **Madam** – [Drinks.]

     ...

4   [Alicia] And I hope you will finde your money so well bestowd

5   **Madam**, that you will vouchsafe always to know the Shop.

6   [Lady] Ever upon the like occasion, **Mistris Saleware**, so most

7   kindly farwell **sweet Mistris Saleware**.

8   [Alicia] The humblest of your servants **Madam**.

     ...

9   [Lady] ... but beware of old Knights that have young Ladies of their

10   owne. Once more adieu **sweet Mistris Saleware**.

11   [Alicia] **Most courteous Madam**. (Brome, C3V-C4R, my emphasis)

After shopping, Lady Thrivewell asks for a glass of beer. In the first three lines, the two women seem to converse as customer and tradesperson normally would. Here the default forms are used (cf. Table 4). But in fact, Lady Thrivewell is triumphant because she has just put Alicia down by her well-planned revenge. Alicia, on the other hand, is furious with good reason. From l. 4 to l. 5, Alicia throws Lady Thrivewell a bluff with a default vocative in mid-sentence. Alicia pretends to be calm as she makes an ironic utterance, but the vocative in the middle of her statement reveals her resentment towards Lady Thrivewell. Alicia inserts a vocative in her utterance to confirm that Lady Thrivewell is getting her message. In other words, this vocative is used as a discourse marker to reinforce the illocutionary force of the utterance. The vocative here seems to express the speaker's emotion and attitude towards the addressee. Lady Thrivewell responds to Alicia's challenge as if nothing untoward has occurred. When Lady Thrivewell bids Alicia farewell in ll. 6-7, she cannot help expressing joy at her victory over Alicia. Lady Thrivewell does so by using very polite language. Here, the strain in the relationship becomes more apparent. Lady Thrivewell adds the premodifier of endearment, *sweet*, to the default form, *Mistris Saleware*, which is supported by the phrase, *most kindly farewell*, thus the politeness vector moves even further towards positive politeness. Here then, Lady Thrivewell's utterance is rather complicated, because it is oriented both to negative and positive politeness. *Mistris Saleware* is oriented to negative politeness and *sweet* is oriented to positive politeness. Lady Thrivewell's use of the deferential vocative is a default form for a customer to address a tradesperson, and *most kindly* and *sweet* would in other circumstances be supposed to add a sense of endearment to her greeting. However, this should be interpreted as a sarcastic re-emphasis of hierarchical order between these two women, rather than any sense of solidarity. Lady Thrivewell's higher position here depends not on social roles or status but on the power struggle between two hostile women. Here Lady Thrivewell, the winner, is basking in her victory over Alicia.

In ll. 9-10, Lady Thrivewell advises Alicia to 'beware of old Knights that have young Ladies of their owne'. The plural forms of *old knights* and *young Ladies of their owne* make the advice sound as if it were generally applicable. However, *old knights* here specifically refers to Lady Thrivewell's husband and *young Ladies* to Lady Thrivewell herself. Thus this is actually an injunction and a threat: never meet or seduce my husband again. Lady Thrivewell repeats an overpolite farewell, this time with *adieu*, reinforcing her ironic stance. Her farewell is a resolute word of parting: I shall not see you again. Lady Thrivewell's utterances are artificial and too polite to be perceived as polite. They sound, in fact, impolite and scathing.

Alicia, on the other hand, responds to these artificially polite utterances with extremely polite answers: 'The humblest of your servants Madam' in l. 8, and 'Most courteous Madam' in l. 11. In the former, Alicia uses the superlative form, *the humblest* to put herself in an inferior position by humiliating herself. In the latter, she uses the superlative form, *most courteous*, to modify the honorific vocative in order to elevate Lady Thrivewell by paying her respect. By doing so, Alicia is trying to keep her distance from her. Alicia is also 'polite' to the point of impoliteness. The third axis of contextual condition is useful in explaining their use of vocatives, as Figure 8 illustrates.

The relationship between Lady Thrivewell and Alicia is different from the usual customer-tradesperson situation observed in Figure 5. On the solidarity axis, their relationship is pushed further towards the negative side, whilst their emotional condition is on the negative side, because they hate each other. The hierarchical axis of social roles and status is also valid. Thus their relationship is complicated and dramatised in terms of politeness.

Figure 8 Lady and Alicia on the three axes

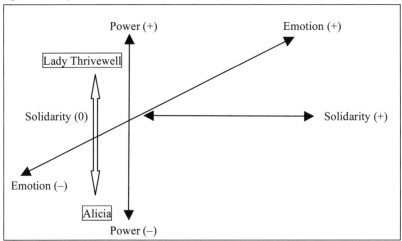

From a stylistic point of view, these overpolite vocatives are foregrounded. What are they doing here with these reciprocal greetings of super politeness with opposite vectors? What is the implication of this extremely polite use of vocatives? These two women's exchanges are superficially very polite, but their implication is extremely bitter and ironic due to the background of adultery and financial trickery. What is implicitly conveyed is contempt and hatred. In plain words, Lady Thrivewell does not hide the fact that she despises Alicia and that she never wants Alicia to come near her husband again. Alicia also shows that she hates Lady Thrivewell. The implication of the dialogue is just the opposite of what it literally means. On the third axis, which represents emotion and attitude, Lady Thrivewell uses a positive politeness strategy paradoxically to display her hatred and contempt towards Alicia, and Alicia uses a negative politeness strategy ironically to show her disrespect for and hatred of Lady Thrivewell. Although the vectors of their strategies are opposite, they serve to fulfil the same purpose: they are off-record strategies to send impolite messages (Brown & Levinson 1987). Overpolite vocatives and over-humble greetings are both beyond the conventional range of politeness to be perceived as politic behaviour

(Watts 1992). This excessively polite verbal exchange, in fact, destroys the relationship between the interlocutors.

6. Conclusion

Now that the default vocative form in the English-speaking world is the first name (Leech 1999), it is difficult to detect hierarchical and horizontal relationships between people in their use of vocatives. As the conventional vocative forms are limited, it is hard to see how vocatives exert manipulative power in the interpersonal relationship. However, it has not always been so. In the Early Modern English period, class, status, and social roles can be more clearly recognised in vocative use. The playwrights of the 17th and 18th centuries are aware of this, and exploit a variety of vocatives as a linguistic and literary device to construct the character relationships in their dramatic worlds, and also manipulate them as the plot unfolds. Especially in comedies, vocatives fluctuate around comic characters and help to enhance comic effects. As tiny a linguistic item as it may seem, a vocative is a useful tool to analyse drama texts in terms of pragmatics and stylistics. I hope to have demonstrated that computer-assisted linguistic research can further reveal the craftsmanship and creativity of playwrights of the past.

Source text

Brome, Richard. 1653. 'A Mad Couple Well Match'd' in Kytö, Merja, and Jonathan Culpeper (eds). Unpublished. *Corpus of English Dialogues 1560-1760.*

References

Archer, Dawn, and Jonathan Culpeper. 2003. 'Sociopragmatic Annotation: New Directions and Possibilities in Historical Corpus Linguistics' in Wilson, Andrew, Paul Rayson and Tony M. McEnery (eds) *Corpus Linguistics by the Lune: A Festschrift for Geoffrey Leech.* Frankfurt/Main: Peter Lang, 37-58.

Brinton, Laurel J. 1996. *Pragmatic Markers in English: Grammaticalization and Discourse Functions.* Berlin: Mouton de Gruyter.

Brown, Penelope, and Stephen C. Levinson. 1987. *Politeness: Some Universals in Language Usage.* Cambridge: Cambridge University Press.

Brown, Roger, and Albert Gilman. 1960. 'The Pronouns of Power and Solidarity' in Sebeok, Thomas A. (ed.) *Style in Language.* New York: Technology Press of The Massachusetts Institute of Technology and John Wiley: 253-76.

Culpeper, Jonathan, and Merja Kytö. 1997. 'Towards a Corpus of Dialogues, 1550-1750', in Ramisch, Heinrich, and Kenneth Wynne (eds) *Language in Time and Space: Studies in Honour of Wolfgang Viereck on the Occasion of his 60th Birthday.* Stuttgart: Franz Steiner: 60-73.

Leech, Geoffrey. 1999. 'The Distribution and Function of Vocatives in American and British English Conversation', in Hasselgård, Hilde, and Signe Oksefjell (eds.) *Out of Corpora: Studies in Honour of Stig Johansson*. Amsterdam: Rodopi: 107-18.

Milroy, Lesley. 1987. *Language and Social Networks*. Oxford: Blackwell.

Raumolin-Brunberg, Helena. 1996. 'Forms of Address in Early English Correspondence' in Nevalainen, Terttu, and Helena Raumolin-Brunberg (eds) *Sociolinguistics and Language History: Studies Based on the Corpus of Early English Correspondence*. Amsterdam: Rodopi: 168-81.

Shiina, Michi. 2002. 'How Spouses Used to Address Each Other: A Historical Pragmatic Approach to the Use of Vocatives in Early Modern English Comedies' in *Bulletin of the Faculty of Letters* 48: 51-73. Tokyo: Hosei University.

Wales, Kathleen. 1983. '*Thou* and *You* in Early Modern English: Brown and Gilman Re-Appraised' in *Studia Lingustica*, 37: 107-25.

Watts, Richard J. 1992. 'Linguistic Politeness and Politic Verbal Behaviour: Reconsidering Claims for Universality' in Watts, Richard J., Sachiko Ide and Konrad Ehlich (eds) *Politeness in Language: Studies in its History, Theory and Practice*. Berlin: Mouton de Gruyter: 43-70.

Collocational Style in the Two Narratives of *Bleak House*: A Corpus-based Analysis

Masahiro Hori

Abstract

In the light of research on collocation in Charles Dickens (1812-70) I would like to make clear various collocational characteristics of the third-person narrative and Esther's narrative in Dickens' *Bleak House* (1852-53), both quantitatively and qualitatively. Certain characteristics of collocation in this text are analysed from two viewpoints: usual and creative collocations. Regarding usual collocations there is an obvious difference between the two narratives in the collocations of frequent words. Unique and creative collocations in both narratives are discussed under three types: metaphorical, transferred, and oxymoronic collocations. As a result of this research, there is apparently a structural difference in collocation between the two narratives. In order to carry out a thorough investigation into this subject and provide further consideration of Dickens' language within the context of the development of the language of fiction and the history of English, I have made use of the CD-ROMs of the *OED 2*, *Eighteenth-Century Fiction,* and *Nineteenth-Century Fiction* as well as electronic texts and concordances of Dickens' works.*

Key words: Dickens; *Bleak House*; usual collocation; creative collocation; corpus-based analysis.

1. Introduction

The major peculiarity of Dickens' *Bleak House* is that the story is narrated by two distinct voices, the third-person narrator who is 'anonymous, objective, and presumably masculine and stands outside the action' (Page 1990: 54) and the first-person narrator, Esther Summerson, who is 'subjective, feminine, and a major character in the story' (ibid.). Dickens hoped to achieve by means of such a technique 'the possibility of our seeing the story from radically different angles

*This is a modified version of chapter 5 of my book, *Investigating Dickens' Style: A Collocational Analysis*, (Basingstoke: Palgrave 2004), and is reproduced here with the permission of the publisher.

of objectivity and subjectivity' (Smith 1974: 8). Accordingly, the differences of style between the third-person narrative (34 chapters) and Esther's narrative (33 chapters) can be discerned easily from the viewpoints of vocabulary and sentence structure as well as of person and tense. The aim of this paper is to show that there is, additionally, a difference of lexical collocation between the two narratives in terms of usual collocations and that there are many linguistically experimental unusual collocations in Esther's narrative (EN) as well as the third-person narrative (TN). As a result of this research, I would like to emphasise the necessity and importance of collocational studies of literary language; there have been few such satisfactory investigations to date, although Firth (1957: 195) and Greenbaum (1970: 81) encouraged the study of common, unique, or peculiar collocations in literary works.

2.1. Usual collocations in Esther's and third-person narratives

In this section I will examine usual collocations in narratives written by the third-person narrator and Esther, the first-person narrator. The following is a table of word-totals, as well as the total number of different words[1] in the Dialogue and Non-dialogue of the two narratives:

Table 1 Total number of words and different words in dialogue and non-dialogue of the two narratives

Bleak House: 356,931 words, 15,412 different words (Dialogue 140,591; Narrative 216,340 words)			
Third-person Narrative (TN) (164,455 words) (11,985 different words)		**Esther's Narrative (EN)** (192,476 words) (10,036 different words)	
Dialogue	Non-dialogue	Dialogue	Non-dialogue
63,320 words	101,135 words	77,271 words	115,205 words
5,579 different words	10,982 different words	6,543 different words	8,183 different words

As Table 1 illustrates, TN has fewer words in total than EN, but a greater number of different words. The ratio of different words per 10,000 words in TN is 1.4 times as many as those of EN (723 different words in TN and 521 different words in EN). The ratio between Dialogue and Non-dialogue in both narratives is almost the same (1:1.6 in TN and 1:1.5 in EN). Regarding different words per 10,000 words in the dialogue, there are 881 words in TN and 847 words in EN. There is little difference in the dialogues of the two narratives. However, an obvious difference can be recognised in different words contained in the non-dialogues of the two narratives; the different words per 10,000 words in the non-dialogue indicate 1,086 words in third-person non-dialogue and 710 words in Esther's non-dialogue. Therefore, it can be said that Esther's phraseology is more dependent upon repetition than that of the third-person narrator.

Among a list of the 100 most frequent words in EN and TN, from which function words and proper names have been removed, 79 words are common between both narratives. John Jarndyce, one of the main characters, is referred to as a *guardian* (Rank 14) 395 times in EN but only once in TN. In contrast the word *trooper* usually referring to George Rouncewell appears 145 times in TN but only nine times in EN. Some words such as *seemed* (185 times in EN, but only 10 times in TN) and *poor* (173 times in EN, but only 57 times in TN) may reflect Esther's personal style. In this way the differences between both narratives can be discerned easily on the level of vocabulary, as well as of person and tense.

On the other hand, there is also the difference between the two narratives in the collocations of frequent words, although collocational differences are not recognised as easily as are vocabulary, person, and tense. For example, let us consider the collocations of *little* and *so*, which are frequently used in both narratives.

Little shows a very high frequency in both narratives (Rank 5 in EN and Rank 9 in TN). What is interesting in the collocates of *little* is the combination with *poor.* This collocation *poor little* (such as *the poor little things* for Mrs. Jellyby's children and *the poor little creature* for Miss Flite) appears 14 times in EN and all these instances of the collocations of *poor little* except one example in Mr. Snagsby's dialogue are used in Esther's non-dialogue. This reveals Esther's pity or sympathy for Mrs. Jellyby's children and Miss Flite in EN. On the other hand, among the four instances of *poor little* in TN, three instances are in the characters' dialogues but not in the third-person non-dialogue. This difference of collocations of *little*, as observed in *poor little* in EN and *little woman* in TN, shows each narrator's attitude toward the characters and at the same time implies the difference in the meaning of *little*, that is, Esther's *little*, as: 'an implication of endearment or of tender feeling on the part of the speaker';[2] the third-person narrator's *little*, as: 'a small body'.

The frequency of *so* is also very high in both narratives (Rank 3 in EN and Rank 4 in TN). The word *so* frequently co-occurs with many words; therefore the difference in the use of *so* between both narratives is not easily discerned. However, the collocation *so very* is distinctive in both narratives. Among the 32 instances of *so very* in EN, 24 instances are used by Esther (22 times in her narration and two times in her dialogue), while in TN there is a total of 12 instances (seven times in the narration and five times in the dialogues). The use of *so very* by male characters occurs only in Prince Turveydrop's dialogue in EN, and in Smallweed's and Guppy's dialogues in TN. The fact that the collocation of similar intensive words of *so very* are never used by other male characters (such as Jarndyce, Woodcourt, and Bucket) may imply that Dickens dealt with *so very* as a style of diction women are inclined to use. The following is a list of collocates of *so very* in EN and TN (non-dialogues):

> *so very* (22) in EN:
> good, cold, clear, military, embarrassing, ridiculous, anxious, pretty, gallant, often, watchful, much, chatty and happy, likely, earnest, sorry (twice), solicitous, ill, long, far, indignant.
>
> *so very* (7) in TN:
> bad, remarkable (twice), large, trying, disagreeable, nomadically.

The collocates of *so very* in the above list are more emotional in EN, as observed in adjectives such as 'embarrassing, anxious, sorry, solicitous, and indignant' than in TN.

The collocations that have been treated in this section are usual and familiar but we are able to realise differences in the use of usual collocations between Esther's narrative and the third-person narrative.

2.2. Usual collocations in Esther's and third-person non-dialogues

The distinctive formal style of collocation in the third-person non-dialogue (which does not occur in Esther's non-dialogue) is the collocation of '*the* + adjective + proper name', while the collocational type in Esther's non-dialogue is the collocation 'adjective + proper name' without a definite article (which does not occur in the third-person non-dialogue). This type of collocation '*the* + adjective +

proper name' is classified into three heads according to the semantic meaning of adjectives in context: a relatively long-term, stable aspect of character or situation, a temporal emotion or situation, and 'others'. Within this collocational type referring to the characters' personality or situation, I find the following collocations:

> the hapless Jo / the eloquent Chadband / the sagacious Smallweed (twice) / the active Smallweed / the susceptible Smallweed / the trusty[3] Smallweed / the venerable[4] Mr. Smallweed / the eminent Smallweed / the Elfin Smallweed / the unoffending Mrs. Smallweed / the snappish Judy / the blooming Judy / the perennial Judy / the fair Judy / the grim Judy / the imperturbable Judy / the sportive Judy / the virtuous Judy / the Honourable[5] William Guppy / the audacious Boythorn / the innocent Mr. Snagsby / the devoted Mr. Snagsby / the unfortunate George / the sanguine George / the fair Dedlock / the great old Dedlock family / the handsome Lady Dedlock / etc.

The following collocations express the temporal emotions or situations of characters:

> the injured Guppy / the afflicted Mr. Guppy / the disconsolate Mr. Guppy / the admiring Mrs. Snagsby / the watchful Mrs. Snagsby / the sprightly Dedlock / the irascible Mr. Smallweed / the scornful Judy / the gentle Judy / the triumphant Judy / the interesting Judy / the placid Vholes / the equable Vholes / the astounded Tony / the careful Phil

The following are collocations which lack judgemental or emotional adjectives:

> the late Mr. Krook's / the late Mr. Tulkinghorn / the present Lady Dedlock / the present Sir Leicester Dedlock / the superannuated Mr. and Mrs. Smallweed

All of the collocations of the type '*the* + adjective + personal name' quoted above occur in the third-person non-dialogue.

With respect to this type of collocation in Esther's non-dialogue, however, there are only two examples of the third type of collocation: *the elder Mr. Turveydrop* and *the identical Peepy*.[6] On the other hand, regarding the type of collocation 'adjective + personal name' (which lacks the definite article), there are many instances in Esther's non-dialogue:

> poor Peepy / poor little Peepy / poor Miss Jellyby (twice) / poor Caddy (four times) / little Miss Flite (three times) / poor Miss Flite / poor little Miss Flite / poor Mr. Jellyby (four times) / poor Charley / poor little Charley / waking Charley / poor dear Richard (twice) / poor Gridley / poor Jo / poor crazed Miss Flite

The adjectives *poor*, *little*, and *dear* in these collocations do not describe the characters' personalities, situations, or temporal emotions but rather reveal Esther's spontaneous emotions towards them.

One of the functions of the definite article is as a specific reference, which 'can be identified uniquely in the contextual or general knowledge shared by speaker and hearer' (Quirk et al. 1985: 265), but a proper name itself functions as a specific reference. In fact, the use of the definite article *the* is not absolutely necessary in order to add an adjective to the proper name. According to Quirk et al. (1985: 290):

> nonrestrictive premodifiers are limited to adjectives with emotive colouring, such as:
>
> | | | |
> |---|---|---|
> | *old* Mrs. Fletcher | *dear little* Eric | *poor* Charles |
> | *beautiful* Spain | *historic* York | *sunny* July. |
>
> In a more formal and rather stereotyped style, the adjective is placed between *the* and a personal name:
>
> the *beautiful* Princess Diana ['Princess Diana, who is beautiful']
> the *inimitable* Henry Higgins ['Henry Higgins, who is inimitable'].

Therefore, the collocational pattern '*the* + adjective + personal name' in the third-person non-dialogue, which tends to convey a relatively long-term, stable aspect of character or situation, rather than a temporal emotion, reveals a more formal style as well as the omnipotent attitude of the narrator toward characterisation.

3. Unusual collocations of EN and TN

Most readers of *Bleak House* have the impression that the third-person narrative is apparently more unusual or deviant than Esther's narrative in its use of language. For example, Page (1990: 55-56) points out language differences between the two narratives as follows:

> Her [Esther's] language is for the most part simple and at times even banal, and her tone informal and confidential; the other narrative by contrast is rhetorical, linguistically experimental, and dramatic. . . Language and style apart, there are further differences between the two narratives. Esther's, for instance, is more consistently serious; most of the comedy in this novel (and there is a good deal) is found in the more imaginative and highly colored third-person narrative.

W. J. Harvey (1969: 226) also mentions Esther's simple and invariable narrative by using negative expressions 'even at the risk of insipidity and dullness' and 'plain, matter-of-fact, conscientiously plodding'. Is this difference reflected in the collocations as well? What is it about

Esther's narrative that leaves us unable to describe her language and style as linguistically experimental, dramatic, lively, etc.? Keeping these issues in mind, I would like to consider some language differences between the third-person narrative and the first-person narrative, in terms of unusual collocations. The unusual collocations to be dealt with in this section are only those collected from Esther's non-dialogue and the third-person non-dialogue, not appearing in any other dialogues.

In *Bleak House* I find many unusual collocations which are not found in other 18th- or 19th-century fiction.[7] Over 700 examples were collected for this research. Among these examples there are (minimally) over 300 unusual collocations in EN. In this section these unusual collocations in the non-dialogues of each narrator will be compared and discussed according to three types of collocations (that is, metaphorical collocations, transferred collocations, and oxymoronic collocations) with consideration for syntactic patterns, though some of the unusual collocations may also belong to other types.

3.1. Metaphorical collocations

The first type of unusual collocation I will examine is metaphorical. One typical metaphorical collocation is personification.[8] As observed in the scene of fog at the beginning of *Bleak House*, natural phenomena, such as *sunshine* and *moon,* are often given animate attributes and anthropomorphic characteristics with the collocational pattern of 'noun + verb'. Such personifications are found in both narratives:

Esther's non-dialogue
The purblind *day was feebly struggling* with the fog, . . . (Ch. 4)
the night was very slowly stirring (Ch. 59)
the houses frowned at us, *the dust rose* at us, *the smoke swooped* at us, nothing made any compromise about itself, or wore a softened aspect. (Ch. 51)
the morning faintly struggled in (Ch. 59)

Third-person non-dialogue
the clear cold *sunshine glances* into the brittle woods, and approvingly *beholds* the sharp wind scattering the leaves and drying the moss. (Ch. 12)
The moon has eyed Tom with a dull cold stare, . . . (Ch. 46)
the long vacation saunters on towards term-time, like *an idle river* very leisurely *strolling down* a flat country to the sea. (Ch. 20)

There are also personifications having the collocational pattern 'adjective + noun'. The following are a list of personified collocations in Esther's non-dialogue:

> cheerful lodging / cheerful town / healthy shore / hospitable jingle / hungry garret / inexpressive-looking books / miserable corner / smiling country / over-ripe berry / pleasant footpath / ripening weather / ungrown despair

In the above list of metaphorical collocations there are many adjectives expressive of sensory perception, such as *cheerful, healthy,* and *hungry*.

Personified collocations 'adjective + noun' in the third-person non-dialogue show only a slight difference from those of Esther's:

> argumentative back-fall[9] / benighted[10] England / deathlike hue / discontented goose / idle river / inconsolable carriages / invigorating pail / penitential sofa-pillows / pertinacious oil lamps / ravenous little pens / upstart gas / welcome light / perplexed and troublous valley of shadow of the law

In comparison to the personified collocations in Esther's non-dialogue, animistic metaphorical collocations, 'which attributes animate characteristics to the inanimate' (Leech 1969: 158) are dominant in the third-person narrative. Esther also tends to use favourable or neutral words such as *cheerful* and *ripening* in the personified collocations *cheerful town* and *ripening weather*, while the third-person narrator uses not only favourable words but unfavourable or negative and judgemental words as well: *benighted, discontented, idle, penitential, ravenous, perplexed, troublous*.

The following are visualised collocations which attribute an image to an abstraction or add a sharp image to concreteness or physical existence. The following occur in Esther's non-dialogue:

> chivalrously polite / colossal staircases / colourless days / fish-like manner / flaming necklace / full-blown girl / musty rotting silence

In the third-person non-dialogue I find additional visualised collocations:

> buttoned-up half-audible voice / clouds of cousins / crooked knife of his mind / dazed mind / elephantine lizard / feline mouth / foggy glory / icy stare / iron bow / leaden lunches / reservoir of confidences / nomadically drunk / shadowy belief / skeleton throats / sparkling stranger / swarm of misery / swelling pride / as hollow as a coffin / unwholesome hand (i. e. the suit, Jarndyce and Jarndyce)

The third-person non-dialogue not only has more visualised collocations but also a greater variety of visual images than Esther's.

Additional metaphorical collocations are:

Esther's non-dialogue

Examples of metonymy: my guardian's delicacy had soon perceived this / as if his natural generosity felt a pang of reproach / her quickness anticipated what I might have said presently

Other interesting metaphorical collocations: calendars of distress / crisp-looking gentleman / dead glove / divine sunshine / gleam of welcome / ruin of youth / summer joke / my vanity should deceive me

Third-person non-dialogue

Examples of metonymy: her head concedes / Mrs. Rouncewell's hands unquiet

Other interesting metaphorical collocations: deadened world / deadly meaning / forensic lunacy / imperial luxury / infernal stables / official cat / unsavoury shelter / imperturbable as Death / imperturbable as the hearthstone

3.2. Transferred collocations

There are collocations which are not contradictory in literal meaning or connotative meaning but are considered as transferred or dislocated collocations, in which an adjective or adverb grammatically qualifies a noun, adjective, or verb but literally or semantically applies to a different word. Among transferred collocations, in both the non-dialogues, collocations of 'an adjective + a body part' are the ones most frequently found. These unusual collocations of body parts are divided into two types: (1) a transferred collocation referring to a temporary emotion of the possessor of a body part; and (2) a transferred collocation referring to a relatively permanent character of the possessor of a body part. The following are transferred collocations of 'an adjective + a body part' in both the non-dialogues:

Esther's non-dialogue (20 examples)

(1) a transferred collocation referring to a temporary emotion of the possessor of a body part: care-worn head / darkened face / disdainful face / pleasant eyebrows / quiet hands / sudden eye / surprised eyes / too-eager eyes / troubled hands / warning feet (10 examples)

(2) a transferred collocation referring to a relatively long-term, stable aspect of character of a body part: gracious hand (Jesus Christ's hand) / quick face (Jarndyce's careful attention to people) / resolute face (Esther's strong-willed aunt) / trusting face (Ada) / mad lips (Miss Flite) / rustic faces / sprightly eyes (Skimpole) / sprightly forehead (one of Skimpole's daughters) / sulky forehead (Prince Turveydrop's girl student) / well-remembered finger (Inspector Bucket) (10 examples)

Third-person non-dialogue (20 examples)

(1) a transferred collocation referring to a temporary emotion of the possessor of a body part: admonitory finger / angry hands / anxious hand / busy face / cruel finger / disdainful hand / unconscious head / wary hand (8 examples)

(2) a transferred collocation referring to a relatively long-term, stable aspect of character of the possessor of a body part: admonitory hand (Chadband) / calm hands (Mrs. Rouncewell) / decent hand (Lady Dedlock) / dreadful feet / gracious head (Lady Dedlock) / knowing eyes (Inspector Bucket) / maternal foot / murderous hand / relentless head / so-genteel fingers (Lady Dedlock) / stately breast (Sir Leicester) / venerable eye (young Smallweed) (12 examples)

These transferred collocations of body parts are of nearly equal number and nearly equally used for both temporary emotions (e. g. *angry hands*) and relatively long-term, stable aspects of character (e. g. *decent hand*) in both the non-dialogues. What is different between them is that the persons to whom these transferred collocations of body parts are applied in Esther's non-dialogue are different from those of the third-person non-dialogues (though exceptionally, Inspector Bucket's finger is described in both non-dialogues).

The transferred collocations of 'an adjective + a human behaviour' are also interesting:

Esther's non-dialogue
attentive smile / dejected bow / dull thoughtfulness / hopeless gesture / observant smile / sulky jerk / sunburnt smiles / triumphant rub

Third-person non-dialogue
angry nods / apologetic cough / comprehensive wave / deferential cough / emaciated glare / explanatory cough / fat smile / gloomy yawn / majestically interpose / majestic sleep / persuasive action / sarcastic nods / shrewd attention / stately approval / undisguisable yawns

The third-person non-dialogue shows a greater variety of adjectives and behaviours in this type of transferred collocation than Esther's non-dialogue.

Other transferred collocations are as follows:

Esther's non-dialogue
affable dignity / agreeable candour / agreeable jocularity / amiable importance / bashful simplicity / captivating gaiety / delightful confidence / delightful gaiety / delightful weather / deplorable home / dreary passage / engaging candour / fearful wet / gentle seriousness / guileless candour / overweening assumptions / painful belief / playful astonishment / pleasant footpath / pleasant weeks / serene composure / surly stop / timid days / thoughtful amazement / timid tenderness / vivacious candour

Third-person non-dialogue
angry reasons / boastful misery / disappointing knobs / grinning silence / inconsolable carriages / melancholy trees / restless pillow / stately gloom / stately liking / uncomfortable tightness / worn-out heavens

Concerning other types of transferred collocations, I find more examples in Esther's non-dialogue. In addition, Esther tends to use transferred epithets with favourable adjectives such as *captivating* and *pleasant*, while the third-person narrator shows a tendency to use adjectives more unfavourable in meaning, such as *boastful* and *uncomfortable*.

3.3. Oxymoronic collocations

Oxymoronic collocations are often used by both Esther and the third-person narrator. In terms of semantic construction there are three types of oxymoronic collocations: (1) 'a word of favourable meaning + a word of unfavourable meaning'; (2) 'a word of unfavourable meaning + a word of favourable meaning'; and (3) 'others':

Esther's non-dialogue (26 examples)
(1) 'a word of favourable meaning + a word of unfavourable meaning':
benignant shadow / captivating looseness / cheerful gravity / curious indifference / delightfully irregular / friendly indignation / good-humoured vexation / good-natured vexation / loving anxiety / modest consciousness / pleasant absurdity / pleasantly cheated / pleasantly irregular / professions of childishness / resolutely unconscious / respectful wretchedness / serene contempt / smiling condescension (18 examples)
(2) 'a word of unfavourable meaning + a word of favourable meaning':
absent endeavours / disagreeable gallantry / haughty self-restraint[11] / mournful glory / old-faced mite / plaintive smile / rapacious benevolence (7 examples)
(3) Others: thoughtful baby (1 example)

Third-person non-dialogue (24 examples)
(1) 'a word of favourable meaning + a word of unfavourable meaning':
affectionate distress / affectionate lunacy / exalted dullness / harmonious impeachment / magnificent displeasure (5 examples)
(2) 'a word of unfavourable meaning + a word of favourable meaning':
awful politeness / cold sunshine / dismal grandeur / dull repose / exhausted composure / foggy glory / frosty fire / frowning smile / gloomy enjoyment / gloomy relief / mechanically faithful / stolid satisfaction / stunned admiration / wicked relief / worn-out placidity (15 examples)
(3) Others: boastful misery / official den / interminable brief / waking doze (4 examples)

Of interest in the above list of oxymoronic collocations is that Esther's non-dialogue surpasses the third-person non-dialogue quantitatively (though a few more examples might be discovered in the third-person non-dialogue). Even more striking is that with respect to the semantic construction of oxymoronic collocations there is a distinctive contrast between Esther's and the third-person non-dialogue. That is to say, 'a word of favourable meaning + a word of unfavourable meaning' is dominant in Esther's non-dialogue while 'a word of unfavourable meaning + a word of favourable meaning' shows an overwhelming majority in the third-person non-dialogue. Such a difference of a semantic word order of oxymoronic collocations seem to be attributed to each narrator's difference of attitude towards the events and characters. To put it another way, Esther's oxymoronic collocations are used in a more generous, less judgemental manner than those of the third-person narrator.

4. Conclusion

As seen in the foregoing sections, collocational characteristics in Esther's narrative and the third-person narrative have been analysed both quantitatively and qualitatively from two viewpoints: usual and creative collocations. With respect to usual collocations, there are various patterns of collocational difference in common words between the two narratives. These differences of collocational pattern are closely connected with the narrators' attitudes and emotional tone. As far as creative or unusual collocations are concerned, this text has a flood of new collocations not to be found in other 18th- and 19th-century fiction. Esther's language or style in her narrative is generally said to be simple, plain, and matter-of-fact; however, there are many unusual collocations in Esther's narrative, including numerous types of unusual collocations (metaphorical, personified, transferred, and oxymoronic collocations). Therefore, it could be said that collocations in Esther's narrative are linguistically experimental and satisfactorily creative. As well, examining differences between Esther's narrative and the third-person narrative, qualitative differences relating to 'unusuality' or types of unusual collocations seem more apparent than differences relating to the quantity of particular collocations. Such differences between unusual collocations leads us to an awareness that the third-person narrator is more deeply involved in and in more direct control of his narration than Esther, who intends to narrate in an unobtrusive manner, as observed in her remark, 'I mean all the time to write about other people, and I try to think about myself as little as possible' (Ch. 9).

Endnotes

[1] 'Different words' indicates morphologically distinct words (e. g., *say, says, saying,* and *said* are each counted as different words).

[2] *OED* s. v. 'little', adj. 3.

[3] The adjective *trusty* is used ironically.

[4] The adjective *venerable* is used ironically.

[5] The adjective *Honourable* has the narrator's ironical tone.

[6] Mr. Guppy, Mr. and Mrs. Snagsby, Smallweed, Chadband, George, etc. also appear in Esther's narrative but the collocational pattern '*the* + adjective + personal name' is not used.

[7] Cf. *Eighteenth Century Fiction* and *Nineteenth Century Fiction* on CD-ROM.

[8] Regarding personification, Leech (1969: 158) points out the following three categories: [a] *The Concretive Metaphor*, which attributes concreteness or physical existence to an abstraction: 'the *pain* of separation', 'the *light* of learning', 'a vicious *circle*', '*room* for negotiation'. [b] *The Animistic Metaphor*, which attributes animate characteristics to the inanimate: 'an *angry* sky', 'graves *yawned*', '*killing* half-an-hour', 'the *shoulder* of the hill'. [c] *The Humanising Metaphor*, which attributes characteristics of humanity to what is not human: 'This *friendly* river', '*laughing* valleys'. As Leech admits, these three categories overlap and especially, the distinction between animistic metaphor and humanising metaphor is not clear.

[9] As an example of *backfall* to mean 'A fall or throw on the back in wrestling. Often *fig.*', the *OED* quotes from *Bleak House* (*OED* s. v. 'backfall', 2).

[10] Here *benighted* is used to mean '*fig.* Involved in intellectual or moral darkness' (*OED* s. v. 'benighted', 2).

[11] *Haughty self-restraint* referring to Lady Dedlock is used in the phrase 'the absence of her haughty self-restraint' (Ch. 36).

References

Firth, J. R. 1957. *Papers in Linguistics, 1934-51*. Oxford: Oxford University Press.

Eighteenth-Century Fiction [CD-ROM]. 1996. Cambridge: Chadwyck-Healey.

Goatly, Andrew. 1997. *The Language of Metaphors*. London: Routledge.

Greenbaum, Sidney. 1969. *Studies in English Adverbial Usage*. London: Longman.

___. 1970. *Verb-Intensifier Collocation in English: An Experimental Approach*. The Hague: Mouton.

Harvey, W. J. 1969. '*Bleak House*: The Double Narrative' in Dyson, A. E. (ed.) *Dickens: Bleak House*. London: Macmillan: 224-34.

Hori, Masahiro. 1999. 'Collocational Patterns of Intensive Adverbs in Dickens: A

Tentative Approach' in *English Corpus Studies* 6: 51-65.

___. 2002. 'Collocational Patterns of *-ly* Manner Adverbs in Dickens' in Saito, Toshio, Junsaku Nakamura and Shunji Yamazaki (eds) *English Corpus Linguistics in Japan*. Amsterdam: Rodopi: 149-63.

___. 2004. *Investigating Dickens' Style: A Collocational Analysis*. Basingstoke: Palgrave.

Hunston, Susan, and Gill Francis. 1999. *Pattern Grammar: A Corpus-Driven Approach to the Lexical Grammar of English*. Amsterdam: John Benjamins.

Leech, Geoffrey. 1969. *A Linguistic Guide to English Poetry*. London: Longman.

McBride, Christopher. 1998. 'A Collocational Approach to Semantic Change: The Case of Worship and Honour in Malory and Spenser' in *Language and Literature* 7(1): 5-19.

Nineteenth-Century Fiction [CD-ROM]. 2000. Cambridge: Chadwyck-Healey.

Page, Norman. 1990. *Bleak House: A Novel of Connections*. Boston: Twayne.

Partington, Alan. 1998. *Patterns and Meanings: Using Corpora for English Language Research and Teaching*. Amsterdam: John Benjamins.

Quirk, Randolph, et al. 1985. *A Comprehensive Grammar of the English Language*. London: Longman.

Sinclair, John. 1991. *Corpus, Concordance, Collocation*. Oxford: Oxford University Press.

Smith, Grahame. 1974. *Charles Dickens: Bleak House*. London: Arnold.

Sørensen, Knud. 1985. *Charles Dickens: Linguistic Innovator*. Aarhus: Arkona.

Stubbs, Michael. 2001. *Words and Phrases: Corpus Studies of Lexical Semantics*. Oxford: Blackwell.

Yamamoto, Tadao. 1950. *Growth and System of the Language of Dickens* (3rd ed.). Hiroshima: Keisuisha.

Bibliography

Alexander, Jonathan. 2000. Review of *The Emerging Cyberculture: Literacy, Paradigm, and Paradox* ed. Stephanie Gibson and Ollie Oviedo (Cresskill, NJ: Hampton Press, 2000) in *Kairos* 6(1). Online at http://english.ttu.edu/ kairos/6.1/reviews/alexander/.

Anderson, Byron. 1998. 'The World Wide Web and the Humanities: Superhighway to What? Research, Quality, and "Literature"' in *Humanities Collections* 1(1): 25-40.

Archer, Dawn, and Jonathan Culpeper. 2003. 'Sociopragmatic Annotation: New Directions and Possibilities in Historical Corpus Linguistics' in Wilson, Andrew, Paul Rayson and Tony M. McEnery (eds) *Corpus Linguistics by the Lune: A Festschrift for Geoffrey Leech*. Frankfurt: Peter Lang: 37-58.

Austin, Timothy R. 1984. *Language Crafted*. Bloomington: Indiana University Press.

__. 1994. *Poetic Voices: Discourse Linguistics and the Poetic Tradition*. Tuscaloosa: University of Alabama Press.

Bakhtin, Mikhail M. 1981. *The Dialogic Imagination: Four Essays*. Austin: University of Texas Press.

Banfield, Ann. 1982. *Unspeakable Sentences: Narration and Representation in the Language of Narrative*. Boston: Routledge & Kegan Paul.

Bard, Alexander, and Jan Söderqvist. 2002. *Netocracy: The New Power Elite and Life after Capitalism*. London: Reuters.

Barthes, Roland. 2000. 'Camera Lucida: Reflections on Photography' in Thomas (2000): 54-62.

Bell, Allan. 1991. *The Language of News Media*. Oxford: Blackwell.

Benjamin, Walter. [1936] 1966. 'The Work of Art in the Age of Mechanical Reproduction' in Arendt, Hannah (ed.) *Illuminations*. New York: Schocken: 217-51.

Benson, D. F. 1981. 'Alexia and the Neuroanatomical Basis of Reading' in Pirozzolo, Francis J., and Merlin C. Wittrock (eds)

Neuropsychological and Cognitive Processes in Reading. New York: Academic Press: 69-92.

Berger, John. 1972. *Ways of Seeing*. London: BBC and Penguin Books.

Berkenkotter, Carol, and Thomas Huckin. 1995. *Genre Knowledge in Disciplinary Communication*. Hillsdale, NJ: Lawrence Erlbaum Associates.

Bernstein, Basil. 1981. 'Codes, Modalities and the Process of Cultural Reproductions: A Model' in *Language and Society* 10: 327-63.

Berutti, Eliane Borges. 2001. 'Gays, Lésbicas e AIDS: uma Perspectiva Queer' in Oliveira Lima & Monteiro (2001): 98-109.

__. 1999. 'Gays e Lésbicas: Vozes da Literatura Norte-Americana Contemporânea' in *Matraga* 12: 1-7.

Biber, Douglas, Susan Conrad and Randi Reppen. 1998. *Corpus Linguistics: Investigating Language Structure and Use*. Cambridge: Cambridge University Press.

Bolter, Jay. 1991. *Writing Space: The Computer, Hypertext, and the History of Writing*. Hillsdale, NJ: Lawrence Erlbaum Associates.

Bonačić, Mirjana. 1998. 'Context, Knowledge, and Teaching Translation' in de Beaugrande, Robert, Meta Grosman and Barbara Seidlhofer (eds) *Language Policy and Language Education in Emerging Nations: Focus on Slovenia and Croatia and with Contributions from Britain, Austria, Spain, and Italy*. Stamford, CT: Ablex: 37-48.

__. 1999. *Tekst Diskurs Prijevod: o Poetici Prevođenja* (Text Discourse Translation: On the Poetics of Translating). Split: Književni krug.

Bray, Joe. 2002. 'Embedded Quotations in Eighteenth-Century Fiction: Journalism and the Early Novel' in *Journal of Literary Semantics* 31: 61-75.

Brinton, Laurel J. 1996. *Pragmatic Markers in English: Grammaticalization and Discourse Functions*. Berlin: Mouton de Gruyter.

Brockmeier, Jens, and Rom Harré. 1997. 'Narrative: Problems and Promises of an Alternative Paradigm' in *Research in Language and Social Interaction* 30(4): 263-83.

Brown, Penelope, and Stephen C. Levinson. 1987. *Politeness: Some Universals in Language Usage.* Cambridge: Cambridge University Press.

Brown, Roger, and Albert Gilman. 1960. 'The Pronouns of Power and Solidarity' in Sebeok (1960): 253-76.

Bruner, Jerome. 1997. *Atos de Significação.* Porto Alegre: Artes Médicas.

Burke, Michael. 2003. 'Literature as Parable' in Gavins, Joanna, and Gerard Steen (eds) *Cognitive Poetics in Practice.* London: Routledge: 115-28.

Bush, Vannevar. 1945. 'As We May Think' in *The Atlantic Monthly* 176: 101-08.

Butler, Judith. 1990. *Gender Trouble.* New York: Taylor & Francis.

___. 2000. *Antigone's Claim.* New York: Columbia University Press.

Caldas-Coulthard, Carmen Rosa. 1994. 'On Reporting Reporting: The Representation of Speech in Factual and Factional Narratives' in Coulthard (1994): 295-308.

___. 1996. 'Women Who Pay for Sex and Enjoy It: Transgression versus Morality in Women's Magazines' in Caldas-Coulthard & Coulthard (1996): 250-70.

___. 2002. 'Cross-cultural Representation of "Otherness" in Media Discourse' in Weiss & Wodak (2002): 272-96.

Caldas-Coulthard, Carmen Rosa, and Malcolm Coulthard (eds). 1996. *Texts and Practices: Readings in Critical Discourse Analysis.* London: Routledge.

Caldas-Coulthard, Carmen Rosa, and Theo van Leeuwen. 2001. 'Baby's First Toys and the Discursive Construction of Childhood' in Wodak, Ruth (ed.) *Critical Discourse Analysis in Post Modern Societies.* Special issue of *Folia Linguistica* 35(1-2): 157-82.

___. 2002. 'Stunning, Shimmering, Iridescent: Toys as the Representation of Gendered Social Actors' in Litosseleti, Lia, and Jane Sunderland (eds) *Gender Identity and Discourse Analysis.* Amsterdam: John Benjamins: 91-110.

Castells, Manuel. 1997. *The Power of Identity.* Oxford: Blackwell.

Catford, John C. 1965. *A Linguistic Theory of Translation.* Oxford: Oxford University Press.

Chauí, Marilena. 2000. *Cultura e Democracia: o Discurso Competente e Outras Falas*. Campinas: Cortez.

Chouliaraki, Lilie, and Norman Fairclough. 1999. *Discourse in Late Modernity: Rethinking Critical Discourse Analysis*. Edinburgh: Edinburgh University Press.

Coleman, Allan D. 1998. *Depth of Field: Essays on Photography, Mass Media and Lens Culture*. Albuquerque: University of New Mexico Press.

Coulthard, Malcolm (ed.). 1994. *Advances in Written Text Analysis*. London: Routledge.

Crowston, Kevin, and Marie Williams. 1997. 'Reproduced and Emergent Genres of Communication on the World-Wide Web' in *Proceedings of the 30th Annual Hawaii International Conference on System Sciences*. Maui (Hawaii): 30-39.

Culpeper, Jonathan, and Merja Kytö. 1997. 'Towards a Corpus of Dialogues, 1550-1750', in Ramisch, Heinrich, and Kenneth Wynne (eds) *Language in Time and Space: Studies in Honour of Wolfgang Viereck on the Occasion of his 60th Birthday*. Stuttgart: Franz Steiner: 60-73.

Davis, Lennard. 1983. *Factual Fictions: The Origins of the English Novel*. New York: Columbia University Press.

Derrida, Jacques. 1977. 'Signature Event Context' in *Glyph* 1: 172-97.

Dirven, René. 1985. 'Metaphor as a Basic Means for Extending Lexicon' in Paprotté & Dirven (1985): vii-xix.

Dobrovolsky, Dmitrij O. 1998. 'Vnutrennyaya forma idiom i problema tolkovaniya' in *Izvestiya AN. Seriya literaturi i yazika* 57(1): 36-44.

Durrant, Geoffrey. 1969. *William Wordsworth*. Cambridge: Cambridge University Press.

___. 1970. *Wordsworth and the Great System*. Cambridge: Cambridge University Press.

Eagleton, Terry. 1982. *The Rape of Clarissa*. Minneapolis: University of Minnesota Press.

Eaves, T. C. Duncan, and Ben D. Kimpel. 1971. *Samuel Richardson: A Biography*. Oxford: Clarendon Press.

Eco, Umberto. 1976. *A Theory of Semiotics*. Bloomington: Indiana University Press.

Emmott, Catherine. [1997] 1999. *Narrative Comprehension: A Discourse Perspective*. Oxford: Oxford University Press.

Evans, Jessica, and Stuart Hall (eds). 1999. *Visual Culture: The Reader*. London: Sage.

Fairclough, Norman. 1992. *Discourse and Social Change*. Oxford: Blackwell.

Fielding, Henry. 1882. 'An Essay on the Knowledge and Characters of Men' in *The Works of Henry Fielding*, Vol. VI (ed. Leslie Stephen). London: Smith, Elder & Co.: 327-53.

Firth, J. R. 1957. *Papers in Linguistics, 1934-51*. Oxford: Oxford University Press.

Fludernik, Monika. 1993. *The Fictions of Language and the Languages of Fiction*. London: Routledge.

Foucault, Michel. 1970. *The Order of Things*. London: Tavistock.

__. [1973] 1983. *This is Not a Pipe* (tr. James Harkness). Berkeley: University of California Press.

__. 1987. *A Arqueologia do Saber*. Rio de Janeiro: Forense-Universitária [original French ed. 1969].

Fowler, Roger (ed.). 1966. *Essays on Style and Language*. London: Routledge & Kegan Paul.

Freeman, Margaret H. 2000. 'Poetry and the Scope of Metaphor: Toward a Cognitive Theory of Literature' in Barcelona, Antonio (ed.) *Metaphor and Metonymy at the Crossroads: A Cognitive Perspective*. Berlin: Mouton de Gruyter: 253-81.

Freire Costa, Jurandir. 2002. *A Inocência e o Vício. Estudos sobre o Homoerotismo* (4th ed.). Rio de Janeiro: Relume Dumará.

Gauntlett, David. 2002. *Media, Gender and Identity: An Introduction*. London: Routledge.

Gee, James Paul. 1990. *Social Linguistics and Literacies: Ideology in Discourses*. London: Falmer Press.

Gerber, Philip L. 1982. *Robert Frost* (rev. ed.). Boston: Twayne.

Gibbs, Raymond W. Jr. 1990. 'The Process of Understanding Literary Metaphor' in *Journal of Literary Semantics* 19: 65-79.

__. [1994] 1999. *The Poetics of Mind: Figurative Thought, Language and Understanding*. Cambridge: Cambridge University Press.

Giddens, Anthony. 1991. *Modernity and Self-Identity*. Cambridge: Polity Press.

___. 1992. *A Transformação da Intimidade. Sexualidade, Amor e Erotismo nas Sociedades Modernas.* São Paulo: Editora da Unesp.

Goatly, Andrew. 1997. *The Language of Metaphors.* London: Routledge.

Goffman, Erving. 1959. *The Presentation of the Self in Everyday Life.* New York: Doubleday.

Goodman, Sharon. 1996. 'Visual English' in Goodman, Sharon, and David Graddol (eds) *Redesigning English: New Texts, New Identities.* London: Routledge: 38-72.

Green, Keith (ed.). 1995. *New Essays in Deixis.* Amsterdam: Rodopi.

Greenbaum, Sidney. 1969. *Studies in English Adverbial Usage.* London: Longman.

___. 1970. *Verb-Intensifier Collocation in English: An Experimental Approach.* The Hague: Mouton.

Greenbaum, Sidney, and Randolph Quirk. 1990. *A Student's Grammar of the English Language.* London: Longman.

Greenberg, Robert A., and James G. Hepburn (eds). 1961. *Robert Frost: An Introduction.* New York: Holt, Rinehart & Winston.

Guedes, Peônia Viana. 2001. 'Desafiando Mitos de Feminilidade: o Grotesco e o Erótico em *Nights at the circus* e em *The passion*' in Oliveira Lima & Monteiro (2001): 100-15.

Habermas, Jürgen. 1979. *Communication and the Evolution of Society.* London: Heinemann Educational.

Hall, Geoff. 2001. 'The Year's Work in Stylistics: 2000' in *Language and Literature* 10(4): 357-68.

Hall, Stuart (ed.). 1997. *Representation: Cultural Representations and Signifying Practices.* London: Sage.

Hall, Steven. 1998. 'Literature Online – Building a Home for English and American Literature on the World Wide Web' in *Computers and the Humanities* 32(4): 285-301.

Halliday, M. A. K. 1978. *Language as Social Semiotic.* London: Arnold.

Haraway, Donna. 1991. *Simians, Cyborgs and Women: The Reinvention of Nature.* New York: Routledge.

Harvey, W. J. 1969. '*Bleak House:* The Double Narrative' in Dyson, A. E. (ed.) *Dickens: Bleak House.* London: Macmillan: 224-34.

Hayles, N. Katherine. 1999. *How We Became Posthumans: Virtual Bodies in Cybernetics, Literature and Informatics*. Chicago: University of Chicago Press.

___. 2000. 'Flickering Connectivities in Shelley Jackson's Patchwork Girl: The Importance of Media-Specific Analysis'. Online at: http:// jefferson. village. virginia. edu / pmc. contents. all. html (consulted 22.02.2002).

Hoey, Michael. 1983. *On the Surface of Discourse*. London: Allen & Unwin.

___. 1991. *Patterns of Lexis in Text*. Oxford: Oxford University Press.

Hori, Masahiro. 1999. 'Collocational Patterns of Intensive Adverbs in Dickens: A Tentative Approach' in *English Corpus Studies* 6: 51-65.

___. 2002. 'Collocational Patterns of -*ly* Manner Adverbs in Dickens' in Saito, Toshio, Junsaku Nakamura and Shunji Yamazaki (eds) *English Corpus Linguistics in Japan*. Amsterdam: Rodopi: 149-63.

___. 2004. *Investigating Dickens' Style: A Collocational Analysis*. Basingstoke: Palgrave.

Hunston, Susan. 1994. 'Evaluation and Organisation in a Sample of Written Academic Discourse' in Coulthard (1994): 191-218.

___. 2000. 'Evaluation and the Planes of Discourse: Status and Value in Persuasive Texts' in Hunston & Thompson (2000): 177-206.

Hunston, Susan, and Gill Francis. 1999. *Pattern Grammar: A Corpus-Driven Approach to the Lexical Grammar of English*. Amsterdam: John Benjamins.

Hunston, Susan, and Geoff Thompson (eds). 2000. *Evaluation in Text: Authorial Stance and the Construction of Discourse*. Oxford: Oxford University Press.

Iser, Wolfgang. 1995. 'On Translatability: Variables of Interpretation' in *The European English Messenger* 4(1): 30-38.

Ivir, Vladimir. 1981. 'Formal Correspondence vs. Translation Equivalence Revisited' in *Poetics Today* 2(4): 51-59.

Jakobson, Roman. 1960. 'Closing Statement: Linguistics and Poetics' in Sebeok (1960): 350-77.

___. 1962. (with Claude Lévi-Strauss) '"Les Chats" de Charles Baudelaire' in *L'Homme* 2: 5-21. English tr. by Katie Furness-Lane in Lane (1970): 202-26.

__. 1970a. 'On the Verbal Art of William Blake and Other Poet-Painters' in *Linguistic Inquiry* 1: 3-23.

__. 1970b. (with Lawrence Jones) *Shakespeare's Verbal Art in 'Th'Expence of Spirit'*. The Hague: Mouton.

Johnson, Eric. 1996. 'Professor-Created Computer Programs for Student Research' in *Computers and the Humanities* 30(2): 171-79.

Jones, Peter. 1995. 'Philosophical and Theoretical Problems in the Study of Deixis: A Critique of the Standard Account' in Green (1995): 27-48.

Jones, Rodney H. 2001. 'Beyond the Screen – A Participatory Study of Computer Mediated Communication among Hong Kong Youth'. Paper presented at the annual meeting of the American Anthropological Association (Nov. 28-Dec. 2, 2001).

__. 2002. 'The Problem of Context in Computer Mediated Communication'. Paper presented at the Georgetown Roundtable on Language and Linguistics (Georgetown University, March 7-9, 2002).

Kafka, Franz. 1925 [posthum.]. *Der Prozess*. Berlin: Verlag Die Schmiede.

Kaplan, Caren. 1996. *Questions of Travel: Postmodern Poetics of Displacement*. Durham, NC: Duke University Press.

__. 2002. 'Transporting the Subject: Technologies of Mobility and Location in an Era of Globalization' in *PMLA* 117(1): 32-41.

Keymer, Thomas, and Peter Sabor (eds). 2001. *The* Pamela *Controversy: Criticisms and Adaptations of Samuel Richardson's* Pamela, *1740-1750*. Vol. I: *Richardson's Apparatus and Fielding's* Shamela. London: Pickering & Chatto.

Kintsch, Walter, and Teun A. van Dijk. 1978. 'Toward a Model of Discourse Comprehension and Production' in *Psychological Review* 85: 363-94.

Klein, Naomi. 1999. *No Logo: Taking Aim at the Brand Bullies*. New York: Picador.

Kövecses, Zoltán. 2002. *Metaphor*. Oxford: Oxford University Press.

Kohut, Heinz. 1959. 'Introspection, Empathy and Psychoanalysis: An Examination of the Relationship Between Modes of Observation and Theory' in *Journal of the American Psychoanalytic Association* 7: 459-83.

__. 1971. *The Analysis of the Self.* New York: International Universities Press.

Kress, Gunther. 1989. *Linguistic Processes in Sociocultural Practices.* Oxford: Oxford University Press.

__. 1996. 'Representational Resources and the Production of Subjectivity: Questions for the Theoretical Development of Critical Discourse Analysis in a Multicultural Society' in Caldas-Coulthard & Coulthard (1996): 15-31.

Kress, Gunther, and Theo van Leeuwen. 2001. *Multimodal Discourse: The Modes and Media of Contemporary Communication.* London: Arnold.

__. 1996. *Reading Images: The Grammar of Visual Design.* London: Routledge.

Kress, Gunther, Regina Leite-Garcia and Theo van Leeuwen. 1997. 'Discourse Semiotics' in van Dijk, Teun A. (ed.) *Discourse as Social Interaction.* London: Sage: 257-91.

Kuper, Peter. 1997. *Gibs auf! und andere Erzählungen von Franz Kafka.* Hamburg: Carlsen Verlag.

Labov, William, and Joshua Waletsky. 1967. 'Narrative Analysis: Oral Versions of Personal Experience' in Helm, June (ed.) *Essays on the Verbal and Visual Arts.* Seattle, WA: University of Washington Press: 12-44.

__. 1968. 'Narrative Analysis: Oral Versions of Personal Experience' in Labov, William, et al. (eds) *A Study of the Non-Standard English of Negro and Puerto Rican Speakers in New York City.* New York: Columbia University Press: 286-338.

Lacqueur, Thomas. 2001. *Inventando o Sexo. Corpo e Gênero dos Gregos a Freud.* Rio de Janeiro: Relume Dumará [original English ed. 1992].

Lakoff, George. 1986. 'A Figure of Thought' in *Metaphor and Symbolic Activity* 1: 215-25.

Lakoff, George, and Mark Johnson. 1980. *Metaphors We Live By.* Chicago: University of Chicago Press.

Lakoff, George, and Mark Turner. 1989. *More than Cool Reason: A Field Guide to Poetic Metaphor.* Chicago: University of Chicago Press.

Lancashire, Ian, et al. 1996. *Using TACT with Electronic Texts.* New York: Modern Language Association.

Lane, Michael (ed.). 1970. *Structuralism: A Reader.* London: Jonathan Cape.

Langacker, Ronald W. 1990. *Concept, Image, and Symbol: The Cognitive Basis of Grammar.* Berlin: Mouton de Gruyter.

Leech, Geoffrey. 1969. *A Linguistic Guide to English Poetry.* London: Longman.

__. 1999. 'The Distribution and Function of Vocatives in American and British English Conversation' in Hasselgård, Hilde, and Signe Oksefjell (eds) *Out of Corpora: Studies in Honour of Stig Johansson.* Amsterdam: Rodopi: 107-18.

Leech, Geoffrey, and Short, M. H. 1981. *Style in Fiction: A Linguistic Introduction to English Fictional Prose.* London: Longman.

Lemke, Jay L. 2002. 'Texts and Discourses in the Technologies of Social Organization' in Weiss & Wodak (2002): 130-49.

Levinson, Stephen. 1983. *Pragmatics.* Cambridge: Cambridge University Press.

Lévy, Pierre. 1997. *Collective Intelligence.* New York: Plenum.

Linell, Per. 1982. *The Written Language Bias in Linguistics.* Linköping: University of Linköping Press.

Locke, John. 1975. *An Essay Concerning Human Understanding* (ed. P. H. Nidditch). Oxford: Clarendon Press [based on 4th ed., 1700].

Lynch, Deirdre S. 1998. *The Economy of Character: Novels, Market Culture, and the Business of Inner Meaning.* Chicago: University of Chicago Press.

Lynen, John F. 1960. *The Pastoral Art of Robert Frost.* New Haven: Yale University Press.

Mackenzie, Henry. 1967. *The Man of Feeling* (ed. Brian Vickers). Oxford: Oxford University Press.

Maingueneau, Dominique. 1998. *Analyser les textes de communication.* Paris: Dunod.

Mairowitz, David Zane, and Robert Crumb. 1995. *Kafka – kurz und knapp.* Frankfurt: Zweitausendeins.

Manguel, Alberto. 1997. *A History of Reading*. London: Flamingo.

Martin, James. 2000. 'Beyond Exchange: Appraisal Systems in English' in Hunston & Thompson (2000): 142-75.

Mayes, Patricia. 1990. 'Quotation in Spoken English' in *Studies in Language* 14(2): 325-63.

McBride, Christopher. 1998. 'A Collocational Approach to Semantic Change: The Case of Worship and Honour in Malory and Spenser' in *Language and Literature* 7(1): 5-19.

McGann, Jerome J. 1997. 'The Rationale of Hypertext' in Sutherland (1997): 19-46.

McHale, Brian. 1978. 'Free Indirect Discourse: A Survey of Recent Accounts' in *PTL: A Journal for Poetics and Theory of Literature* 3: 249-87.

McLuhan, Marshall. 1994. *Understanding Media: The Extensions of Man*. Cambridge, MA: The MIT Press.

Melerovich, Alina M. 1982. 'Semanticheskaya struktura frazeologicheskih yedinits v sovremennom russkom yazike kak lingvisticheskaya problema'. Doctoral habilitation dissertation. Leningrad: Leningrad University.

Melville, Herman. 1957. *Moby Dick: or The Whale* (ed. Newton Arvin). New York: Holt, Rinehart & Winston.

__. 1988. *Moby-Dick* (ed. Tony Tanner). Oxford: Oxford University Press.

Mills, Jon, and Balasubramanyam Chandramohan. 1996. 'Literary Studies: A Computer Assisted Teaching Methodology' in *Computers and the Humanities* 30(2): 165-70.

Milroy, Lesley. 1987. *Language and Social Networks*. Oxford: Blackwell.

Mischler, Elliott G. 2001. 'Narrative and Identity: The Double Arrow of Time'. Paper presented at *Discourse and Identity Conference*, Rio de Janeiro: PUC.

Mitchell, W. J. T. 1994. *Picture Theory*. Chicago: University of Chicago Press.

Morley, Simon. 2003. *Writing on the Wall*. Berkeley: University of California Press.

Motta-Roth, Désirée. 1998. 'Discourse Analysis and Academic Book Reviews: A Study of Text and Disciplinary Cultures' in Fortanet,

Inmaculada, et al. (eds) *Genre Studies in English for Academic Purposes*. Castelló: Universitat Jaume I. Servei de Publicacions: 29-58.

Naciscione, Anita. 2001. *Phraseological Units in Discourse: Towards Applied Stylistics*. Riga: Latvian Academy of Culture.

Neubert, Albrecht, and Gregory M. Shreve. 1992. *Translation as Text*. Kent, OH: Kent State University Press.

Nida, Eugene A., and Charles R. Taber. 1974. *The Theory and Practice of Translation*. Leiden: E. J. Brill.

Nixon, Sean. 1997. 'Exhibiting Masculinity' in Hall (1997): 291-336.

Noldy, N. E., R. M. Stelmack and K. B. Campbell. 1990. 'Event-Related Potentials and Recognition Memory for Pictures and Words: The Effects of Intentional and Incidental Learning' in *Psychophysiology* 27(4): 417-28.

Oliveira Lima, Tereza Marques, and Conceição Monteiro (eds). 2001. *Representações Culturais do Outro nas Literaturas de Língua Inglesa*. Rio de Janeiro: Vício de Leitura.

Page, Norman. 1990. *Bleak House: A Novel of Connections*. Boston: Twayne.

Paprotté, Wolf, and René Dirven (eds). 1985. *The Ubiquity of Metaphor: Metaphor in Language and Thought*. Amsterdam: John Benjamins.

Parkes, Malcom B. 1992. *Pause and Effect: An Introduction to the History of Punctuation in the West*. Aldershot: Scolar.

Partington, Alan. 1998. *Patterns and Meanings: Using Corpora for English Language Research and Teaching*. Amsterdam: John Benjamins.

Pascal, Roy. 1977. *The Dual Voice: Free Indirect Speech and its Functioning in the Nineteenth Century Novel*. Manchester: Manchester University Press.

Poster, Mark. 2002. 'Digital Networks and Citizenship' in *PMLA* 117(1): 98-109.

Potter, Rosanne G. 1996. 'What Computers Are Good for in the Literature Classroom' in *Computers and the Humanities* 30(2): 181-90.

Quirk, Randolph, et al. 1985. *A Comprehensive Grammar of the English Language*. London: Longman.

Rajagopalan, Kanavilil (in press). 'Emotion and Language Politics: The Brazilian Case'. To appear in *Journal of Multilingual and Multicultural Development.*

Raumolin-Brunberg, Helena. 1994. 'Historical Sociolinguistics' in Nevalainen, Terttu, and Helena Raumolin-Brunberg (eds) *Sociolinguistics and Language History: Studies Based on the Corpus of Early English Correspondence.* Amsterdam: Rodopi: 11-37.

Richardson, Samuel. 2001. *Pamela; or, Virtue Rewarded* (ed. Thomas Keymer and Alice Wakely). Oxford: Oxford University Press [based on 1st ed., 1740].

Riffaterre, Michael. 1959. 'Criteria for Style Analysis' in *Word* 15: 154-74.

Robbins, Bruce. 2002. 'The Sweatshop Sublime' in *PMLA* 117(1): 84-97.

Rochester, Eric. 2001. 'New Tools for Analysing Texts' in *Language and Literature* 10(2): 187-91.

Rosler, Martha. 1998. *Positions in the Life World* (ed. Catherine de Zegher). Cambridge, MA: The MIT Press.

Sanders, José, and Gisela Redeker. 1993. 'Linguistic Perspective in Short News Stories' in *Poetics* 22: 69-87.

Sarup, Madan. 1996. *Identity, Culture and the Postmodern World.* Edinburgh: Edinburgh University Press.

Schank, Roger C. 1982. *Dynamic Memory: A Theory of Reminding and Learning in Computers and People.* Cambridge: Cambridge University Press.

Scollon, Ron. 1998. *Mediated Discourse as Social Interaction: A Study of News Discourse.* London: Longman.

__. 2001. *Mediated Discourse: The Nexus of Practice.* London: Routledge.

Scollon, Ron, and Suzie Wong Scollon. 2003a. *Discourses in Place: Language in the Material World.* London: Routledge.

__. 2003b. *Globalization: The Multimodal Shaping of Public Discourse.* http://www.gutenbergdump.net.

Sebeok, Thomas A. (ed.). 1960. *Style in Language.* New York: Technology Press of The Massachusetts Institute of Technology and John Wiley.

Semino, Elena. 1997. *Language and World Creation in Poems and Other Texts*. London: Longman.

Semino, Elena, Mick Short and Jonathan Culpeper. 1997. 'Using a Corpus to Test a Model of Speech and Thought Presentation' in *Poetics* 25: 17-43.

Shepherd, Michael, and Carolyn Watters. 1998. 'The Evolution of Cybergenres' in *Proceedings of the 31st Annual Hawaii International Conference on System Sciences*. Maui (Hawaii): 97-109.

Shiina, Michi. 2002. 'How Spouses Used to Address Each Other: A Historical Pragmatic Approach to the Use of Vocatives in Early Modern English Comedies' in *Bulletin of the Faculty of Letters* 48: 51-73. Tokyo: Hosei University.

Short, Mick. 1989. 'Speech Presentation, the Novel and the Press' in van Peer, Willie (ed.) *The Taming of the Text: Explorations in Language, Literature and Culture*. London: Routledge: 61-81.

Short, Mick, Elena Semino and Martin Wynne. 2002. 'Revisiting the Notion of Faithfulness in Discourse Presentation Using a Corpus Approach' in *Language and Literature* 11(4): 325-55.

Shuttleworth, Mark, and Moira Cowie. 1997. *Dictionary of Translation Studies*. Manchester: St. Jerome.

Sinclair, John. 1986. 'Fictional Worlds' in Coulthard, Malcolm (ed.) *Talking about Text*. Birmingham: ELR Monographs 13: 43-60.

___. 1991. *Corpus, Concordance, Collocation*. Oxford: Oxford University Press.

Sinclair, John, et al. 1998. 'Language Independent Statistical Software for Corpus Exploration' in *Computers and the Humanities* 31(3): 229-55.

Slembrouck, Stef. 1992. 'The Parliamentary Hansard "Verbatim" Report: The Written Construction of Spoken Discourse' in *Language and Literature* 1(2): 101-19.

Smith, Grahame. 1974. *Charles Dickens: Bleak House*. London: Arnold.

Sontag, Susan. [1961] 2001. 'Notes on Camp' in *Against Interpretation and Other Essays*. New York: Picador: 275-92.

___. 1999. 'The Image-World' in Evans & Hall (1999): 80-94.

___. 2000. 'In Plato's Cave' in Thomas (2000): 40-53.

Sørensen, Knud. 1985. *Charles Dickens: Linguistic Innovator*. Aarhus: Arkona.

Squires, Radcliffe. 1969. *The Major Themes of Robert Frost*. Ann Arbor: University of Michigan Press.

Stallabrass, Julian. 1995. 'Empowering Technology: The Exploration of Cyberspace' in *New Left Review* 211: 3-32.

Steen, Gerard. 1992. 'Literary and Nonliterary Aspect of Metaphor' in *Poetics Today* 13: 687-704.

__. 1994. *Understanding Metaphor in Literature*. London: Longman.

__. 2002. 'Identifying Metaphor in Language: A Cognitive Approach' in *Style* 36(3): 386-407.

Steiner, George. 1992. *After Babel: Aspects of Language and Translation* (2nd ed.). Oxford: Oxford University Press.

Sternberg, Meir. 1982. 'Point of View and the Indirections of Direct Speech' in *Language and Style* 15(2): 67-117.

Stone, Allucquere Rosanne. 1995. *The War of Desire and Technology at the Close of the Mechanical Age*. Cambridge, MA: The MIT Press.

Stubbs, Michael. 2001. *Words and Phrases: Corpus Studies of Lexical Semantics*. Oxford: Blackwell.

Sussex, Roland, and Peter White. 1996. 'Electronic Networking' in *Annual Review of Applied Linguistics* 16: 200-25.

Sutherland, Kathryn (ed.). 1997. *Electronic Text: Investigations in Method and Theory*. Oxford: Clarendon Press.

Tabakowska, Elżbieta. 1997. 'Translating a Poem, From a Linguistic Perspective' in *Target* 9(1): 25-41.

Tadros, Angela. 1993. 'The Pragmatics of Text Averral and Attribution in Academic Texts' in Hoey, Michael (ed.) *Data, Description, Discourse*. London: HarperCollins: 98-114.

Tannen, Deborah. 1989. *Talking Voices: Repetition, Dialogue, and Imagery in Conversational Discourse*. Cambridge: Cambridge University Press.

__. 1995. 'Waiting for the Mouse: Constructed Dialogue in Conversation' in Tedlock, Dennis, and Bruce Mannheim (eds) *The Dialogic Emergence of Culture*. Urbana: University of Illinois Press: 198-217.

Thomas, Julia (ed.). 2000. *Reading Images*. Basingstoke: Palgrave.

Toolan, Michael. 1998. *Language in Literature*. London: Hodder.

__. 2001. *Narrative: A Critical Linguistic Introduction* (2nd ed.). London: Routledge.

Toury, Gideon. 1995. *Descriptive Translation Studies and Beyond*. Amsterdam: John Benjamins.

Twain, Mark. 1961. *The Complete Humorous Sketches and Tales of Mark Twain*. New York: Hanover House.

Tytler, Graeme. 1982. *Physiognomy in the European Novel: Faces and Fortunes*. Princeton, NJ: Princeton University Press.

van Dijk, Teun A. 1988. *News as Discourse*. Hillsdale, NJ: Lawrence Erlbaum Associates.

van Dijk, Teun A., and Walter Kintsch. 1983. *Strategies of Discourse Comprehension*. New York: Academic Press.

van Leeuwen, Theo. 1993. 'Recontextualization of Social Practice'. Unpublished manuscript.

Vološinov, Valentin N. [1929] 1986. *Marxism and the Philosophy of Language* (tr. Ladislav Matejka and I. R. Titunik). Cambridge, MA: Harvard University Press.

Wales, Kathleen. 1983. '*Thou* and *You* in Early Modern English: Brown and Gilman Re-Appraised' in *Studia Linguistica* 37: 107-25.

Warner, William B. 1998. *Licensing Entertainment: The Elevation of Novel Reading in Britain, 1684-1750*. Berkeley: University of California Press.

Watts, Richard J. 1992. 'Linguistic Politeness and Politic Verbal Behaviour: Reconsidering Claims for Universality' in Watts, Richard J., Sachiko Ide and Konrad Ehlich (eds) *Politeness in Language: Studies in its History, Theory and Practice*. Berlin: Mouton de Gruyter: 43-70.

Waugh, Linda R. 1995. 'Reported Speech in Journalistic Discourse: The Relation of Function and Text' in *Text* 15(1): 129-73.

Weiss, Gilbert, and Ruth Wodak (eds). 2002. *Critical Discourse Analysis: Theory and Interdisciplinarity*. Basingstoke: Palgrave.

Wertsch, James V. 1991. *Voices of the Mind: A Sociocultural Approach to Mediated Action*. Cambridge, MA: Harvard University Press.

Winter, Eugene. 1982. *Towards a Contextual Grammar of English*. London: Allen & Unwin.

Winterson, Jeanette. 2001. *The PowerBook*. London: Vintage.

Woodward, Kathryn. 1997. 'Identity and Difference' in Woodward, Kathryn (ed.) *Culture, Media and Identities*. London: Sage: 10-22.

__. 2000. 'Identidade e Diferença: Uma Introdução Teórica e Conceitual' in Silva, Tomás Tadeu (ed.) *Identidade e Diferença: a Perspectiva dos Estudos Culturais*. Petrópolis: Vozes: 7-72.

Yamamoto, Tadao. 1950. *Growth and System of the Language of Dickens* (3rd ed.). Hiroshima: Keisuisha.

Index

V

W

Theory into Poetry:

New Approaches to the Lyric.

Edited by Eva Müller-Zettelmann and Margarete Rubik.

Amsterdam/New York, NY 2005. 375 pp.
(Internationale Forschungen zur Allgemeinen und
Vergleichenden Literaturwissenschaft 89)

ISBN: 90-420-1906-9   € 75,-/ US $ 94.-

At the beginning of the 21st century, there is still no generally accepted comprehensive definition of the lyric or differentiated modern toolkit for its analysis. The reception of poetry is largely characterised either by an empathetic identification of critics with the lyric persona or by exclusive interest in formal patterning.

The present volume seeks to remedy this deficit. All the contributors 'theorise' the lyric to overcome the impasse of an impressionistic and narrowly formalistic critical debate on the genre. Their papers focus on a variety of different questions: the problem of establishing a framework for definition and classification; the search for dynamic and potent critical approaches; investigations of poetry's cultural performance and its fundamental relevance for the construction of group cohesion. The essays collected in this volume offer a consciously polyphonic range of theories and interpretations, suggesting to the reader a variety of theoretical frameworks and practical illustrations of how a discussion of poetry may be firmly grounded in modern literary theory.

USA/Canada: 906 Madison Avenue, UNION, NJ 07083, USA.
Call toll-free (USA only)1-800-225-3998, Tel. 908 206 1166, Fax 908-206-0820
All other countries: Tijnmuiden 7, 1046 AK Amsterdam, The Netherlands.
Tel. ++ 31 (0)20 611 48 21, Fax ++ 31 (0)20 447 29 79
Orders-queries@rodopi.nl   **www.rodopi.nl**
Please note that the exchange rate is subject to fluctuations

Contemporary Pragmatism

Edited by John Shook,
Oklahoma State University, USA
Paulo Ghiraldelli, Jr.,
Centro de Estudos em Filosofia Americana, Brazil

ISSN: 1572-3429

Contemporary Pragmatism is an interdisciplinary, international journal for discussions of applying pragmatism, broadly understood, to today's issues. This journal will consider articles about pragmatism written from the standpoint of any tradition and perspective, but it will concentrate on original explorations of pragmatism and pragmatism's relations with humanism, naturalism, and analytic philosophy. The journal welcomes both pragmatism-inspired research and criticisms of pragmatism. We cannot consider submissions that principally interpret or critique historical figures of American philosophy, although applications of past thought to contemporary issues are sought. Contributions may deal with current issues in any field of philosophical inquiry. CP encourages interdisciplinary efforts, establishing bridges between pragmatic philosophy and, for example, theology, psychology, pedagogy, sociology, medicine, economics, political science, or international relations.

USA/Canada: 906 Madison Avenue, Union, NJ 07083, USA.
Call toll-free (USA only)1-800-225-3998, Tel. 908 206 1166, Fax 908-206-0820
All other countries: Tijnmuiden 7, 1046 AK Amsterdam, The Netherlands.
Tel. ++ 31 (0)20 611 48 21, Fax ++ 31 (0)20 447 29 79
info@rodopi.nl   www.rodopi.nl
Please note that the exchange rate is subject to fluctuations